LAYING OUT THE BONES

Irish Studies
James MacKillop, *Series Editor*

Select titles in Irish Studies

Irish Women Dramatists: 1908–2001
Eileen Kearney and Charlotte Headrick, eds.

Israelites in Erin: Exodus, Revolution, and the Irish Revival
Abby Bender

Joyce/Shakespeare
Laura Pelaschiar, ed.

Political Acts: Women in Northern Irish Theatre, 1921–2012
Fiona Coffey

*Relocated Memories: The Great Famine in Irish
and Diaspora Fiction, 1846–1870*
Marguérite Corporaal

*Revolutionary Damnation: Badiou
and Irish Fiction from Joyce to Enright*
Sheldon Brivic

Seamus Heaney as Aesthetic Thinker: A Study of the Prose
Eugene O'Brien

Standish O'Grady's Cuculain: A Critical Edition
Standish O'Grady; Gregory Castle and Patrick Bixby, eds.

LAYING OUT THE BONES

DEATH AND DYING IN THE MODERN IRISH NOVEL

BRIDGET ENGLISH

SYRACUSE UNIVERSITY PRESS

Excerpts from "Three Novels" by Samuel Beckett, English translation copyright © 1955 by the Estate of Patrick Bowles and the Estate of Samuel Beckett. Used by permission of Grove/Atlantic, Inc. Any third party use of this material, outside of this publication, is prohibited.

Excerpts from *The Gathering* by Anne Enright. Published by Jonathan Cape, 2007. Copyright © Anne Enright. Reproduced by permission of the author c/o Rogers, Coleridge & White Ltd., 20 Powis Mews, London W11 1JN

Copyright © 2017 by Syracuse University Press
Syracuse, New York 13244-5290

All Rights Reserved

First Edition 2017

17 18 19 20 21 22   6 5 4 3 2 1

∞ The paper used in this publication meets the minimum requirements of the American National Standard for Information Sciences—Permanence of Paper for Printed Library Materials, ANSI Z39.48-1992.

For a listing of books published and distributed by Syracuse University Press, visit www.SyracuseUniversityPress.syr.edu.

ISBN: 978-0-8156-3548-2 (hardcover)
978-0-8156-3536-9 (paperback)
978-0-8156-5414-8 (e-book)

Library of Congress Cataloging-in-Publication Data

Names: English, Bridget, author.
Title: Laying out the bones : death and dying in the modern Irish novel / Bridget English.
Description: First edition. | Syracuse, New York : Syracuse University Press, 2017. | Includes bibliographical references and index.
Identifiers: LCCN 2017043145 (print) | LCCN 2017043151 (ebook) | ISBN 9780815654148 (e-book) | ISBN 9780815635482 (hardcover : alk. paper) | ISBN 9780815635369 (pbk. : alk. paper)
Subjects: LCSH: English fiction—Irish authors—History and criticism. | Death in literature. | Death—Ireland.
Classification: LCC PR8803 (ebook) | LCC PR8803 .E54 2017 (print) | DDC 823/.91099417—dc23
LC record available at https://lccn.loc.gov/2017043145

Manufactured in the United States of America

For Patrick and Kathleen English

*In memory of
Rita Peters (1919–2014)
and Robert Soldat (1933–2014)*

Contents

Acknowledgments · ix

INTRODUCTION
"Traversing the Dismal Fields"
Death and Dying in Modern Ireland · 1

1. Death and Narrative Regeneration
James Joyce's *Ulysses* · 23

2. The Eve of All Souls and the Death of Desire
Kate O'Brien's *The Ante-Room* · 56

3. Deathbed Confessions and Unraveling Narration
Samuel Beckett's *Malone Dies* · 87

4. Ritual and Denial in a World Stripped of Illusion
John McGahern's *The Barracks* · 119

5. Death without Resurrection and the Modern Wake
Anne Enright's *The Gathering* · 150

CONCLUSION
"As You Were before You Rested"
Death and the Afterlife of the Irish Wake · 180

Notes · 193
Bibliography · 213
Index · 229

Acknowledgments

This project grew out of my research in the Department of English at Maynooth University, Ireland, where I was fortunate enough to benefit from the expertise, general collegiality, and good humor of many friends and colleagues. My thanks especially to Joe Cleary, without whose guidance and intellectual generosity this book would not have been possible and who continues to be an invaluable source of lively commentary, inspiration, and exchange. My deepest gratitude to Conor McCarthy, who likewise contributed immensely to the completion of this study and whose solidarity, advice, and support continue to be a sustaining force. Thanks also to Emer Nolan for her incisive commentary on various drafts and for her good counsel and encouragement. For their inspirational discussions and practical advice, thanks to Amanda Bent, Íde Corley, Michael G. Cronin, Luke Gibbons, Colin Graham, Sinéad Kennedy, Tracy O'Flahery, and Stephen O'Neill. Special gratitude is owed to Oona Frawley, who provided sage commentary at particularly vexed times and whose insight, kindness, and friendship continue to be a much-valued resource.

Declan Kiberd not only offered his time and astute commentary in reading a draft of the book, but has also remained a constant source of cheerful encouragement and wisdom. A conversation with Margaret Kelleher provided an idea for a much-needed theoretical framework for this project, and I am grateful for her support throughout. Early feedback from Chris Morash was likewise crucial in structuring this project.

At Syracuse University Press, thanks especially to Deborah Manion, Lisa Kuerbis, and Annette Wenda for their encouragement and care with the manuscript. It has been a pleasure to work with all the staff at Syracuse, and I am grateful for their support. I would also like to acknowledge the anonymous readers for Syracuse University Press, whose rigorous, detailed reports, suggestions, and challenges were tremendously useful in revising the manuscript.

Intellectual exchanges and debates with many friends across several countries have shaped the words on these pages and have proved a sustaining source of joy over the years. My deepest thanks to Claudia Luppino, Joanne McEntee, Michaela Marková, Lauren Clarke, Matt Fogarty, Declan Kavanagh, Orla Fitzpatrick, Theresa Harney, Ciara Gallagher, Deirdre Quinn, Maggie O'Neill, Alan Carmody, Marion Quirici, Feargal Whelan, and Katie Mishler. Thanks to Elizabeth Mannion for her keen editorial skills and all her help in manuscript preparation and beyond. Not only did Sonia Howell proofread parts of the manuscript, but she and John Dillon have proved endlessly generous in support of all kinds.

Finally, my greatest debt is to my family, without whose care and encouragement none of this would have been possible and whose humor relieved some of the grimmer aspects of researching death and dying. Many thanks to Joan Janis; Maureen and Mary Soldat; Dan, Gail, Daniel, Stephen, and Allison Peters; and the extended Hyland family. Colleen English deserves special thanks for her practical help, feedback, friendly skepticism, and lively debates about death. Deepest gratitude to my parents, Kathleen and Patrick English, who instilled in me a love of learning and a passion for books and whose love and support are unfailing. To them and to the memory of Rita Peters and Robert Soldat, who are not here to see the completion of this project but each of whose steadfast love and unfailing support contributed to its completion in innumerable ways, this book is dedicated.

LAYING OUT THE BONES

INTRODUCTION

"Traversing the Dismal Fields"

Death and Dying in Modern Ireland

In a now famous interview hosted by Marian Finucane and broadcast on RTÉ radio on Saturday, April 12, 2008, Nuala O'Faolain revealed that she was dying of lung cancer and had refused chemotherapy.[1] The Irish public listened in rapt attention as O'Faolain declared that there was no religious consolation to be had for her because she did not believe in God or an afterlife. This rawly emotional interview was significant for publicly voicing private fears and emotions about dying, but also because O'Faolain was relating a very harrowing account of a secular life and death to a once famously Catholic nation. She was giving public voice to what is commonly a very private or at most familial experience, and the powerful reactions the interview provoked revealed the extent to which modern Irish society generally silences and marginalizes the voices of the dying.[2] Perhaps the most shocking part of the interview was O'Faolain's brutal honesty about her unmitigated despair and the lack of solace she derived from the idea of God or from the promise of an afterlife. O'Faolain was not only making her private death public and declaring the wholly secular nature of her encounter with her end, but also expressing her sense of her death as inconsolable tragedy. In her view, the pleasures, memories, and wisdom that she had accumulated over her lifetime would all disappear without a trace at her passing. The interview was brutally honest and utterly uncompromising in its sense of the finality of death, and it left in its wake many questions about how we make sense of death in an increasingly secular world.

After telling Finucane that she could not be consoled by mention of God, O'Faolain referred to the modern Irish song "Thíos i lár an ghleanna" that she had heard at the Merriman Summer School and suggested that Finucane might play it at the end of the program, particularly for dying people. O'Faolain noted, "The last two lines are two things, asking God up there in the heavens, even though you don't believe in him, to send you back, even though you know it can't happen. Those two things sum up where I am now."[3] It is curious that O'Faolain explains her refusal to take solace in the idea of God before suggesting that her host broadcast a song about man's request to God to give him new life. Significantly, in her description of the song, O'Faolain reveals that her own deepest desire is to be given a second chance at life. The beauty of the song that O'Faolain recommended might well justify its inclusion in the program in any case, but the request also suggested that even after we have ceased to (fully) believe in the things we inherit from tradition, those things can continue to move us and to mold our emotional sense of our most profound experiences.

O'Faolain also expressed a vivid historical sense of the nature of death and dying throughout the course of the interview. Though she underlined the terrific feeling of "aloneness" of her own personal encounter with death, she also drew attention to the fact that she was dying a relatively comfortable death, surrounded and helped by friends and family and with enough money to support herself and to meliorate the worst features of the process of dying. In that sense, she said, she considered herself fortunate compared to the multitudes who died in Ireland during the Famine or to the millions of people throughout the twentieth century who had been condemned to die in the most atrocious circumstances imaginable. Despite her acknowledgment of this difference, the distinction she made between her own protected affluence and the totally unprotected mass deaths suffered by so many others across history did not ease O'Faolain's emotional suffering. The point she seemed to be making was that in modern affluent societies, middle-class people can be spared at least some of the more harrowing forms of death and can thus meet their ends with some degree of personal control and dignity. Nevertheless, the unrelieved anguish that she so graphically expressed about her own dying indicated that even the most comfortable death was ultimately a shattering experience.

Near the end of the interview, O'Faolain expressed the hope that she would die a "good death" and described her conception of this kind of death as "some kind of fading away, that you lay on your bed and you were really a nice person and everyone came and said goodbye and wept and you wept and you meant it and you weren't in any pain or discomfort and that you didn't choke and didn't die in a mess of diarrhea and you just go weaker." This description evokes the deathbed scene associated with the Christian "good death" that requires the dying to receive the last rites, to repent of their sins, to mend family relations, and to sort their worldly affairs before passing away peacefully. However, as a secular person, O'Faolain did not mention the elements of faith and salvation conventional to traditional ideas of a "good death" in her description. For a modern unbeliever, O'Faolain indicated, what constitutes a "good death" is the absence of the grosser forms of pain and suffering, the presence of loved ones, and the avoidance of bodily unpleasantness. Her stress on the messy physicality of death highlights that even this kind of secular "good death" may be almost as elusive as the religious kind. Religious or secular conventional versions of what a "good death" might mean persisted in O'Faolain's imagination and colored her sense of her own passing. But they persisted for her largely as a kind of afterimage, as something rather fictional and awkwardly out of kilter with the actualities of death in twenty-first-century Ireland.

In modern Western societies, death most often occurs in private places such as hospital wards or bedrooms. The dying are seldom interviewed by a media more inclined to stress youth and place great emphasis on how people might strive to live longer, healthier, happier lives. Contemporary Ireland is no different from the rest of Europe or North America in this respect. The only public part of most contemporary deaths is the funeral ceremony, but such ceremonies rarely deal with the process of dying itself. Instead, funerals offer polite retrospectives on the life of the deceased person, or they try to express solidarity with the grief of the mourners. The most unique aspect of O'Faolain's interview was that a discussion of dying itself became a media event, her words of despair making the front page of the *Sunday Independent* the following day.

By opening up discussions of death to include the conventionally unmentionable aspects of the process such as gross physical suffering and the possibility of ending life without hope or meaning, O'Faolain's interview stands as one of the most important moments in contemporary Irish cultural history in relation to death and dying.[4] Lacking the quality of celebration or hopeful anticipation of an afterlife that characterizes traditional Irish wakes and Christian death rituals, O'Faolain laid bare the new challenges of dying at the heart of modern secular Irish society.

As the communal belief systems provided by religious or ancient myths weaken, modern men and women have to rely on their own private emotional and intellectual resources to understand the meaning of their lives in the harsh glare of death. This modern Western condition is not unique to Ireland, but Ireland makes a particularly interesting study, as Irish attitudes toward death and dying are shaped by a cultural and literary experience that includes Roman Catholicism, the Famine years, and the rhetoric of self-sacrifice and martyrdom that characterized its struggle for independence.

Catholicism has been a crucial part of the history of death in Ireland for centuries. O'Faolain's interview revealed a sense that the Catholic Church's monopoly over the rituals of dying and burial might be receding, and it highlighted the challenges of dying without the sureties of religious hope. O'Faolain forced listeners to confront radically antagonistic conceptions of death and to attempt to reconcile the Catholic promise of heaven with a liberal-humanist emphasis on human life and personal fulfillment. This marked a watershed in Irish culture, as it conveyed an unadorned and complex understanding of death and dying that did not simply construe the end of life as either a punishment or a reward but rather as a final end that could be neither escaped nor transcended. O'Faolain's dying interview was a visceral moment in Irish culture that signaled a willingness to openly address conflicting and changing conceptions of death, but the issues she raised have long been absorbed by Irish writers, particularly twentieth-century novelists.

The five novels that inform this study—James Joyce's *Ulysses*, Kate O'Brien's *The Ante-Room*, Samuel Beckett's *Malone Dies*, John McGahern's *The Barracks*, and Anne Enright's *The Gathering*—have been chosen as the centerpieces because of how death informs and structures their narratives, revealing conflicts between religious and secular conceptions of death. These novels engage both with traditional literary depictions of death and dying (such as the Victorian deathbed scene or the notion of the "good death") and with the Irish context, in which residual pagan elements have been blended with Catholic rituals that then come into conflict with the secularizing thrust of modernization.

Ulysses, the most famous twentieth-century Irish novel, opens with a young mourning-suited Stephen Dedalus grieving the recent death of his cancer-afflicted mother and tormented by the fact that in order to assert his own secular identity, he has had to aggravate his mother's physical suffering with a further anguish about her son's loss of faith. The narrative shape of *The Ante-Room*, generally considered to be one of the most accomplished realist novels to emerge in twentieth-century Ireland, is also governed by the experience of death. Teresa Mulqueen's adult children gather on the Eve of All Saints to prepare for her death. They must wrestle not only with their mother's passing but also with the conflicts arising from their own inabilities to reconcile earthly passions with the demands of their inherited and deeply ingrained religious feelings. Death inhabits the very title of Beckett's grimly comic *Malone Dies*. The novel savagely parodies all ideas of a "good death" and explores how the desire to manage death by writing about it exposes the futility of all narrative endeavors to assert control over existence and acknowledges the human necessity for narrative as a way of easing the fear of death.

McGahern turned obsessively to the experience of the death of a mother, a preoccupation that began in his very first novel, *The Barracks*. *The Barracks* tells the story of Elizabeth Reegan, a lonely woman dying of cancer who outwardly conforms to Catholic rituals of dying and has evident parallels with *Ulysses* and *The Ante-Room*. But McGahern's narration of the experience of dying from the perspective of a dying woman, rather than from the point of view of the children who will outlive her, is a departure in Irish fiction. Here, the mother figure is not a representative of a dying generation; she is an individual meeting death as best she can and with little assistance from her family or community.

Enright's novels have engaged with the secular world of modern late-capitalist Ireland, and in this sense there are obvious differences between her Ireland and that of the poorer rural farming worlds depicted by McGahern and by so many other Irish writers of a previous generation. But in *The Gathering*, Enright too constructs an entire novel about how to come to terms with death in an era when the old rituals have lost their power but in which no meaningful alternatives have come together to take their place. Enright's novelistic style is, as might be expected, quite different from the approach of her predecessors, but the continuity of concern between *The Gathering* and the novels just mentioned is all the more remarkable for it.

Spanning the best part of a century, we find in all of these works an abiding preoccupation with the idea that there can be no meaningful engagement with the business of modern living without a corresponding engagement with the significance of death in modern times.

From the nineteenth century onward, the culture surrounding death and dying in Ireland has been distinguished by the influence of the Catholic Church and by the incorporation of pagan customs into Catholic religious practice. As Tom Inglis observes, what separates Ireland from other Western societies is not strictly the inclusion of these practices, but the "variety and frequency with which pagan practices are enacted as part of Catholic religious behavior." Nowhere is this more evident than in the phenomenon of the Irish wake, which is both a site of opposition to Catholic control and a place where pagan and Catholic beliefs coexist. In the eighteenth and nineteenth centuries, the Irish "merry wake" along with pilgrimages and pattern festivities were not simply "marginalized vestiges of archaic Irish culture" but "alternative to and co-existent with orthodox Christian values, beliefs, and rituals."[5] The wake, then, is a particularly important trope in Irish literature and culture as a means of understanding the ways that Catholic and pagan beliefs surrounding death influenced larger cultural conceptions of death and dying.[6]

According to Gearóid Ó Crualaoich, the traditional wake and funeral "together constituted a central institution of popular Irish rural culture which had both great symbolic and behavioral significance in people's lives. The institution articulated for those involved . . . their collective response to their life experience." The social significance of the traditional Irish wake and its accompanying sexually explicit games, dancing, singing, and keening posed a threat to the authority of the Catholic Church. As early as 1641, the Synod of Armagh objected to mortuary rituals that involved obscene songs and suggestive games, a complaint that was still repeated centuries later in the Maynooth Synod of 1927. Regardless of the church's objections, the wake tradition enjoyed a continued popularity in Irish culture because it eased the transition between life and death and provided the living with a way of expressing their sorrow while reminding them of their own vitality. This kind of communal response to death, as Ó Crualaoich argues, served the dual function of "mourning a transition and also resolving and removing social tension."[7]

The Catholic Church could not entirely condemn or forbid the wake because it served an important social purpose. The custom was therefore assimilated into Catholic practice, combining some of the old pagan traditions with religious rituals. During the Devotional Revolution (1850–75), Catholic authorities attempted to shift religious practice from the home to the church. Accordingly, the First Synod of Maynooth in 1875 required parish priests to put an end to unchristian wakes. Though it was not formally required that all funeral ceremonies take place in the church rather than the home until the new Code of Canon Law in 1971, there was a considerable effort to transform the "merry wake" into a somber mourning ritual. Even though the traditional wake persisted into the twentieth century, particularly in rural counties, the elements of clerical satire and paganism had essentially been removed from its practice by then.[8]

The Catholic attempts to control attitudes toward death also pertained to funerals and burial. At the beginning of the twentieth century, Roman Catholic canon laws regarding funeral rites and burials for suicide victims, unbaptized children, and others who died outside of the church had a harshly unforgiving influence on larger cultural attitudes to death.[9] Until the 1960s, Irish suicide victims were buried in *Cillíní* (also known as *killeens* or *kyles*), the term used for disused burial grounds employed for the burial of unbaptized children, Jews, peddlers, and paupers. Suicide itself was regarded as evidence of the sin of despair and remained a criminal offense to state law until the Criminal Law (Suicide) Act of 1993.[10] Yet for all its authority, the Catholic Church could never completely control the attitudes of the people toward death. This point is evidenced by the persistence of the wake as well as the widespread sympathy for political deaths, such as of the Hunger Strikes, even though some clergy termed these deaths voluntary or irreligious suicides. As explored in later chapters, Irish attitudes toward death during the nineteenth and early twentieth centuries were informed by a mix of Catholic rituals and folk superstitions. Communal and folk practices such as the wake and customs surrounding the dead—the opening of windows at the time of death, covering all the mirrors in the house, stopping the clocks, and sitting up all night with the corpse—persisted well into the twentieth century, and some continue today.[11]

Even though the Catholic Church's control over death was probably at its height in Ireland in the decades after independence, its power began to decrease as Ireland became more secular. There were many positive aspects to these wider shifts. In an attempt to keep pace with the changing attitudes to such matters in wider society, the Catholic Church has, for example, adopted a more forgiving attitude toward suicide, cremation, and the funeral rights for unbaptized infants.[12] Though these changes were generally welcomed by the Irish public and viewed as beneficial, the wider cultural shifts also brought some negative consequences. As the Catholic Church liberalized its attitudes toward death, the country also became more affluent and consumerist, further diminishing the earlier importance attached to death in Christian societies.

Historians have suggested that death in modern culture has become removed from daily life, hidden and sealed away in hospital rooms rather than being discussed publicly as a natural part of human life. Philippe Ariès argues, "The dying man's bedroom has passed from the home to the hospital.... The hospital is the only place where death is sure of escaping a visibility—or what remains of it—that is hereafter regarded as unsuitable and morbid." It follows that because death is not as visible in society, it becomes an unmentionable topic and, as Geoffrey Gorer maintains, now replaces sex as a taboo topic. The reason that death becomes forbidden, according to Ariès, is partly attributable to a more widespread shift away from a communal lifestyle after the First World War. The privatization and denial of death, Ariès contends, result in death becoming artificial, arranged, and controlled by bureaucrats.[13] Throughout the twentieth century, modern technologies and medical advancements made it possible to live longer. But they also made it more difficult for modern individuals to come to terms with death. One of the most profound effects of this shift was that death became culturally invisible and unreal. Furthermore, as religious or mythic narratives declined, modern societies had few alternatives to make sense of death. This lack of meaning increased fear of the end of life, as Western cultures became focused instead on how to live longer.

Death can occur unexpectedly, but the funeral is something that can be controlled and regulated, thus serving to ease the pain of loss by offering the bereaved the illusion of control over death. Thomas Long and Thomas Lynch argue that the modern funeral has become devalued not only because of the commercialization of the funeral business but also because the corpse is often absent from the ceremony. Without the structures or rituals that inform the traditional funeral, the modern secular "memorial service" or "celebration of life" becomes, in Long's words, "a potpourri of made-up pageantries and sentimental gestures combined with a few leftover religious rites that have broken loose from their moorings and floated downstream." According to Long and Lynch, there are several elements required for a "good funeral," whose purpose is, Lynch argues, "to get the dead and the living where they need to be."[14] These elements are the presence of the corpse, the attendance of survivors who cared about the deceased, some way of registering the change of status between living and dead, and the disposition of the dead body.

Narrative serves as a way of mediating between the corpse and the mourners by describing the way that death has altered reality and constitutes an essential response to mortality. This need for narrative often takes religious expression, but it need not. Long claims that the act of participating in the funeral procession itself—transporting the dead to the grave—is to "enact a ritual story with a beginning, middle and an end."[15] The narrative shape of the funeral acts as a way of giving a human life coherence and wholeness, restoring the fracturing effects of death. Narrative, then, serves to mediate between the individual and the communal, offering a way to cope with death and loss. Long and Lynch argue that communal rituals such as the funeral procession have lost some of their significance in modern times and that a restoration of these basic human rituals is necessary in order to cope with grief.

Most funeral rituals in Ireland still feature the presence of the corpse and a procession in which the living transport the dead to the grave. Nevertheless, Lynch and Long's model provides a valuable link between the sociological changes in death practices and the way that these alterations are processed in novelistic narrative. This notion of the funeral as a narrative that tells the story of a person's movement from birth to death becomes particularly important in the last and most recent novel in this study, *The Gathering*, whose structure is informed by Veronica's journey to retrieve her brother's body from England for an Irish burial.

As secular humanist conceptions of death have vied with Catholic ones in recent decades, funeral rituals in Ireland became more hybrid or eclectic. Very few deaths, whether of believers or nonbelievers, are conducted outside of Christian churches altogether. Thus, most people still have church funeral services and are buried in consecrated graveyards. But the Catholic rituals of death also slowly ceded ground to new practices. It has become more common for a family to personalize religious rituals by incorporating aspects of the deceased person's life into the ceremony. Some bereaved families deliver their own eulogy, where once the priest was the only person allowed to perform this task. Others insist on the incorporation of secular songs into the service, where once religious hymns dominated. Additionally, personal items that held special meaning for the deceased are commonly integrated into the memorial service. For some mourners, the addition of such songs and items makes the funeral service more "personal" and meaningful; for others, including disapproving clergy, it represents an unwelcome return of "pre-Christian" or "pagan" elements into the sacred rituals of the church.

These changes in Irish attitudes toward death and dying were invariably complex and rarely linear. It is often assumed in both social and cultural criticism that early-twentieth-century Ireland was a wholly and homogeneously Catholic society and that contemporary Ireland is an almost wholly secular society: this conception represents a serious simplification of the reality. The assumption that Ireland was once wholly Catholic separates Ireland from the wider developments in post-Enlightenment Europe and approaches matters as though scientific and secular humanist developments made no impact on the Irish world before the 1960s. Irish Catholicism has always contended with competing Protestant versions of Christianity, various forms of neopaganism espoused by Yeats and other Revivalists, and forms of socialism and republicanism that were sometimes strongly antireligious in cast. By the same token, even though Irish Catholicism may be in steady recession today, a great many Irish people remain devoutly practicing Catholics, and even "lapsed" or "nonpracticing" Catholics turn to the church to mediate important moments in their lives, especially birth and death. Thus, this book contends that the transition from religious to secular worldviews in Ireland was a radically uneven process, one in which religious and secular systems have competitively overlapped with each other in complex ways throughout the century.

These developments can best be conceptualized by using Raymond Williams's notion of "dominant," "emergent," and "residual" forms of cultural expression. Viewed in Williams's terms, one can argue that the Roman Catholic worldview was the dominant worldview in Ireland at the beginning of the twentieth century, but even then that dominance was contested to various degrees by residual forms of pagan belief or practice (as most obviously embodied in the wake customs mentioned above) and by emergent forms of secular humanist ideology and atheist conviction. As Ireland became more deeply embedded in global capitalism and in new political realities such as the European Economic Community (now European Union), and as the country was exposed to foreign and domestic modes of mass culture, religious and secular worldviews entered into much more open and vocal conflict with each other. It is generally held that the Catholic Church fought against these secularizing forces, but it also tried to accommodate them into its own worldview where possible. By the end of the twentieth century, the relative force of religious and secular elements in Irish society would appear to be of nearly equal weight, creating a situation in which neither the secular humanist view nor the Catholic worldview could claim to be wholly dominant. This awkward coexistence of secular and religious worldviews is further complicated by what Williams argues is the capacity of declining or residual elements of a culture to remain active as "an effective element of the present." Even a once dominant worldview, such as Catholicism in this instance, can still exert a critical function by challenging the norms and values of the culture that has displaced it.[16] Williams's model allows us to check the tendency to assume that every society is becoming or destined to become wholly secular (or wholly religious, for that matter), and it reminds us that transitions are always complex nonlinear affairs. Most of all, Williams's model emphasizes that these apparently whole or solid cultural blocks that we designate as residual, emergent, or dominant are porous, permeable, and constantly seeping into one another.

❦

Scholars addressing Western representations of death in the novel—including Garrett Stewart, Elisabeth Bronfen, Frederick Hoffman, Alan Warren Friedman, and, more recently, David Sherman—focus on what portrayals of death and dying reveal about repressed desires, human anxieties surrounding mortality, and the separation between fiction and reality.[17] Inevitably, as Hoffman and Friedman suggest, novelistic portrayals of death are shaped by philosophical, literary, cultural, and historical developments. Thus, these studies provide a general framework for understanding death in modern Western culture. But the specific historical and cultural context of the Irish novel complicates these models considerably.

The novel is a fascinating medium through which to rethink changing conceptions of death in Irish culture, since the form often tries to reconcile or mediate the social structures of feeling that shape how we think about the end of life. By its very nature, death poses exceptionally acute problems for the meaning of existence, which is equally true for religious and secular societies. The novel tries to give structure and meaning to human life, and therefore it must by definition incorporate some attitude toward the meaning of life or death, even when these matters are not specifically engaged as primary plot points. In the Irish case, matters are complicated by the fact that nineteenth-century Ireland experienced particularly traumatic encounters with death. The Great Famine, which resulted in the death and emigration of millions, is the starkest example. The inability of the weakened Famine victims to bury or attend to their dead undoubtedly impacted conceptions of death and dying, particularly in terms of the living dead, the undead, and increased anxieties surrounding improper burial. This single episode left a lasting legacy that many cultural historians find continued to affect Irish society well into the twentieth century.[18] The nature of this legacy was most obviously discernible in Irish attitudes toward the exceptionally high rate of emigration that followed for decades after the Famine. These departures were often marked by "American wakes" that constructed emigration as a kind of social death. Such wakes continued after the availability of air travel, indicating how strongly the wake persisted as a mode for negotiating death and departure.

If the Irish historical experience of death is a very particular one, how does the Irish novel deal with the complexities of this experience? Peter Brooks argues that the emergence of novelistic plot as a way of ordering human experience can be attributed to the process of secularization. Brooks explains that during the Renaissance and the Enlightenment, religious plots such as the Chosen People, Redemption, and the Second Coming began to lose their earlier hold, and people therefore needed a new way of making sense of their individuated time-bounded mortal existence. Likewise, Ian Watt emphasizes the importance of an emergent middle-class worldview for the development of the novel as form. This middle-class worldview, Watt argues, takes the fate of the individual's relationship to a historically conceived society rather than to the eternity of the next world as its primary focus of interest.[19] Thus, although most British novels were generally respectful of Christianity and might even be strongly Protestant in many of their fundamental assumptions, the novel as a species had a strongly secularizing thrust owing to its focus on worldly pursuits and its adherence to the conventions of realism.

Nevertheless, while the novel as form may indeed have contributed to the shaping of a modern secular worldview, the medium is also, as Mikhail Bakhtin and others argue, an intrinsically dialogic form. It is not a pure form—such as the religious sermon, philosophical tract, sonnet, or elegy—but rather a heterogeneous and composite medium composed of many different types of discourses or idiolects (social, philosophical, legal, moral, religious, secular, and so forth) that mold the devices of character and plot. In Bakhtin's view, these different discourses are seldom easily reconciled with each other, opening up the possibility of their mutual contestation of each other's assumptions.[20] From this standpoint, even if the novel as form is, as argued earlier, generally secular in orientation, there is also scope within the form for at least some contestation of the secular. Thus, the novel tends to be a largely secular form, but a tension between religious and secular modes of discourse can be expected to inform the "raw materials" from which the novel constitutes itself. Many scholars have noted, for example, that the secular thrust of the nineteenth-century English or French realist novel does not hold true for the wider spectrum of the novel as a whole. Hence, the rise of the English realist novel runs alongside Gothic and other "romantic" or "evangelical" modes that retain a strong interest in the supernatural. Likewise, the strongly anticlerical grain of the French realist novel coexists alongside a distinguished French Catholic novel tradition.[21] The novel may, in the main, be a secular form, but secular ideologies can be expected to enter into relation with religious ideologies that retain considerable force.

Brooks's argument that novelistic plots compel a reader because the latter is driven by the need to understand death is particularly important to this study. According to Brooks, narrative is connected to man's "time-boundedness," and plot is "the internal logic of the discourse on mortality."[22] Brooks further argues that Sigmund Freud's theories of *Eros* and *Thanatos*, as outlined in "Beyond the Pleasure Principle," can be mapped onto the psychic functioning of narrative plot itself, which is bound and regulated by these tensions between the life and death instincts. The process of reading compulsively forward through the pages of a novel is, Brooks says, charged by the reader's desire to know the ending, at which point the tensions of the plot are relieved and the narrative that leads to the ending acquires meaning by virtue of the retrospective view. In this sense, the process of reading resembles the death drive or the desire to relieve tension by bringing things to a conclusion.

But novels also need to defer the pleasure of meaning, in order to create suspense and stimulate the reader. In this sense, they also resemble *Eros*, or the life instinct. The novel, as Brooks sees it, plays the life and death instincts against each other. Both are fundamental to the pleasures of novelistic narrative, but the one cannot sustain itself without the other. These conflicting desires for life and death are connected by their arrangement into plot, which Brooks views as the organizing line or intention of narrative. Narratives, Brooks argues, are life-giving in that they arouse and sustain desire, but they also reveal the human desire to tell and to implicate the listener in the "thrust of desire that can never quite speak its name."[23] This desire can never fully be realized, as it would mean the death of desire itself. Thus, even as the plots of novels are driven by this desire to know or understand death, they also possess a contrary urge to delay it. The end of a novel serves in some way to release these tensions between the life and death instincts but does not fully satisfy the reader's desire for meaning.

Brooks's model provides an intriguing starting point from which to examine the way that death shapes the form and structure of the novel in general and contributes both to the desire of the reader to linger in pleasurable if also frustrated suspense and to get to the end of things in order to discover the ultimate meaning that only knowledge of the end can confer. Nevertheless, for all the attention he pays to death and the need for meaning as propulsions that motivate both the forward motion of the novelistic plot and the psychology of the reader, Brooks's insistence on the secularity of the novel disqualifies competing conceptions of death. His understanding of the novel as a form is deeply psychoanalytic and largely ahistorical, and it operates beyond political or cultural difference. But to consider how the novel negotiates competing religious and secular worldviews or ideas of death, cultural history is paramount. Therefore, one of the goals of this study is to extend Brooks's model beyond what it can tell us about the reading process generally so as to deal with more directly historical engagements in the Irish novel with rival conceptions of death.

The five Irish novels in this study have been selected as representations of the wider engagement with death and dying in the modern Irish novel. These works allow us to think about the different ways in which the Irish novel has engaged with ideas of death and dying and to get some sense of how novelistic modes of narrating death have changed over the course of the past century. My object is to examine some moments in which the intersection of death and the Irish modern novel might have broader symptomatic cultural interest.

The approach adopted here is one that views the novel as an elastic literary form that assimilates residual, emergent, and dominant discourses and ideas in a society and fashions these materials into plots or stories of human interest. But as it assimilates these various forces, the novel cannot help but put them into mutual dialogue with each other. The form thus allows scope for critique of these forces as well as for discussion of the ways that these matters are forced into "resolutions" or "endings." It may well be the case, as Brooks argues, that readers read for the end because the end is the only vantage point from which we can gain some sense of transcendent meaning. But in an age in which secular and religious conceptions of what death or "the end" means vie with each other, the meaning of "the end" is itself inevitably in flux. The novel may offer a more definitive sense of closure than social narratives do, but it is debatable whether this sense is necessarily what draws readers to novels or what makes novelistic endings seem increasingly arbitrary or provisional. In any case, if the Irish novel does not offer us a simple window onto Irish society, it does, in this conception of things, try to draw the conflicting worldviews or structures of feeling operative within a society into its narrative fold. The ways in which the novel succeeds—or fails—to do so can tell us interesting things about the society more generally.

This discussion of death and dying in the modern Irish novel begins in chapter 1 with James Joyce's *Ulysses* not only because of that novel's decisive influence on the twentieth-century Irish novel that followed, but also because of the central importance of death to Joyce's most famous work. The deaths encompassed in this work are various: they include the death of Gaelic language and culture; the death of Stephen's belief in Catholicism; the death of Bloom's father and his son, Rudy, and the lingering death of his marriage; perhaps even in a certain way the death of the realist novel as such. If *Ulysses* is viewed in this manner, one might argue that it shares many concerns with the nineteenth-century Irish novel, which was more often preoccupied with the death of Gaelic culture or with the collective deaths of larger communities, such as the Anglo-Irish Ascendancy or the impoverished peasantry, than with individual death. Though these wider communal concerns are always in the background in *Ulysses*, Joyce's focus is nevertheless quite firmly fixated on the individual experience of death as mediated in particular through the characters of Stephen Dedalus and Leopold Bloom.

Beginning the novel with Stephen remembering the tormented dying of his mother, Joyce integrates death throughout the narrative, inserting it into the midst of life. Joyce sees Catholic and liberal secular worldviews as intrinsically linked in terms of their incapacity to make any meaningful sense of death. In the novel Stephen, a secular "lapsed Catholic," and Leopold, a nonreligious Jew, may not share the Catholic convictions of middle-class Dublin society generally, but their lack of religious conviction does not entirely free them from guilt or represent complete liberation. Rather, the younger and older men are unable to resolve their mourning for lost loved ones and therefore cannot fully connect with each other. If, for Joyce, there is any resolution to the problem of death in the modern world, then that solution comes in the form of the novel itself whose plot can be rearranged and its elements recomposed to form new meanings. In the course of *Ulysses*, Catholic rituals are mocked and desacralized but nevertheless absorbed into the novel, and their reordering provides the text with new vitality. The dead are not simply memorialized in Joyce's novel but, rather, work to disturb the narrative order. In this way, death disrupts fixed meanings and destabilizes narrative authority, opening the imaginative possibilities that are shut down by normative novelistic endings, ensuring that death functions as a point of reinvention or rebirth.

The Irish novelists following Joyce do not share his faith in literary narrative to restore life or to overcome the finitude imposed by death. Chapter 2 discusses the complicated relationship between Catholic obligation and human desires in Kate O'Brien's *The Ante-Room*. Like Joyce's *Ulysses*, *The Ante-Room* is steeped in a deeply Catholic world. As the title of *The Ante-Room* suggests, it is a novel that hovers in the waiting chamber between two spaces—life and death—and O'Brien's narrative explores how these forces interpenetrate each other. Set on the three consecutive November holidays that commemorate the dead, the Eve of All Souls, All Souls' Day, and All Saints' Day, the novel's structure suggests that the boundaries between these two worlds are particularly porous on Catholic feast days. There is a strained sense throughout the novel that despite the fact that the worlds of life and death have temporarily converged by means of the observation of the sacred calendar, the Mulqueens cannot inhabit both worlds and must choose between the two. In *The Ante-Room* death does not relieve the tensions between religious and secular worldviews but highlights their incompatible and mutually destructive natures. In refusing to make these worldviews cohere, O'Brien forces the characters, and in turn her readers, to assess what is gained and what is lost when one of these competing ways of being in the world is privileged over the other.

This purgatorial sense of being trapped between life and death finds further and narratively more experimental elaboration in Samuel Beckett's *Malone Dies*. Rather than seeking to transcend death by means of narrative rearrangement as Joyce does, or to compel the reader to weigh the merits of secular and spiritual commitments in the manner of O'Brien, Beckett pushes the idea that death defeats every worldly ambition to such an extreme that the novel itself begins to implode, and all forms of narrative eventually come to seem mere exercises in futility. As Beckett's Malone attempts to narrate his own demise, he initially finds himself following the religious models laid out for him in genres such as the *ars moriendi*, as exemplified by the Anglican Jeremy Taylor's *Rules and Exercises of Holy Dying*. However, Malone soon finds that he cannot adhere to these protocols because he cannot recall any sins to confess, has no memory of his origins, and fails to fully separate himself from his own fictional re-creations. The novel ends with an unfinished sentence, leaving its readers with a sense of dissolution. *Malone Dies* at once reworks the concerns raised by Joyce and O'Brien about how to reconcile religious conceptions of death with the inherently secular form of the novel, while also suggesting that despite the fact that death will always disastrously thwart the human compulsion to find meaning in existence, a human desire for structure and meaning will nevertheless stubbornly, if futilely, persist. Beckett's use of macabre humor works to highlight the pointlessness of attempting to find meaning and order through novelistic narrative, while paradoxically indicating that narrative is the only way of confronting the reality of death and accepting mortality.

Chapter 4, on John McGahern's *The Barracks*, returns to the Catholic-dominated social reality depicted by Joyce and O'Brien, but also shows evidence of its post-Beckettian status in its denial of transcendence and in its refusal of the consolation provided by Catholic notions of eternity. The dead or dying mother depicted in Joyce, O'Brien, and Beckett returns in McGahern's work as a decisive trope in the figure of Elizabeth Reegan, a former nurse and now a housewife in her forties dying of cancer in the rural Midwest of Ireland. Elizabeth's life is strongly tied to her family's welfare and her sense of self tightly bound up with her position in the local community, yet the prospect of dying separates her from all that surrounds her. Death forces Elizabeth to reevaluate her beliefs, causing her to recall the existentialist philosophies that she encountered as a young woman living in London during the Second World War. Elizabeth can neither accept her life in wholly existentialist terms nor yet return to some earlier unthinking faith in God. In *The Barracks* Christianity may help the living to console themselves in the face of death, but it also overwhelms the actuality of death for the dying person and thus serves to negate any really meaningful encounter with the end. McGahern's novel is unique in this study in that it is narrated from the perspective of a dying woman and moves from the individual to the communal, indicating the failures of society to accommodate personal suffering. By contrasting an existentialist focus on the individual quest for meaning with Elizabeth's social reality, McGahern suggests that the individual life is lived socially and that this reality must be taken into account when attempting to make sense of death. Novelistic narrative has an important role in mediating between the individual and the social world in which that individual's life is lived.

Chapter 5 elaborates this conception of death as a force that reveals things that society would prefer to keep hidden. Anne Enright's *The*

Gathering begins with the narrator, Veronica Hegarty, receiving news of her brother Liam's suicide in England. To cope with her loss, Veronica travels to England to recover the body of her brother and to return him to his family in Ireland for burial. As she takes on this task, Veronica tries to write down her family history as a way of making sense of her trauma. In the absence of well-established rituals that bestow meaning on the dead, the act of writing provides Veronica with a way to figuratively experience death in order to help her to reengage with life. Veronica's commitment to writing recalls both Joyce's faith in the endless narrative possibilities of the novel as well as Beckett's Malone as he tries in frustration to order his life through narrative in the face of death's undoing. The Irish wake features prominently in *The Gathering*, but in this instance it is an event transformed from its earlier-nineteenth-century or even Joycean manifestations. The characters in *The Gathering* adhere to the rituals of the Catholic wake not because they believe in any religious or pagan cosmology but out of a sense of obligation to their family and to the dead; it is, as the title suggests, a way of gathering the bereaved and assembling shared memories. Even in the largely secular Ireland of Enright's novel, the wake still serves a social function of passage from this world to the beyond, and adhering to its rituals provides Veronica with a structure for her narrative, allowing her to collocate forgotten memories. *The Gathering* depicts an Ireland in which Catholic and liberal humanist worldviews coexist. Death does not force these views into opposition but rather uncovers shared traumas of the past. In the absence of any strong religious or mythic narrative to bind communities together, it is the process of retrieving and disposing of the dead that supplies a narrative structure that allows the bereaved to process their grief and move on with life.

Despite the prevalence of wakes, death, and dying in Irish novels, the topic has as of yet yielded no major critical studies. The Irish novel has long been wrestling with the meaning of death and dying in a world where religious and secular conceptions of the nature of existence and the end of life have uneasily coexisted and mutually interrogated each other for a long time. As such, the topic of death in the

Irish novel not only is worthy of study but can also contribute to a much deeper understanding of larger cultural shifts. These five novels do not provide answers to the meaning of life or death in modern Ireland, but how they narrate death reveals something of the way that humans conceive of mortality. In order to understand how we live, these novels suggest, we must first come to terms with how we die.

1

Death and Narrative Regeneration

James Joyce's *Ulysses*

The central importance of death to Joyce's *Ulysses* (1922) tends to be overlooked by readers and critics who focus instead on the novel's famous ending, with Molly Bloom's vitalist affirmation of life summed up in the word "Yes."[1] But one might argue that the plot of *Ulysses* is equally driven by a sense of death and loss, its narrative motivated by a desire for understanding of the end of life, a concern evidenced from the first chapter's focus on Stephen Dedalus as he broods over the death of his mother. Joyce's novel confirms death's presence in life, thereby emphasizing the circularity of life's natural cycle and also undoing the normative function of novelistic endings. While Joyce's impulse to create *Ulysses* may have been partly motivated by his mother's death, and while there are undoubtedly autobiographical links between Joyce's and Stephen's grief over their mothers' deaths, what is crucial here is the way that death drives the narrative and serves as a motivation for reinventing the form of the Irish novel.[2] Joyce accomplishes this reinvention by employing the narrative structures of Homer's *Odyssey* and parts of the Catholic liturgy in order to highlight the inability of these structures to adequately order human life. By inserting death into the midst of life, Joyce reinvigorates narrative form, bringing the living and the dead into dialogue and submerging his readers in the infinite play of language that mediates between the actualities of lived experience and the meanings endowed upon that experience by death.

Many deaths shadow the narrative of *Ulysses*: the death of Charles Stewart Parnell; the death of the mother in the lives of several characters; the death of Leopold Bloom's father and of his son, Rudy; as well as the death of Paddy Dignam, whose funeral Bloom attends. While this chapter focuses on the human deaths, the metaphoric deaths of the Irish language and of Stephen's belief in Catholicism also contribute to the novel's sense of loss and to Joyce's attempts to offer literary compensation for these losses.[3] Joyce's preoccupation with death does not begin here, however; it is first evidenced in *Dubliners*' framing stories, "The Sisters" and "The Dead." For Joyce, death represents an irrevocable loss that serves as an impetus for artistic invention and as a driving force for creation. In narrative, Joyce sees the possibility of overcoming the notion of death as a final end, and instead he stresses the power of novelistic narrative to provide everlasting life through the arrangement of words and their endless combinations of meanings. Rather than following a linear plot line or tracing the development of a character over time, the plot of *Ulysses* progresses through deviance and error, by wrong turns and endless associations that destabilize narrative authority and undo the function of novelistic endings that fix meaning in place.

Despite his own agnosticism, Joyce's fictional depictions of death were undoubtedly influenced by his Catholic upbringing. Catholicism, like other religious narratives, provides humans with a way of making sense of death, and *Ulysses* foregrounds Catholic death rituals. While Joyce's novel is widely thought to reject Catholicism as ideology, the religious elements in the narrative demonstrate Joyce's admiration for the power of Catholic ritual to alleviate anxieties surrounding death and to bind communities together.[4] The narrative also offers clear disapproval of Catholicism's restrictions on the body and division of mortal and immortal time. Part of Joyce's task, then, is to undo these divisions and, through his incorporation of religious ceremonies into his novel, to interrogate the function of these rituals. As part of that task, Joyce links Catholic rituals with Jewish burial customs and also loosely connects them with Chinese and Egyptian rituals through Bloom's free associations in "Hades." The inclusion of these various cultural references in his novel is illustrative of Joyce's desire to move beyond compartmentalizing categorizations by bringing seemingly disparate ways of coping with death together.

According to Pericles Lewis, the young Joyce was attracted to the idea of a religion of art, a notion that he moved away from in maturity, instead viewing the discovery of sacredness in everyday experience as the central goal of the artist.[5] For Joyce, daily life serves as an inspiration for art, but Irish life is undeniably shaped by Catholic rituals and informed by Catholic theology that provides a structure for understanding death, even for those individuals who do not profess to believe. In particular, Joyce's conception of narrative is informed by the Catholic notion of the Resurrection, and *Ulysses* witnesses the return of the dead in the form of characters from other of Joyce's fictions; *Finnegans Wake* evokes wake rituals and extends them beyond their religious associations. The resurrection of past characters and their incorporation into the *Ulyssean* narrative illustrate Joyce's principle of literary composition by which he seeks to combine a variety of religious and mythic structures into one narrative form.

Divided into episodes that correspond with the books of *The Odyssey* and employing Catholic rituals and liturgy to highlight the way that religion dominates everyday life in Ireland at the beginning of the twentieth century, *Ulysses* is a novel deeply concerned with the narrative structures that order human life. Religious institutions and novels are alike to the extent that they each try to provide ways of ordering experience and tend to conceive of life retrospectively: they look to the end of life to confer meaning from that terminal vantage point on what went on before. In religious belief, a "good death" redeems life and promises eternity after death. Novels often confer meaning onto a protagonist's life from how that life narratively ends.[6] *Ulysses* does not work this way. In that novel death inhabits life from the outset, and there is no definitive ending. The distinguishing feature of Joyce's novel is its extraordinarily protean language. That language is teeming with association; it interlaces past experience with present rumination and desire for the future into a single verbal weave; it meshes past, present, and future into a single passing day. In this way, language itself becomes that which both contains life and assimilates death; it acquires something of the life-giving force that religions ascribe to the condition of holiness or blissful death. Instead of remaining confined to one individual's experience of the world, Joyce uses language to integrate a variety of individual perspectives into one communal consciousness.[7] By using language in this way, Joyce expands the novel form and increases its fictional possibilities, emphasizing the power of narrative to move beyond the limits created by individual bereavement and to create a more communal process of mourning, which transforms endings into beginnings.

Joyce's experiments in narrative form—from newspaper headline to dramatic form—celebrate the ways that these individual experiences can be bound together through the inner thoughts of ordinary men and women whose memories and free associations make up the novel's content. The style of free indirect discourse in "Telemachus" and "Hades" allows the reader access to Stephen's and Bloom's minds and reveals the ways that their perceptions of reality and connections to the community have been shaped by loss. In "Circe" both characters' anxieties are acted out in dramatic form, stressing the power of narrative to give shape to human emotions. "Circe" then marks a reversal in the way that melancholia functions in the novel: it no longer isolates Stephen and Bloom from the world around them, but becomes a way of relating to that social reality.[8]

The plot of *Ulysses* allows diversions in thought to shape the narrative flow as characters attempt to reconcile their individuality with the communities that surround them. These tensions can be better understood through Freud's notion of *Eros*—a drive aimed at reinforcing communal bonds and preserving life—and the destructive death instinct that compels individuals to destroy these bonds in an effort to return to an inorganic state of quiescence.[9] Joyce's novel seems at first glance to act in the service of *Eros* in that it generates new life through the combination of different words and formal structures into larger and larger units of meaning. At the same time, part of Joyce's process of novelistic composition involves destruction—the breaking down of boundaries and the unfixing of meaning. Death, in Joyce's narrative scheme, is necessary for the creation of life as well as for the process of narrative reinvention. Karen Lawrence argues that the most significant change in the style of narration in *Ulysses* is the "abandonment, roughly halfway through the book, of the third-person narrative style with which *Ulysses* begins." This authoritative narrative style, which features characters' attempts to interpret their pasts, is replaced by what Lawrence calls "a series of stylistic masks," eventually giving way to the "breakdown of the novel as a form and the creation of an encyclopedia of narrative choices" following the "Circe" episode.[10] What Joyce offers his readers is not simply the "death" of narrative and the destruction of the novel form, but the opening of creative and novelistic possibilities.

These possibilities are created by the narrative telling that subverts the authority of third-person narrative through the use of free indirect discourse, calling attention to the impossibility of completely objective narration. As Luke Gibbons observes, the vernacular language that characterizes free indirect discourse "simultaneously carries voices from both inside and outside a culture," thus expressing not only a character's own personal traumas but also the larger cultural upheavals from which they have become inseparable.[11] Gibbons's contention that *Ulysses* is "haunted" by the voices of the dead and by missing people, unwritten histories, and unrealized potential exposes the endless possibilities that exist in Joyce's text and indicates the radical ways that Joyce is employing death. Joyce plays on the dual function of death as that which marks an end to human existence as well as that which, according to religious doctrine and ancient beliefs, represents the beginning of a new life and channels the energies of these two contradictory impulses together.

Mourning characterizes the emotional state of many of *Ulysses*'s characters: Simon Dedalus is still grieving over the death of his wife (Stephen's mother), May; Paddy Dignam's family and all the people that attend Dignam's funeral are in mourning; and even Molly Bloom still laments the loss of her son, Rudy, as apparent from the novel's closing episode, "Penelope." Despite the fact that all these characters are bereaved, Stephen and Bloom remain separated from the community as a result of their bereavements, indicating their inability to reengage with life. Though their losses appear clear to readers—Stephen is mourning the loss of his mother, and Bloom's thoughts continually turn back to his father's suicide and his infant son's premature death—these characters embody Freud's theory of melancholia as articulated in his seminal essay "Mourning and Melancholia" (1917), in that they seem unable to overcome their losses. In his 1923 essay "The Ego and the Id," Freud reworks this idea, redefining the self as "a precipitate of abandoned object-cathexes in that it contains a history of those object-choices."[12] This idea of the self as that which contains a "history" of abandoned object choices allows for a much more nuanced view of melancholia, which, unlike mourning, allows the grieving subject to continue living by incorporating the lost object into itself. In a similar way, *Ulysses* charts Stephen's and Bloom's process of coming to life, which involves the incorporation of lost objects in a movement by assimilation that mirrors *Ulysses*'s plot progression, which is shaped by shifting narrative styles, a technique that incorporates death into the living fabric of the novel.[13]

Freud's theories of *Eros* and the death instinct offer insight into the textual dynamics of *Ulysses*, or what Peter Brooks would call its "psychic functioning": the drives and desires that provide impetus for narrative and compel reading. The emergence of novelistic narrative as a dominant mode of ordering life is, Brooks argues, attributable partly to the process of secularization and marks a falling away from religious and mythic master plots.[14] Brooks asserts that novelistic plot provides a way of structuring the human experience of time and of individual consciousness within the limits of mortality. *Ulysses*, a novel confined to a single day, stretches its own temporal boundaries by presenting the inner thoughts of its characters whose memories extend both forward and backward in time. Similarly, Joyce's novel escapes the finality of death by eluding fixed meaning, using narrative as a means for rebirth through the incorporation of older texts, stories, and oral tales. Joyce ends *Ulysses* with Molly Bloom's "Yes," which, in its affirmation of life, works to undo the function of ending, stressing the endless complexity of life rather than resolving its conflicts or illuminating its meaning.[15]

Novelistic narrative in *Ulysses* offers a new perspective on quotidian human activities such as bathing, going to the pharmacy, mailing a letter, or walking around the city. For Joyce, the unending possibilities of words and their continual reorganization through narrative become his way of countering the guarantees offered by Catholicism, for he remains skeptical of national belonging as secular compensation for religion.[16] Novelistic narrative cannot replace religion but instead provides a new perspective on the human experience of death, highlighting its regenerative properties. Joyce's novel is often bawdy and lewd, taking obvious delight in sex and the pleasures of the flesh. This focus on sex and the body seems on the surface to be an affront to Catholicism. But Joyce's issue is not so much with Catholicism as with its puritanical attitude toward sex. If our physical, bodily experiences of life and death are the fundamental things, then *Ulysses* stresses that they are what matter most and that Catholicism needs to be reminded of this fact.[17]

Joyce's concern with bodies—their functions and limitations—is particularly apparent in the appearance of grotesque corpses throughout the novel, which disrupt the flow of the narrative and serve as reminders of death's often unexpected presence in life. The gruesome corpses encountered by Stephen and Bloom in episodes such as "Proteus," "Hades," and "Circe" are presented as rotting and are associated with liminality, marking the point of rupture between tradition and modernity. David Sherman argues that for Joyce, the corpses of the modern dead are "too strange" for either religion or secularism and create an "ethical and existential task for the living's aesthetic powers, a necessary fiction to replot with a new brilliance that can actualize them as a force and presence in the world."[18] While Joyce finds an answer to this ethical imperative through the replotting of his fictional narrative, the corpses function in a different way at the level of character. The appearance of these abhorrent bodies forces Stephen and Bloom to confront their fears of death, but their inability to move on from these losses is indicative of a larger crisis in modern conceptions of mortality.[19] Despite the seeming unsuitability of mythic or religious narratives to contain modernity's bloated corpses or subdue the unquiet dead, Joyce nevertheless employs one of the most well known of these structures—*The Odyssey*—to organize his narrative, indicating the possibility of reinventing these older forms.[20]

One of the ways that Joyce allows the unrealized potentials of the past to leak into the present is through the retrospective setting of his novel in Dublin in 1904, before the start of World War I. Lewis argues that the "fascination with corpses" apparent in the modernist literature of the 1920s can be traced in part to the trenches of the Great War. While the war's influence on Joyce while he was writing *Ulysses* may help to explain the prominence of dead bodies in the novel, he nevertheless chose to set it before the outbreak of war; the sense of loss here cannot, then, be attributed to that war's atrocities, but indicates a deeper crisis in modern society with relation to death. Indeed, the suddenness of death on the battlefield and massive loss of life during World War I profoundly altered the ways that humans conceived of the end of life and, as Lawrence Langer observes, greatly impacted the historical and personal consciousness of the twentieth century.[21] The novel's sense of loss is further complicated by the fact that it is set in Dublin at a time when the city suffered the fifth-highest death rate in the world, and Catholicism provided a widely shared structure for understanding death and the afterlife.[22] While British and American medical and technological advancements of the early twentieth century resulted in major shifts in death practices—death was now handled by doctors and funeral directors, state bureaucracies controlled burials, and embalming was popularized in the United States—these changes were not as strongly felt in Ireland, where the pattern of modernization was considerably less even.[23] *Ulysses* depicts Ireland at a crossroads: its traditional patterns of life disrupted but not destroyed by modernization, it remains for much of the twentieth century a country neither fully modern nor wholly traditional.

In *Ulysses* the coexistence of these old and new belief systems is apparent in the characters of Stephen and Bloom: the former is attempting to establish himself as an artist but is haunted by his memories of his mother's death, and the latter is Jewish but has been baptized both as Protestant and as Catholic and is religious in outward appearance but secular in belief. These characters create a sense of universality—people are broadly similar in the ways that they live and die—while also focusing on individual perceptions of reality.[24] Bloom's Jewish background enables him to draw parallels between different religions and to make sense of death by imagining it as an equalizer, as he does in "Hades": "Funerals all over the world everywhere every minute. Shoveling them under by the carload doublequick. Thousands every hour. Too many in the world."[25] In contrast, Stephen's semi-secular worldview is at odds with his mother's devout Catholicism, and he struggles to make sense of death, ultimately relying on art to do so. The dominance of Catholic conceptions of heaven is apparent throughout *Ulysses*, but it is the narrative points of view of Bloom and Stephen that reveal the tension between individual experience of the world and Catholic structures that are meant to impart meaning to these experiences.

Aside from Reverend Conmee and Father Coffey, whom Bloom observes performing the Masses in "Lotus-Eaters" and "Hades," very few of the characters in the novel are devout Catholics. However, despite these characters' lack of devotion, the historical weight of Catholicism is so substantial and its interiorization so pervasive that they nonetheless depend almost entirely on Catholicism for their emotional responses to the meaning of life and death. In "Hades" Stephen's father, Simon Dedalus, stands over his wife's grave and expresses a desire to join her in death. When Mr. Powers assures him that she is in a better place now, he responds: "I suppose she's in heaven if there is a heaven."[26] Mr. Dedalus doubts the Catholic promise of heaven, but he can make sense of his grief only with reference to the Catholic doctrine in which his wife believed. This adherence to Catholicism even in the absence of real conviction in its teachings produces a fractured subjectivity, one that is neither devout nor atheistic. Joyce seeks to bind these dualisms together, combining them into a narrative that weaves individual thoughts into a collective story.[27]

The interweaving of Stephen's and Bloom's narrative strands and their ultimate intersection in "Circe" demonstrate the way that Joyce uses death as a point of novelistic reinvention. Beginning with "Telemachus," the first section of this chapter focuses on Stephen's inversion of Catholic rituals in an attempt to structure his experience of loss. This reinvention is most apparent in the repetition of Stephen's vision of his mother's deathbed scene, which features most prominently in "Telemachus," "Proteus," and "Scylla and Charybdis" and comes to a head in "Circe" and acts as an expression of Stephen's guilt for not praying for his mother. This vision is accompanied by lines from the Catholic last rites as well as by W. B. Yeats's poem "Who Goes with Fergus?," indicating the ways the Stephen attempts to make sense of his mother's death through religious ritual and literature. Stephen's conception of death and its connection with literary narrative are important for an understanding of Joyce's own vision of the relationship between death and novelistic narrative. For Joyce, death is both an impetus for narrative creation and expressive of the paralysis that can result from an overly restrictive society unable to move on from its losses. In order to overcome this inertia, Joyce removes the association between death and ending by integrating death throughout the novel.

The second section examines Bloom's observations of the rituals surrounding Paddy Dignam's death in "Hades." This episode foregrounds the theme of the individual's struggle to reconcile personal experience with the moral obligations of society. Bloom's interpretation of the funeral Mass and burial is presented in a quasi-anthropological fashion, indicating his interest in human nature as well as serving to defamiliarize the rituals. In particular, Bloom tends to blur the lines between the sacred and the profane. Working against the contention of sociologists such as Émile Durkheim, who argues that religion binds together a moral community through the practices that distinguish the sacred from the profane, Joyce seeks to bring them together.[28] What unites individuals in *Ulysses* is not their mutual sense of the sacred but their shared experience of the world, the very fact of their human, mortal bodies moving through the routines of everyday life.[29] These shared experiences include those of living bodies as well as those of the dead, such as Dignam, whose corpse threatens to disrupt social order by spilling out onto the road, but also serves as food for new life as it undergoes the process of decomposition.

Section 3 considers the narrative shift from the free indirect discourse of the earlier chapters to dramatic form in "Circe" as the interior thoughts of Stephen and Bloom are enacted. The return of deceased characters such as May Dedalus, Paddy Dignam, and Rudy Bloom marks a turning point where memory is actualized. In this episode, Dignam returns in the form of a beagle, while Stephen's mother appears "emaciated" and "green with gravemould," indicating both the horror of death and the idea of metempsychosis, by which a spirit migrates from one body to the next.[30] Most important, the return of the dead forces Stephen and Bloom to confront their own mortality and to reengage with life.

The fourth section focuses on the novel's last episode, "Penelope," which concludes with Molly Bloom's orgasmic climax that, while appearing simply to affirm life, is also a kind of death in its realization of desire. This ending brings the novel to conclusion by releasing its textual tensions but also, in its emulation of sexual orgasm, returns the reader to the origins of life in its mirroring of the process of conception. Death marks a divide between earthly existence and nonexistence, but Joyce seeks to undo this division. Instead, he depicts life's continuity by creating a text that defies notions of bodily restriction, moving from one character's mind to the next. Joyce at once fulfills the reader's desire for knowledge by allowing access to the thoughts of the characters and frustrates this desire by writing an ending that defers meaning. In *Ulysses* Joyce submerges the reader in the experience of a single day, and his novel ends with an orgasmic release of textual tensions that confirms death's presence in life.

"Telemachus," the opening chapter of *Ulysses*, establishes both death and Catholicism as two of the novel's primary concerns. As the novel begins, Buck Mulligan, bearing "a bowl of lather on which a mirror and a razor lay crossed," holds the bowl in the air and says: *"Introibo ad altare Dei."*[31] The Latin, which translates as "I will go up to God's altar," is said by the priest at the opening of the traditional Catholic Mass and indicates Mulligan's intention to mock Catholic rituals.[32] However, more than simply poking fun at the Mass, Mulligan is attempting to find a way to reach Stephen and to bring him back to reality. While Stephen rejects Catholic teachings, he is grieving over his mother's death and struggling with the guilt he feels at not praying for her on her deathbed. Mulligan's reversal of the Mass provides Stephen with a way to begin to make sense of his grief by connecting religion with everyday life. It also stirs memories of his mother.

As Stephen gazes out at the Irish Sea, he becomes aware of his own need to break with the past. The sea becomes a "bowl of bitter waters" and reminds him of his mother's deathbed and the words *"Liliata rutilantium te confessorum turma circumdet: iubilantium te virginum chorus excipiat,"* part of the Latin Prayers for Dying cited in the Catholic *Layman's Missal*, which translates as "May the glittering throng of confessors, bright as lilies gather about you. May the glorious choir of virgins receive you." According to Gifford, this Latin phrase was offered to commend a dying person to God and could be read in the absence of a priest by any responsible man or woman.[33] According to Catholic doctrine, Stephen, by uttering these words, could have saved his mother from eternal damnation by blessing her before her death in lieu of a priest. His refusal to do so prevents him from moving on with his life. Religious rituals have lost their meaning for Stephen, but his way of thinking about the world remains informed by Catholicism.

In this initial episode, death is ghastly and is associated with the Catholic Church and stasis. As Stephen struggles to shake off any association with the church, he remains haunted by the memory of his mother: "In a dream, silently, she had come to him, her wasted body within its loose graveclothes giving off an odour of wax and rosewood, her breath, bent over him with mute secret words, a faint odour of wetted ashes."[34] Stephen has repressed his own grief and attempted to move on without acknowledging what he has lost in his mother's death.[35] This dream vision of May Dedalus envisions her as a ghost in "brown graveclothes" reminiscent of a monk's brown robe, suggesting that she was a member of the Third Order of St. Francis, a Catholic lay organization. May's Catholic devotion, signified by the grave clothes, is further clarified by the odor of rosewood—a popular wood for rosary beads and crosses—and wax, associated with the candles that are burned during the Catholic Mass. May's ghost is frightening because her wasted body is clearly trying to tell him something that he does not understand. For Stephen, her words are "mute" and "secret," both because he cannot relate to her Catholic devotion and because she now belongs to the world of the dead. In any case, she represents something unknown to Stephen, and throughout the novel he struggles to discover the secret of her words. Death simultaneously draws Stephen back into the past, while the fear of it impels him forward, pushing him to fulfill his goal of becoming an artist.

Stephen's dead mother is also his only connection to the social world he inhabits, and if he banishes her memory, he will lose the understanding of life's mysteries that it provided. Stephen's response to the appearance of her ghost is "Ghoul! Chewer of corpses! No mother! Let me be and let me live!"[36] His identification of his mother as a ghoul—an evil spirit, especially one that robs graves and feeds on dead bodies—and a chewer of corpses indicates an association between the bodies of the dead and sustenance. The phrase "Chewer of corpses" refers to the Catholic ritual of communion in which bread, symbolizing the body of Christ, is consumed. This association of Catholicism with his mother's corpse reminds Stephen of his own liminal position as a lapsed Catholic in a Catholic-dominated world. It also connects Catholicism with stasis, as it is not the living who feed on the dead but the dead themselves who gain nourishment.

Stephen's memories of his mother threaten to impede his engagement with life. Mulligan, with his playful parody of the Catholic Mass, offers a way for Stephen to move forward through the reinvention of Catholic rituals. Stephen admits that he begrudges Mulligan for saying, "*O, it's only Dedalus whose mother is beastly dead*" after his mother died. Mulligan responds, "And what is death, he asked, your mother's or yours or my own? You only saw your mother die. I see them pop off every day in the Mater and Richmond and cut up into tripes in the dissecting room. . . . You wouldn't kneel down and pray for your mother on her deathbed when she asked you. Why? Because you have the cursed jesuit strain in you only it's injected the wrong way." Mulligan attempts to ease the pain of Stephen's mother's death by making light of it: death is everywhere because, as a medical student, he sees so much of it. As Emer Nolan notes, Mulligan's cavalier attitude toward death has the effect of reducing the gravity of Stephen's mother's death and, indeed, "prefigures Bloom's demystifying reflections at Paddy Dignam's funeral."[37] By reducing death to an everyday occurrence, Mulligan desacralizes it. Stephen, however, cannot so easily adopt the idea that his mother's death lacks meaning—hence Mulligan's comment that Stephen has the "cursed jesuit strain" in him, only "it's injected the wrong way." Stephen is unable to pray for his mother on her deathbed because the rituals still hold significance for him and to perform them would be hypocritical. For Mulligan, death is mundane and rituals meaningless, and they can therefore be performed without thought. Mulligan's description of the dead bodies that are "cut up like tripes" in the dissecting room of the hospital offers an image of the corpse not as sacred and whole but as fragmented. The word "tripe" itself could refer to the animal stomach, which is used as food or, used as slang, could refer to writing or speech that is worthless. These meanings are related to Joyce's process of novelistic composition that involves the redeployment of words that might otherwise be considered worthless and uses them as fuel for new art. Joyce's ultimate goal, however, is to restore the fracturing effects of death and to reincorporate it into a narrative whole. This process manages to retain death's mystery by shattering traditional structures of meaning and incorporating them into the narrative of *Ulysses*.

"Telemachus," then, establishes death as one of *Ulysses*'s most prominent themes and also links this theme to Catholicism through the haunting image of May Dedalus, whose death is presented as an improper death in the novel as it defies the Christian notions of a "good death" by which a person accepts their death, sets their affairs in order, and prepares for penance.[38] Stephen's memories of his mother's death, while steeped in Catholic imagery, are characterized primarily by pain and suffering. His refusal to pray for his mother on her deathbed is at once a rejection of Catholicism as well as of the *ars moriendi*, or "art of dying," that underlies the Christian concept of a "good death."[39] While May died of natural causes, Stephen views her death as improper because of his refusal to pray for her and because of Buck Mulligan's contention that this denial constitutes a form of matricide. Mulligan mocks Stephen: "Etiquette is etiquette. He kills his mother but he can't wear grey trousers."[40] Despite his repudiation of the Catholic customs that require him to pray for his mother, Stephen clings to the cultural practice of wearing black mourning clothes after the death of a loved one. Mulligan's mockery of the church highlights Stephen's reverence for ritual and inadvertently provides a way for Stephen to reengage with the world around him.

For Stephen, art replaces religion, providing a way of understanding death by aestheticizing it. This aestheticizing of death is particularly apparent in Stephen's memories of reciting Yeats's "Who Goes with Fergus?" to his mother on her deathbed. The poem was included in the first version of Yeats's play *The Countess Cathleen*, which is set in Ireland during a famine and portrays Cathleen as a female martyr figure. Richard Ellmann describes Joyce's profound interest in the poem and how "its feverish discontent and promise of carefree exile were to enter his own thought, and not long afterwards he set the poem to music and praised it as the best lyric in the world." The poem is sung in the play "to comfort the Countess, who has sold her soul to the powers of darkness so that the people might have food." Similarly, Stephen compensates for his refusal to pray by offering his mother the words of the poem: "She was crying in her wretched bed. For those words, Stephen: love's bitter mystery." Joyce's brother Stanislaus claims that Joyce sang this lyric to their dying brother, George, in 1902, a biographical detail that helps explain why Joyce might have had Stephen sing the poem to his dying mother. For Stephen, art and religion can be brought together through narrative, but it is art, rather than religion, that has power over death. In Stephen's view, life must ultimately be sacrificed for art. But he is burdened by the conflict between his rarefied intellect and his earthly body that is mortal and subject to decay. As Jean Kimball notes, "This is Stephen's problem on Bloomsday: to establish a loving tie to the flesh so that he can become capable of immortalizing that flesh in art."[41] Stephen's love for his mother provided him with a connection to the earthly world, a link he must reestablish if he is to become capable of creation. Whether Stephen is capable of fulfilling his role as artist is a question the novel never fully resolves, but there is a strong suggestion that Bloom provides the connection to the flesh that Stephen seeks.

Stephen's need to establish a bond with the living is evident from his expression of loneliness and desire for human contact in "Proteus": "Touch me.... I am lonely here.... O touch me soon, now. What is the word known to all men?" This question returns in "Circe" when Stephen asks the ghost of his mother, "Tell me the word, mother, if you know now. The word known to all men."[42] Here Stephen assumes that death has provided his mother with an answer to his question. However, Stephen does not know the word, and it is also kept from the reader. Stephen's desire for meaning is left unsatisfied, and he continues to wonder about the word; critics have speculated that the word is either "love" or "death."[43] Kimball concludes that the "word known to all men" is neither "love" nor "death" but the relationship between the two: "Love makes life possible, and Stephen, if he accepts Bloom as the flesh in him, can solve his problem and conquer death through life and art, for Bloom is the flesh that completes the spirit in Stephen, a psychic fact that is made visual in the Gilbert schema where the first three episodes are shown with no corresponding organs."[44] The tension between life-love and death compels the plot of *Ulysses*, but this tension cannot be resolved by one overpowering the other. Joyce seeks a word that can encompass both love and death, indicating his desire to bring together beginning and ending. Since Stephen lacks replacements for the religious structures that offer consolation and cannot incorporate his mother's memory into his own consciousness without accepting Catholicism, he remains unable to move on with life. Bloom, with his demystification of religious ritual and obsession with the body, provides the connection to life that Stephen needs in order to reengage with life. The reappearance of Stephen's mother's ghost throughout *Ulysses* becomes indicative of Joyce's process of narrative recomposition, which brings together sacred and profane through narrative reordering that borrows the forms of religion and myths to tell the tale of daily life.

~

Joyce's desire to reverse traditional novelistic plot in order to reinvent it is particularly apparent in "Hades," where the distinctions between sacred and profane begin to break down. The reversal of these distinctions is made possible through the consciousness of Leopold Bloom. Bloom's thoughts about the rotting corpses in Glasnevin cemetery, in particular, concern death's ability to generate new life, acting as impetus for narrative and positioning death as a beginning. "Hades" begins with Bloom stepping into the funeral carriage that will carry him, along with Simon Dedalus, Martin Cunningham, and Jack Power, to Prospect (Glasnevin) cemetery for the funeral of Paddy Dignam, who has died of alcoholism. The rituals surrounding death bring these men together, yet Bloom's unfamiliarity with Catholic practices and his modern ideas about burial further distance him from this community.

The contrast between traditional customs and modern innovations is established by Simon Dedalus's comment that the funeral procession passing through the center of Dublin in order for everyone to pay respect is "a fine old custom" and that he is "glad to see it has not died out."[45] Dedalus's comment suggests that there is a danger that old customs are being lost but that public funeral processions such as Dignam's still hold communal value.[46] Bloom does not hold the custom in the same reverence as Dedalus, and his observations of the procession make the ritual strange to readers, forcing into relief the living's obligation to the dead and the obstacles modernity poses to that duty. As Sherman argues, "Because of the dead, modernization cannot unfold its narrative of progress as seamlessly as it desires, but must awkwardly double-back in its plot toward some Elpenor-like presence it cannot account for." When the carriage encounters a drove of cattle headed to the slaughterhouse, Bloom remarks, "And another thing I have often thought, is to have municipal funeral trams like they have in Milan, you know. Run the line out to the cemetery gates and have special trams, hearse and carriage and all."[47] Bloom seeks the most efficient way to transport the corpse to its resting site, hinting at the power of technology to remove the dead from everyday life.[48] Bloom's thoughts about technology's efficiency are contrasted with the narrative progress of the "Hades" episode itself, which oscillates between the present (the conversation in the funeral carriage), the past (Bloom's memories as he passes streets he once lived), and the future (the anticipation of arriving at Glasnevin), while remaining largely focused on the funeral procession.

Joyce's choice to put the reader inside the funeral procession instead of outside of it makes him or her a participant rather than an observer. At the same time, our impressions of the procession are filtered through Bloom, who, though he is inside the carriage, focuses on the life outside the window as well as on the conversation around him, thereby linking public and private. This focus on individual consciousness throughout the novel breaks with traditional narrative forms that feature moments of free indirect discourse in an otherwise consistent narrative style and point of view. Ultimately, this interior focus allows the novel to express forgotten voices from the past and to connect them with innovative modern thought.[49] Bloom's observations of Dublin are extremely detailed in his descriptions of shops, houses, and monuments, but also incredibly personal in the memories and associations these places evoke in him. This mode of narration grounds the novel in social reality while also having a defamiliarizing effect, representing common objects in a new light. This method of making the old new through narrative perspective is made especially apparent when Bloom observes the social rituals of Dignam's funeral and finds links between Irish Catholic, Jewish, and pagan rituals.

Throughout "Hades" Bloom remains focused on the cleanliness of his own body in contrast to Dignam's decaying corpse. As he listens to the conversation around him, he notices how clean his nails are and remembers the cake of soap in his pocket. These observations are contrasted with Bloom's earlier comments that the laying out of the corpse is an "unclean job" and his later comparison of the smell of the decaying corpse to the odor of rotted cheese.⁵⁰ Dignam's funeral reminds Bloom of his own mortality; the cake of soap, as a symbol of purity, soothes him. Bloom considers the practicalities of physical demise and what will happen to Dignam's body: he thinks about how death has transformed it, what will happen to it as it decays, and what it will smell like.⁵¹ Bloom's thoughts about those who deal with the dead, such as the women who lay out the body and the Glasnevin groundskeeper, John O'Connell, associate them with the earth and the unclean. This association is characteristic of Jewish belief that the corpse is a source of pollution and transmits uncleanliness.⁵² Joyce sets up this contrast between cleanliness and decay to emphasize the way that death separates the unclean body from the supposedly pure soul. The process of bodily decomposition then breaks down this distinction and has a purifying effect.

The sense of reinventing old forms is furthered by the contrast between Bloom's unorthodox views on death and the traditional views held by the others in the funeral carriage. When Mr. Dedalus comments that Dignam "went" very suddenly and Cunningham and Powers lament his passing, Bloom tries to be optimistic: "—The best death, Mr. Bloom said. Their wideopen eyes looked at him.—No suffering, he said. A moment and all is over. Like dying in sleep. No one spoke." Bloom's conception of sudden death as "the best death" defies many of the Christian rules on dying a "good death" as elaborated in documents such as the medieval *Tractatus*—a six-chapter treatise on rituals and practices of death—as well as the *Ars Moriendi*, which features illustrations of the dying surrounded by temptation. As Alan Warren Friedman argues, "The ideal text of ideal dying, the *ars moriendi*, can be written and performed only in a world with sufficient time and attention for ritual endings."⁵³ Dignam's sudden death does not offer time for an "ideal dying": it is random and chaotic. Bloom's reinterpretation of Catholic funeral rituals indicates a need for an alternate way of making sense of the end, not by abandoning the old structures but by merging them.

Dignam's seemingly random and meaningless death achieves greater significance in Bloom's mind by association with the monument that commemorates the Irish Protestant nationalist leader Charles Stewart Parnell, who also died of a heart attack.[54] Just after he comments on sudden death as being the best kind, Bloom observes the sights out of the window of the carriage: "Dead side of the street this," before noting, "Foundation stone for Parnell. Breakdown. Heart."[55] Again, as in Stephen's search for a word to encompass love and death, Bloom associates death with the heart—the human organ most associated with love. Dignam is linked to Parnell through the words "Breakdown. Heart," as these are the exact words that Martin Cunningham has earlier used to describe Dignam's own death. When Bloom notes that the street is "dead," he simply means that there is no one on it, but the image of a dead street further enhances the episode's prevalent mood of otherworldliness. Paradoxically, the Dublin streets are "dead" to Bloom, while the cemetery is full of life.[56] The foundation of a memorial to Parnell is being constructed, but in Bloom's mind this structure is associated with collapse. Instead of building a community around an idealization of the dead—one that elevates them to a heroic status beyond that of ordinary men—Joyce seeks to integrate the memories of the dead into life, forging a community through a shared sense of life's ability to rejuvenate.[57]

Like Dignam's inauspicious demise, nearly all the deaths alluded to in *Ulysses* are improper, either because they are unexpected or owing to the fact that the rituals surrounding them are indecorously executed. Beginning with May Dedalus's death from cancer whose "good death" was compromised by Stephen's failure to pray for her on her deathbed, all the deaths in the novel fail in some way to achieve the status of a "good death."[58] The various improper deaths in the novel include Dignam's sudden death from alcoholism, Bloom's father's suicide and his infant son Rudy's premature death, and the child's funeral that Bloom passes on the way to Glasnevin.[59] Bloom thinks of how the Friendly Society helped to pay for Rudy's funeral: "Our. Little. Beggar. Baby. Meant nothing. Mistake of nature. If it's healthy it's from the mother. If not from the man."[60] Bloom's sadness after Rudy's death is enhanced by his inability to pay for the burial. He feels further humiliation concerning his sense of masculinity because in ancient Jewish belief, the health of the child is said to be a reflection of the male's virility.[61] As a modern man, Bloom rationally knows that his young son's death has no bearing on his own manhood, but he cannot shake the old beliefs that emasculate him. Again, *Eros*—the sexual love-life instinct—is intimately connected to death, and, in this example, Rudy's death threatens Bloom's desire for life and harms his sexual relationship with Molly. Rudy's death, as well as the other deaths and corpses littered throughout *Ulysses*, works to disrupt social order in the novel, revealing the underlying old customs, superstitions, and religious beliefs that inform conceptions of life and death.

Death's ability to disrupt social order is nowhere more apparent than in the "Hades" funeral procession when Bloom envisions Paddy Dignam's corpse spilled out on the road: "Red face: grey now. Mouth fallen open. Asking what's up now. Quite right to close it. Looks horrid open. Then the insides decompose quickly. Much better to close up all the orifices. Yes, also. With wax. The sphincter loose. Seal up all."[62] Bloom both captures the gross physical realities of death and also points out how a corpse becomes a "memory picture."[63] Death is a loss evident in the emptiness of Dignam's body and his gaping mouth. Society desires to seal up the corpse's orifices in order to make it look lifelike. While wax to Stephen recalls the devotional candles used during Catholic ceremonies, wax for Bloom is a tool for sealing things up.[64] Bloom sees the need of society to keep death sanitized. Sherman argues that this example confirms the corpse as a "site where things can happen," and while it is indeed true, Dignam's corpse does more than "reintroduce narrativity."[65] Death disturbs the novel's order, causing an overflow of memories that run backward and forward across the novel's temporal boundaries. Rather than filling in the gaping holes of meaning in the body of his text, Joyce allows them to remain open as a reminder of absence, inviting the reader to participate in the text's construction by imagining what might have happened.

At Dignam's funeral Mass, Bloom recognizes the burial rituals but fails to comprehend their liturgical meaning. As the priest sprinkles holy water on the coffin, Bloom thinks, "As you were before you rested. It's all written down: he has to do it." Bloom finds the ritual comic because he does not believe in life after death, and "rest" is for him an absurd euphemism for death. Bloom then notes, "Holy water that was, I expect. Shaking sleep out of it. He must be fed up with that job, shaking that thing over all the corpses as they trot up. . . . All the year round he prayed the same thing over them: sleep. On Dignam now." Bloom trivializes the sacred water by referring to the aspergillum, the vessel used in Catholic ceremonies to sprinkle holy water, as "that thing" and calls the finality of death into question by suggesting that the holy water will put everyone under the spell of sleep. Stephen, on the other hand, associates water with the nightmarish vision of drowning and references the sea as "bitter water."[66] To Stephen, the supposedly purifying water reminds him of the failure of ritual. In Bloom's reinterpretation of ritual, the holy water retains the magical ability to unite all in sleep, from which there is the possibility of awakening.

The sense of the dead as lying just beneath the surface of the earth, waiting to awaken, is furthered by Bloom's description of burial, which is focused on the way the corpse feeds new life. When imagining the women who might be willing to marry John O'Connell and live in the cemetery, Bloom thinks: "You might pick up a young widow here. Men like that. Love amongst the tombstones. Romeo. Spice of pleasure. In the midst of death we are in life. Both ends meet. Tantalising for the poor dead. Smell of grilled beefsteaks to the starving."[67] Bloom imagines the dead as hungry for life, thus Stephen's earlier reference to his mother as a "chewer of corpses." Bloom's inversion of this image—from the living feeding off of Christ to the dead feeding off the living—functions in a similar way to his descriptions of the Mass: they return the focus from the religious to everyday life. Even more important, it suggests a means of resurrection outside of the institution of the Catholic Church. The dead of Glasnevin cemetery are restless in their graves and, like the corpse that rises from the sea in "Proteus" or Dignam's overturned casket, threaten to rise up and disturb the social order, refiguring death as ghoulish rebirth.

In *Ulysses* this connection between birth and death is embodied in the figure of the woman who both delivers a child and, in the Irish tradition, also has the job of laying out the corpse.[68] Bloom muses on the women who prepared Dignam's body: "Extraordinary the interest they take in a corpse. Glad to see us go we give them such a trouble in coming. Job seems to suit them. Huggermugger in corners. Slop about in slipperslapper's for fear he'd wake. Then getting it ready. Laying it out." As R. M. Adams notes, "the word 'slipper-slapper' gets double resonance here from the circumstances under which it appears nearly four hundred pages later in 'Circe.'" In "Circe" Bloom asks, "Is this Mrs. Mack's?" And Zoe answers, "No, eightyone. Mrs. Cohen's. You might go farther and fare worse. Mother Slipperslapper. (familiarly) She's on the job herself tonight with the vet her tipster that gives her all the winners and pays for her son in Oxford." Adams interprets this repetition of the word to indicate that Bloom in "Circe" has returned to a house of death, but he also notes the connotations with Old Cohen's bed as a place both of conception and birth and of sleep and death. Gifford also comments that the phrase "slipper-slapper" is often attributed to a song entitled "The Fox" or "Old Mother Slipper-slapper" in which the mother is a surrogate for Ireland.[69] Joyce builds on this association of Ireland and mother to further his idea of it as a place of resurgence. Burial is particularly important to this transformation, as "huggermugger" is used to refer to the secret way that Polonius was interred in Shakespeare's *Hamlet*. Polonius is buried without ceremony to hide the fact that it is Hamlet who has killed him. The word "huggermugger" implies secrecy and a lack of ceremony. In Bloom's mind, however, the secrecy attached to the women's laying out the corpse is owing not to a lack of ceremony but to an adherence to ritual. The women are described as sneaking around because of their fear of waking the dead. For Joyce, the body's ability to regenerate offers the possibility of the dead returning in altered form, linking the revival of the corpse with the Catholic resurrection.

The dead who have been threatening to return finally do reemerge in "Circe," which serves as a climax to the plot of the novel as the inner consciousnesses of Stephen and of Bloom converge in a hallucinatory phantasmagoria. "Circe" is set in a brothel in the red-light district of Dublin known as Nighttown. The dramatic form of this episode is unique to the novel, suggesting that Stephen's and Bloom's inner thoughts are no longer being presented as monologue but are being acted out in contrapuntal dialogue. This formal shift depicts the individual's power to shape his or her social reality through the acting out of repressed desires. "Circe," however, does not simply mark Stephen's and Bloom's emergence from their melancholic states; it also involves a blasting apart of boundaries, merging their inner thoughts and desires together. This assimilation of consciousness provides them with a way of overcoming their individual grief communally: by incorporating their memories of the dead into their lives.[70]

In this episode, the dead souls of Rudy, Stephen's mother, and Paddy Dignam all reappear. Additionally, characters from other of Joyce's fictional works are reincarnated as well. These include Tom Kernan, Joe Hynes, Paddy Leonard, Nosey Flynn, Lenehan, Crofton, Mrs. Riorden, and Father Farley as well as characters from history, among them Charles Stewart Parnell's brother John Howard Parnell and the Irish evicted tenants. Joyce also gives dramatic voice to "Old Sins" and even to "the Gramophone." Paddy Dignam reemerges, in the form of a beagle with Dignam's face, to defend Bloom. His reappearance returns to the novel's recurrent theme of metempsychosis, or the "transmigration of souls," the idea that the deceased can return in either animal or human form.

When Bloom asks how it is possible that Dignam should speak with the voice of Esau, Dignam's ghost replies, "By metempsychosis. Spooks." In "Calypso" Molly asks Bloom what "metempsychosis" means, and Bloom replies, "It's Greek: from the Greek. That means the transmigration of souls." When Molly asks him to explain it in a simpler way, Bloom thinks, "Bone them young so they metempsychosis. That we live after death. Our souls. That a man's soul after he dies, Dignam's soul." "Circe," then, offers a direct manifestation of Bloom's earlier thoughts about metempsychosis. Joyce uses the theme of metempsychosis as a fictional technique that, through free indirect discourse, enables the narration to move from the consciousness of

Stephen on to the consciousness of Bloom and Molly. For Joyce, the novel form not only provides access to the inner consciousness of the individual but also brings together these various voices through imagination. As Karen Lawrence observes, in this episode, "The omitted is now committed."[71] "Circe," then, is a manifestation of the desires that impel the novel itself. If the novel is driven by a need to know or understand death, the resurrection of the dead in this episode promises a fulfillment of that desire. However, the dead provide no answers about the meaning of life or the hereafter, and the focus of the text after "Circe" shifts to the living.

"Circe" offers a distillation of narrative that slows time from the rapidly moving thoughts of the characters in free indirect discourse to the descriptions of the characters' actions in dialogue form. The formal shift breaks the temporal boundaries of the novel that separate past events from present as the dead return. The reappearance of Stephen's mother, for example, represents the return of the past and with it the Catholic conceptions of sin that Stephen wants to leave behind. Stephen seeks from his mother the "word known to all men," which he believes she knows. The mother does not answer but instead beseeches Stephen to pray. Stephen reacts violently to his mother's benediction: "*He lifts his ashplant high with both hands and smashes the chandelier. Time's livid flame leaps and, in the following darkness, ruin of all space, shattered glass and toppling masonry.*" In doing so, he frees "time's livid flame," indicating that time has been shattered, the divide between mortal and eternal life broken. This break, which results in a temporary lapse into darkness, prepares for the redisposition of narrative structures that will ensue. As the episode progresses, distant voices are heard calling, "Dublin's burning! Dublin's burning!" followed by the description: "*The midnight sun is darkened. The earth trembles. The dead of Dublin from Prospect and Mount Jerome in white sheepskin overcoats and black goatfell cloaks arise and appear to many. A chasm opens with a noiseless yawn.*"[72] These stage directions mimic the description of the aftermath of the Crucifixion: "And the earth did quake, and the rocks rent; And the graves were opened; and many bodies of the saints which slept arose, And came of the graves after his resurrection, and went into the holy city, and appeared unto many" (Matt. 27:51–53). Joyce's evocation of the biblical description of Christ's Resurrection indicates a desire to make the mundane sacred. By borrowing the language of the Bible and applying the description of the aftermath of the Crucifixion to Dublin during a night in the brothel, Joyce stresses the importance of the episode as a turning point in the novel.[73] The dead here rise up out of the earth not owing to Christ's sacrifice but owing to Joyce's narrative recomposition. In "Circe" Joyce conveys the horror of death and the way that trauma inhabits the unconscious imaginations of its characters. But while the scene registers the deep psychic wishes of Stephen and Bloom, it does so in seriocomic fashion. The episode skillfully combines the tragic, the grotesque, the comic, and even the hilarious. The reader is torn between a sense of the episode as tragic and a sense of it as comic roustabout.

As "Circe" nears its conclusion, the reader witnesses a further breakdown of fixed structures of sense making.[74] Stephen's sentences fragment when he cannot remember Yeats's poem "Who Goes with Fergus?" that he recited to his mother on her deathbed: with *prolonged vowels* Stephen murmurs, "Who . . . drive . . . Fergus now And pierce . . . wood's woven shade."[75] Bloom, who has attempted to rouse Stephen, is puzzled by the words. When Stephen continues, " . . . shadows . . . the woods . . . white breast . . . dim sea," Bloom thinks how Stephen looks like his mother and misinterprets his words as alluding to an amorous encounter with a girl. The poem that reminded Stephen of his mother's deathbed in the beginning of the novel now becomes disjointed and, through Bloom's misreading, becomes associated with the promise of romantic love. Here, as elsewhere, Bloom's interpretation makes the old new, reversing previous associations and finding in them new possibilities. "Circe," then, represents a watershed moment in *Ulysses* when the novel begins to remake itself.

At the end of "Circe," Bloom's dead son, Rudy, appears dressed in an "Eton suit with glass shoes and a little bronze helmet," reading a Jewish text. Rudy's resurrection is indicative of a return to innocence: the "white lambkin" he carries is a symbol of sacrifice in the

Jewish context; in the Christian context, it is suggestive of Jesus or the Lamb of God.[76] Rudy's appearance carries with it connotations of redemption from sin, a cleansing of all that has taken place in the brothel. He also, as Lawrence observes, dramatizes possibilities that have been lost to death.[77] Curiously, the innocence associated with the vision of Rudy is contrasted with the event that preceded it: the episode's Black Mass and its reversal of the Catholic Mass. The Black Mass is a satanic ritual, primarily concerning reversal, in which the Christian Mass is perverted and is associated with the Witches' Sabbath.[78] Joyce's use of this ritual indicates a further desire to undo meaning through repetition with a difference. Far from suggesting that Joyce is attempting to endow these rituals with satanic meaning, this reversal instead entails a relaxation of novelistic boundaries, confusing linear notions of plot.

The Black Mass in "Circe" further desacralizes Catholic rituals in order to reverse notions of the sacred and the profane. Here Joyce seeks to reconcile human mortality, the death of the body, with the notion of immortality and the idea of the eternal soul that leaves the body at the moment of death. While many novels depict the linear progression of a protagonist's life from birth to death, *Ulysses* focuses on people's experience of the world. Through his use of free indirect discourse and shifting narrative forms, Joyce creates a novel that offers a view of a communal consciousness bound by a shared experience of the world. The endless recycling of old forms such as the English novel, the Bible, and Shakespearean drama offers a new means of understanding the world, by bringing together these extremes. The function of religion in society is then radicalized, shifting from a prohibitive force to a connective one. "Circe" marks a shift in the novel where instead of moving toward death—the end point that divides mortal and eternal life—the plot of *Ulysses* returns to an earlier time. The episode begins with Bloom's encounter with his deceased mother and father, at which point he finds himself dressed in a blue Oxford suit, indicating a return to his youth. The appearance of Gerty, the young lame girl whom Bloom masturbates to in "Nausicaa," is further indicative of the ways that "Circe" repeats the novel's earlier plot points. The return of the dead and the shift in form serve to reinvigorate the novel's textual energies, creating a narrative with endless meanings.

Ulysses's last episode, "Penelope," functions as a final climax in its orgasmic release of textual tensions, which "Circe" failed to dissipate, but it also uses memories of the past to rejuvenate the present, undoing the normative function of ending by affirming death in life. Molly Bloom's monologue incorporates the novel's various themes into a breathless stream-of-consciousness narrative that serves as both a culmination of textual desire and, paradoxically, the reawakening of textual energies.[79] In its realization of desire, the monologue represents a kind of death, but Molly's persistent use of the word "yes" and the narrative emulation of sexual climax seem to contradict this notion, suggesting that this ending is closer to a burst of new life rather than death. Throughout this episode, Molly's associations run together, linking Dignam's funeral, Stephen's mother, and little Rudy's demise. Violating the traditional rules of punctuation, the episode is divided into eight exorbitant sentences, giving the narrative a sense of movement, indicative of the continuity between beginning and ending. Beginning the novel with the loss of Stephen's mother, Joyce ends with Molly's grief for her dead son, establishing her role as a mother figure who embraces both birth and death in her final "yes."

"Penelope" begins with Molly lying in the bed she shares with Leopold, returning to earlier associations of the bed as a site of conception and death. This setting recalls the end of "Hades," when Bloom leaves the cemetery and thinks, "Plenty to see and hear and feel yet. Feel live warm beings near you. Let them sleep in their maggoty beds. They are not going to get me this innings. Warm beds: warm fullblooded life."[80] Celebrating the triumph of life over death, Bloom associates life with warmth, blood, and human contact. Bloom's affirmation of life prefigures Molly's soliloquy but with a vital difference: in "Penelope" death is not simply escaped but incorporated into life. In Molly's narrative love and death are associated through sexual orgasm—*la petite mort*—which is at once a kind of death in its satisfaction of desire but also carries with it the possibility of conceiving new life.

Molly's monologue defies the rules of grammar and traditional novelistic discourse, but rather than breaking down the structures of the novel form, Joyce employs this strategy to forge a continuity between text and life. The link is apparent not only in the style of the episode—which is written as if Molly were speaking her thoughts aloud—but also in the way that letters and newspapers feature in the monologue itself. Molly considers the possibility that Bloom is cheating on her, "because the day before yesterday he was scribbling something in a letter when I came into the front room to show him Dignams death in the paper as if something told me and he covered up with the blottingpaper pretending to be thinking about business so very probably that was it to somebody who thinks she has a softy in him because all men get a bit like that at his age."[81] Bloom's covering up the letter with blotting paper is suggestive of the ink from texts bleeding together. The news of Dignam's death reveals underlying tensions in the Blooms' marriage. Letters and newspapers serve as a bridge between individual thoughts and the everyday world. Joyce's use of these texts indicates his faith in the possibility of narrative to create continuity between life and death.

The newspaper in particular provides Molly with knowledge of events in the novel that she did not witness: "this is the fruits of Mr. Paddy Dignam yes they were all in great style at the grand funeral in the paper Boylan brought in if they saw a real officers funeral thatd be something reversed arms muffled drums . . . they call that friendship killing and then burying one another and they all with their wives and families at home."[82] Obtaining a glimpse of the men in their funeral attire from the newspaper, Molly scoffs at the idea that Dignam's funeral was stylish. Dignam died of alcoholism, but Molly blames his friends for his death. Molly's musings about Dignam's death multiply her thoughts, leading her from Dignam to May Dedalus to Stephen and then to Rudy. Joyce presents Molly's proliferation of associations to give a sense of death as a force that regenerates. The lack of punctuation and persistent use of the word "yes" give the monologue an incantatory quality, as if Molly is tying these events together and affirming their continuity through her narrative.

Molly's thoughts about Stephen, in particular, link the beginning and the end of the novel. Molly remembers how eleven years ago, she saw Stephen with his father and mother driving to the Kingsbridge station: "I was in mourning thats 11 years ago now yes hed be 11 though what was the good in going into mourning for what was neither one thing nor the other of course he insisted hed go into mourning for the cat I suppose hes a man by now by this time he was an innocent boy then." Molly's thoughts fuse past, present, and future as she remembers that the first time she saw Stephen, she was in mourning for Rudy; in retrospect she considers this mourning pointless and imagines Stephen as a man now. Molly uses the pronoun "he" confusingly in this passage to refer to both Stephen and to Bloom, whom she thinks overly sentimental, as he would mourn the cat if it died. Molly's narrative brings together Stephen and Bloom through an association with mourning, in turn aiding in her recollection of her own grief. Though she seems here to have come to terms with Rudy's death, a few pages later it is evident that she blames herself for the loss. Molly's sense of guilt stems from her belief that she cursed Rudy's birth because she and Bloom conceived him after she became aroused while watching two dogs mate. She goes on to reason: "I shouldn't have buried him in that wooly jacket I knitted crying as I was but give it to some poor child but I knew well Id never have another our 1st death too it was but we were never the same since O Im not going to think myself into the glooms about that any more I wonder why he wouldnt stay the night."[83] Molly's sorrow over Rudy's death overwhelms her practicality. Despite her insistence on moving on, she and Bloom have not been the same since Rudy's death. In contrast to the fragmented sentences that make up Bloom's and Stephen's narratives, Molly's soliloquy ties all these memories into giant sentences, creating a sense of extension rather than breakdown.

Throughout *Ulysses* Joyce portrays women's bodies as the origins of both *Eros* and *Thanatos* in their ability to arouse sexual desire as well as to satisfy it. The feminine role is both to give birth to new life and to tend to and lay out the bodies of the dead. Molly's soliloquy furthers this association as it draws together the fragments of Bloom's and Stephen's narratives and recomposes these snippets of memories into a new textual body. This act of narrative recomposition is associated with the erotic as Molly recalls past lovers and as the chapter builds toward a final orgasmic release when she relives the moment when she agreed to marry Bloom. Molly remembers: "I asked him with my eyes to ask again yes and then he asked me would I yes to say yes my mountain flower and first I put my arms around him yes and drew him down to me so he could feel my breasts all perfume yes and his heart was going like mad yes and yes I said yes I will Yes." This ending to the novel emulates sexual climax by means of an innovative style that submerges the reader in a moment of textual bliss. As Roland Barthes argues, "Bliss may come only with the *absolutely new*, for only the new disturbs (weakness) consciousness"; he further asserts, "Confronting it, the New is bliss (Freud: 'In the adult, novelty always constitutes the condition for orgasm')."[84] Defying the rules of grammar, incorporating taboo topics such as orgasm and menstruation, and employing stream-of-consciousness narrative, Joyce creates an entirely new experience of reading that captures for the reader this feeling of bliss. This ending is exceptional because, while it releases textual tensions and therefore represents a kind of *petite mort*, the reader's desire for meaning does not stop here. In fact, Molly is remembering a moment of pleasure that she may or may not be experiencing.[85] Her memory of Bloom's proposal sends the reader back to a moment that occurred before the text and therefore represents a return to origins rather than a final resting place. *Ulysses* begins with a son mourning for his mother and ends with a mother mourning for her son. The plot of the novel, though driven by death and loss, does not move linearly toward a resolution of mourning. Molly's mourning, unlike Stephen's, serves to create continuity between life and death. In its realization of desire, this ending returns readers to the origins of the novel and results in a sense of rejuvenation of novelistic possibilities rather than in absolute narrative closure.

~

Beginning with a focus on grief and loss, *Ulysses* is a novel concerned not only with the living but also with the dead. Joyce's ability to craft a novel from the fragments of various narrative forms indicates his faith in the ability of narrative to revive the potential futures lost to death. Ending the novel with a rejuvenation of textual energies, Joyce returns to the premodern tradition of the Irish wake that featured amusements for the living, often involving matchmaking and procreation.[86] Thus, Joyce's *Ulysses* contains many reversals and inversions, not simply of Catholic rituals but also of the plot of the novel that is time bound and driven toward an understanding of death. In the themes of death and resurrection, Joyce evokes premodern folklore narratives and the theme of the "revival of the seemingly dead," which Ilana Harlow has observed throughout Irish folktales and oral narratives.[87]

According to Harlow, popular forms of oral narrative that feature tales of people who feign death for the purpose of a joke, as well as certain wake customs that treat the corpse as if it were alive, reveal a deeper premodern belief in the return of the dead.[88] These tales provide more than just another structure for Joyce's novel; rather, they inform his conception of the novel form itself. This notion of revival finds further elaboration in *Finnegans Wake*, Joyce's final novel. *Finnegans Wake* takes its title and initial theme from the Irish American folk song, which describes how Finnegan is brought back from death when a fight breaks out at his wake and whiskey is spilled on his coffin, a revival of the "seemingly dead," similar to those revivals in the oral folk narratives recorded by Harlow. Thus, in Joyce's figuration, the novelistic text is a corpse made up of dead meanings in need of reinvention. If reading is, as Brooks argues, driven by the desire to know death, then Joyce's proliferation of words, his incorporation of different languages, images, songs, and rituals, ultimately precludes any definitive ending that bestows retrospective meaning on the text.

Joyce's goal in incorporating a variety of deaths—accident, illness, and suicide—is not simply to show us that there are many ways of dying as life continues on in a linear stream toward the end. Rather, Joyce seeks to overcome the boundaries of the novel that fix meaning at the end, creating a text that is reborn with each new reading.[89] By fictionally inverting the rituals of the Catholic Church, Joyce attempts to revive a shared meaning attached to death. For Joyce, narrative holds the possibility of salvation through its ability to subvert old meanings. Joyce's reinvention of the Irish novel and its previous associations with a dead tradition has profound implications for the novelists writing in his wake. Blasting open the boundaries of the conventional novel form, Joyce offers a creative freedom to Irish novelists previously confined by conceptions of the past as dead or dying. Yet Joyce's attempts to overcome death by creating a text that highlights life's continuity are not so easily repeated. As religious conceptions of heaven and the afterlife begin to fade, so too does the consolation they once offered. The four remaining authors in this study—Kate O'Brien, Samuel Beckett, John McGahern, and Anne Enright—while undoubtedly influenced by Joyce's reinvention of the Irish novel through death and rebirth, do not share his faith in the possibilities of narrative to restore and rejuvenate. Their differences, as well as their similarities, provide valuable insight into changing conceptions of death and dying in Irish literature and culture.

2

The Eve of All Souls and the Death of Desire

Kate O'Brien's *The Ante-Room*

Kate O'Brien's second novel, *The Ante-Room* (1934), is one of her most accomplished works, presenting a sophisticated reflection on Irish conceptions of death, dying, and the afterlife. Divided into sections that correspond with the three consecutive Catholic feast days commemorating the dead, the novel focuses on the dying Teresa Mulqueen and the effects her imminent death has on her adult children, Reggie, Marie-Rose, and Agnes, whose futures appear bleak. Running parallel to this plot line is another that follows Agnes's moral conflict as she struggles to suppress her amorous feelings for Marie-Rose's husband, Vincent, while also attending to the needs of her dying mother. Agnes wants to remain loyal to her sister and is torn between her devout Catholic upbringing that values personal sacrifice for the good of the community and secular commitments to individual self-realization, which impel her to develop her relationship with Vincent. The novel's extended deathbed scene focuses on agonized emotions, so much so that action is curtailed, but O'Brien's omniscient narrative allows the reader access to Agnes's thoughts as well as to those of more marginal characters such as Vincent and Marie-Rose. This technique allows for a nuanced portrayal of the beneficial aspects of Catholicism as well as offering a disturbing picture of the dangers resulting from its repression of human instincts. While Agnes and Vincent's resolution to sacrifice their happiness for each other for the good of their family suggests the necessity of Catholicism in keeping human desires in check, the ending of the novel implies something very different. In a novel suffused with a sense of anticipation of Teresa's death, Vincent's unexpected suicide defies readerly expectation and calls Catholic values into question. In her portrayal of death and dying, O'Brien suggests that while desire can be destructive, so too can Catholic repression.

Written between the world wars, at a time when the Catholic Church's spiritual hegemony dominated all aspects of Irish life, stifling intellectual freedom and curtailing women's rights, *The Ante-Room* offers a strong liberal Catholic critique of the restrictive aspects of Catholicism, arguing that the consolation it provides is little compensation for the ongoing suffering it causes.[1] *The Ante-Room*'s shift in focus from the plot of the dying mother to the spiritual death of Agnes's desires indicates the ways that O'Brien employs the form of the novel to critique the church's domination of Irish life. Rather than a bildungsroman trajectory of self-development, *The Ante-Room* depicts the opposite: the failure of self-realization, the slow decline of the Catholic bourgeois class, and a running down of textual energies that ends in self-destruction. In this way, O'Brien highlights how the church's restrictions have not simply impacted the life of the individual but also limited artistic expression and the very development of the Irish novel itself.

Some understanding of O'Brien's conflicted attitude toward Catholicism provides insight into her depictions of death and her conception of literary narrative. Born in Limerick in 1897, Kate O'Brien was one of Ireland's most accomplished middle-class female novelists writing in the early twentieth century. Like Joyce, O'Brien was raised Catholic but later identified as an agnostic. After suffering the loss of her mother at an early age, she was sent to a Catholic boarding school.[2] These early experiences shaped O'Brien's literary sensibility and may account for the melancholic tone to her fiction. Her biographer Eibhear Walshe has rightly identified this tone as "the melancholy of the lapsed Catholic at odds with the sexual codes of her religious education, yet still enraptured with the beauty of its ceremonies and its liturgy."[3] This sense of O'Brien as a lapsed Catholic who retains appreciation for the church's rituals while also being critical of religion's stranglehold over Irish society is similar to Joyce's own feelings about the church and is later echoed by John McGahern in *The Barracks*. *The Ante-Room* evokes the familiar trope of the dying or dead mother so apparent in Joyce's *Ulysses*, but while O'Brien's *The Ante-Room* is permeated with nostalgia for a world that is fading away, *Ulysses* is concerned with the new life that arises out of death. O'Brien does not share Joyce's interest in Catholic theology. Rather, she is interested in Catholicism's social function and the spiritual dilemmas that emerge when this function becomes too closely allied with its religious purpose.[4]

In *The Ante-Room*, O'Brien's omniscient narration provides access to Agnes's conflicted consciousness while also depicting her social reality, including the thoughts of other characters. This narrative perspective offers a sympathetic view of the Catholic rituals that give life meaning for believers while also showing, via dissident thought and interiority, the restraints that society can place on personal freedom. Thus, O'Brien does not condemn Catholicism as a wholly negative impediment to personal fulfillment, but she does suggest that the convergence of its social and religious functions results in a repressive environment that stifles personal expression and isolates individuals. Another distinctive feature of O'Brien's fiction is her portrayal of characters who are in some way sexually dissident. While *The Ante-Room* is not as controversial in its depiction of sexuality as O'Brien's last published novel, *As Music and Splendor* (1958), which features a lesbian relationship, her interest in forbidden love and the religious and societal restrictions that limit these desires is clear in her portrayal of Vincent and Agnes's relationship. The novel begins with Agnes attempting to suppress her love for Vincent through prayer. Although this entreaty initially appears to work, Vincent's admission that he loves her proves too much for Agnes, and she confesses her own feeling for him. This love plot contrasts with the death plot that follows Teresa's impending demise, creating a tense atmosphere of expectancy at the family home, Roseholm.

In the narrative, death represents the end of human control, and the experience of watching a loved one die provokes an outbreak of human impulses. Yet even as Vincent and Agnes's feelings for each other threaten to overpower their self-control, they remain aware of the commitments that restrain them. What prevents them from fulfilling their sexual desire for one another is not simply their Catholic faith but the unhappy fact that Vincent is already married to Marie-Rose. Acting on their feelings would not only defy rules surrounding the Catholic sacrament of marriage but also violate their familial bonds. Devout Catholics might view Vincent and Agnes's love as tragic but would argue that the sacrifice of these characters' happiness is necessary for the greater good of the community. O'Brien takes a different view, suggesting that Agnes and Vincent's separation is harmful and that the suffering that is caused by their suppression of desire far outweighs the benefits of maintaining family loyalties and adhering to social conventions.

The Ante-Room is often identified as a Catholic novel, not because of its endorsement of religious belief but because of its sharp criticism of the restrictions imposed by orthodox Catholicism.[5] A distinctive feature of O'Brien's fiction is that it seems on the surface to endorse Catholic belief in its sympathetic portrayals of Catholic characters who find solace in their faith during morally trying times. Yet O'Brien uses these instances of moral conflict to critique the ways in which Irish society and religion were becoming too deeply entwined. The retrospective setting of *The Ante-Room* in the 1880s is significant because it precedes some of the most violent events in Irish history, such as the 1916 Easter Rising, the Irish War of Independence, and the Irish Civil War. Writing in the wake of these events, O'Brien's portrayal of Catholic attitudes toward death, particularly her description of Vincent's suicide, is undoubtedly influenced by the strong relationship between Catholicism, Irish nationalism, and martyrdom that characterized this period of Irish history.

The Ante-Room returns readers to the fictional village of Mellick, the setting of her first novel, *Without My Cloak* (1931), and a place that strongly resembles the Limerick of O'Brien's own upbringing. Additionally, Teresa Mulqueen of *The Ante-Room* is a descendant of the Considine family, whose fortunes were recounted in detail in *Without*

My Cloak. While that novel depicts the rise of the Irish Catholic bourgeoisie, *The Ante-Room* describes its demise, elaborating on the earlier novel's underlying criticism of the oppressive nature of family bonds that limit imaginative and spiritual freedom. *The Ante-Room* is strongly elegiac in tone, a feeling that is enhanced by its 1880s setting. Declan Kiberd describes *The Ante-Room* as "a resigned and minimalist elegy." He argues that "this is a world that is doomed to die even as it is revealed, and one which might be said never to have fully existed at all."[6] The novel's focus on Teresa's deathbed heightens this sense of a dying world, but Kiberd rightly points out that *The Ante-Room*'s pervasive melancholy can also be attributed to the failure of this world and its characters to have ever lived at all, a failure that creates a sense of unfulfilled potential.

The feast days that structure the novel are times when the dead are celebrated, bringing a pervasive sense of death into ordinary life for a period of three consecutive days. This merging of the worlds of the living and the dead is a key motif in the novel as the characters struggle to accept death. They are trapped in a purgatorial state as they await Teresa's demise, an end that promises a new beginning. The "ante-room," or waiting room, of the novel's title is a metaphor for purgatory, suggesting that the characters must all remain trapped in suffering before they can be released to either heaven or hell. As they strive to make sense of mortality, these characters find that the promise of eternal life has the effect of easing the pain of death by denying its finality. While Catholicism seeks to regulate thoughts and action, keeping human desires in check, death threatens to break down this restrained order of things. O'Brien cleverly sets up the novel as being driven by the desire for Teresa's death, which will relieve the painful sense of waiting, and then she maintains the reader's interest by complicating Teresa's progression toward death.

One of the first complications is that Teresa cannot die peacefully until she has ordered her life. Teresa's greatest worry is the fate of her son, Reggie, whose syphilis prevents him from marrying. This failure puts his future in jeopardy, making him solely reliant on his dying mother for support. Teresa's attempts to order her life are richly evocative of the Christian notion of achieving a "good death" so prevalent in nineteenth-century deathbed narratives.[7] However, Teresa's is no ordinary deathbed scene, as her dying occupies the entire novel. *The Ante-Room* is a predominantly realist work, and it is therefore of particular importance that O'Brien avoids describing Teresa's death and that the reader's last view of Teresa is presented through Agnes's eyes as she envies the look of happiness on her dying mother's face. The central conflict of the novel is not whether Teresa will live or die, but the struggle between *Eros*, which seeks to preserve life and to bind the community together, and *Thanatos*, the death instinct, which seeks to dissolve the bonds to community and life in order to achieve restful inertia in death.

This central conflict of *The Ante-Room*, between love and death, is best understood through a closer examination of Sigmund Freud's theory of the death drive and civilization's control of that destructive human impulse through guilt and punishment. Freud argues that it is the struggle between these two contradictory impulses—one that seeks to preserve life, the other that seeks to return things to their primeval state of rest—that constitutes human life. This tension manifests itself in the individual mind as a sense of guilt that creates a need for punishment. Civilizations then use this guilt to establish laws and create punishments to keep human impulses in check.[8] However, when this guilt increases in an individual without a corresponding feeling of connection with the community, as it does for Vincent in *The Ante-Room*, it can result in self-destruction.

Religions, according to Freud, claim to "redeem mankind of this sense of guilt, which they call sin. From the manner in which, in Christianity, this redemption is achieved—by the sacrificial death of a single person, who in this manner takes upon himself a guilt that is common to everyone—we have been able to infer what the first occasion may have been on which this primal guilt, which was also the beginning of civilization, was acquired."[9] In Catholicism redemption is achieved through self-sacrifice and through sacrificial death. This focus on sacrificial death further complicates the relationship between death and Catholicism. Christianity supposedly controls the human impulse toward death and destruction in order to promote feelings of love and unity, but it accomplishes this sense of community through the sacrificial death of one man. In the Irish context, this relationship is even more problematic, as Irish nationalism during the late nineteenth and early twentieth centuries relied heavily on Catholic images and rhetoric of self-sacrifice.

Freud's theory is particularly helpful in understanding Vincent's suicide in *The Ante-Room*. Vincent's self-destructive impulse can be attributed to the overwhelming sense of guilt that comes from his need to suppress his love for Agnes. His Catholic faith is of little use in controlling this impulse; in fact, he confuses the symbolism of Christ's sacrificial death with his own destructive instincts. Vincent dies believing that he is sacrificing his life for the greater good of the community and under the illusion that his sin will be overlooked and that he will be delivered to heaven. In this instance, the guilt resulting from the repression of desire has not warded off destructive human impulses; it has, rather, directed these impulses to disastrous ends. Narrated from Vincent's perspective, O'Brien uses this last death scene to return readers to the source of man's primal guilt and the origins of the Catholic religion, at once highlighting the dangers inherent in Catholic dominance over society while indicating a need to return religion to its symbolic function.

Vincent's suicide brings together the novel's parallel plot lines and reverses their trajectory. Agnes and Vincent's love, which according to traditional novelistic marriage plots should end in nuptials, ends in death, while Teresa's illness, which should end in death, ends inconclusively, with Teresa finding happiness in the news that Reggie is engaged to Nurse Cunningham.[10] The sense of closure that Teresa's "good death" would have provided is undone by Vincent's death, which does little to resolve any of the novel's central conflicts. The novel's last lines—"Darling Mother. He pulled the trigger, his thoughts far off in boyhood"—establish Vincent's belief that he will be reunited with his mother in heaven. These lines both sound a false note and are also, as Kiberd notes, "melodramatic" and "richly sceptical."[11] Ending the novel in this way, O'Brien not only defies the expectations surrounding the fictional deathbed scene but in her depiction of the failure of the love plot and the death plot also offers her strongest critique of Catholicism.[12] What is perhaps most revealing about the radical nature of this ending is the negative way it was received by critics and, indeed, the way O'Brien herself regarded it later in life.

O'Brien thought *The Ante-Room* to be the greatest of her novels, despite the fact that it was not as popular as *Without My Cloak*.[13] It is curious, then, to discover that she doubted the strength of its ending. According to Walshe, at the end of her writing career, O'Brien "wrote of [*The Ante-Room*] as an unappreciated work but her purest, strongest and best-formed, doubting, in hindsight, the wisdom of Vincent's suicide at the end, but still calling it 'a damn good example of a tragic novel.'"[14] O'Brien's own classification of *The Ante-Room* as a "tragic novel" highlights the subversive nature of the ending. Vincent's suicide and Agnes's spiritual death call into question the Catholic privileging of communal over individual needs and underscore the disadvantages of this restrictive environment. O'Brien's feelings about *The Ante-Room* seem contradictory: she calls it her "best-formed" work, but she also doubts the quality of its design as she expresses reservations about the ending.[15]

Lorna Reynolds sees Vincent's suicide as the realization of "the tragic potential of the theme [of Catholic feeling at the level of individual consciousness]" but views such an ending as a "mistake." Reynolds implies that this ending is a mistake because it suggests that Catholicism has such a strong hold that it can be escaped only through death. Adele Dalsimer similarly argues that "although his death preserves Agnes for her family, Vincent's suicide is a weak ending to this powerful book. The final words should be Agnes's. She has made the righteous decision; everything she has known or been taught has led to it. And yet we see her choice of Marie-Rose above all else as we see her mother's love for Reggie and Vincent's passion for his dead mother: as a retreat from the future."[16] While Vincent's death may indeed "preserve" Agnes for her family, she is of little use to them now, as O'Brien has just described her spiritual death. What makes this ending intriguing is the fact that it is not narrated from Agnes's point of view but offered from the perspective of Vincent, an eccentric outsider whose attempts to reconcile the Catholic focus on the community with secular self-fulfillment result in the delusion that suicide will return him to his mother in heaven. This ending may indeed represent a "retreat from the future," but it also serves as a warning for readers to avoid this tragic mistake. Without a loosening of Catholic restrictions in order to account for individual desires and human frailty, there can be no hope of a promising future.

The Ante-Room's ending leaves Teresa on the brink of death, her family still trapped in a state of waiting. Yet Teresa has reached a kind of heaven on earth through the knowledge that Reggie's fate is settled. O'Brien renders the loss of Agnes's soul as a fate worse than death, while the illusion of a Christian heaven provides hope for her mother. Vincent's suicide—the last death in the novel—is the only one that is realized in the narrative time of *The Ante-Room*, making it the most important of all the deaths. The fact that it is a suicide calls into question Catholic values by highlighting the risk inherent in placing the attainment of heaven outside of mortal time, offering eternal life as a reward for a life well lived. Refusing to provide her readers with the expected novelistic closure, O'Brien challenges them to reexamine the religious and social limitations that deny desire and endorse suffering. Using death to expose the dangerous split between secular notions of individual self-fulfillment and Catholic control over human impulses, O'Brien calls for a change in Catholic attitudes toward sin to adapt to an increasingly secular modern society.

O'Brien's critique of Irish middle-class Catholic society is incisive but also ambivalent, and, though her novel is set in the late nineteenth century, it can be applied equally to the early to mid-twentieth century as well. *The Ante-Room*'s portrayal of a society that has been stymied by its uneasy relationship to dogmatic Catholic ideology suggests that while the church's rigid rules may have been necessary to bind society together during one of the most turbulent historical changes in the nineteenth century as Ireland emerged from the devastation of the Great Famine and made strides toward achieving independence from British rule, they now function as a kind of prison in an era of independence. O'Brien's characters find Catholic ideology so powerful because it has enabled the middle class's rise to power, even as it now distorts the lives of these characters. In essence, what O'Brien is suggesting is that although strict adherence to Catholic ideology has been useful for the middle class as a collective, it has been harmful to the individual.[17]

Nevertheless, while O'Brien may be critical of the way that commitments to family and religious codes can smother individual desires, her novel curiously repeats on a narrative level the wider middle-class impasse it diagnoses. In the novel Agnes and Vincent are the most transgressive characters in terms of their illicit love, which not only is a religious sin but also poses a threat to bourgeois society, as it endangers social and familial bonds. Yet no matter how much they emotionally transgress the ideologies that oppress them, Agnes and Vincent ultimately conform to the values they doubt. Agnes's last expressed wish in the novel is to die, and Vincent's last action is to kill himself, an action that he frames in Catholic terms. In this way, *The Ante-Room* portrays conformity as suicidal but fails to narratively conceive of any alternative. In the end, O'Brien's novel suggests that the conflict between Catholicism and secular modernity cannot be resolved. The old world may be dying, but *The Ante-Room* offers no vision of a new world to come.

※

The first of *The Ante-Room*'s three sections, "The Eve of All Saints," is named after a Catholic holiday of pagan origin that traditionally marks the end of the harvest. According to Irish folklore, it is a time when the boundary between life and death becomes permeable and the dead return to their ancestral homes.[18] An awareness of the holiday's origins informs this section, which depicts the restrictive social environment at Roseholm as the Mulqueen family agonizes over Teresa's impending death. Contrasting Teresa's perception of reality with Agnes's, O'Brien sets up a conflict between mortal and eternal time and between the inner and outer realities of the characters. Agnes finds solace in thoughts of heaven and comfort in the structure that Catholicism gives to her life. Her inner joy in her Catholic faith contrasts with the way that Catholic restrictions dominate her outer reality, limiting her self-expression. Death loosens these boundaries, triggering a return of dormant feelings. For Teresa, death awakens concerns over the future, and the Catholic promise of heaven offers her an escape from earthly suffering.

The title of the section, "The Eve of All Saints," rather than the more common secular name, Halloween, indicates that it is a Catholic feast day. Even so, the residual elements of the day's pagan origins are apparent in the ghostly imagery, references to autumn light and to the return of "dead" desires. The section's name has the dual function of reminding the reader of the Catholic rituals that structure the everyday lives of the characters and recalling Ireland's pagan past and the spiritual realm that lies outside the bounds of mortal time. In her assessment of *The Ante-Room*'s structure, Heather Ingman observes, "The feast-days are both inside time, being marked on the Church calendar, and outside, in that they focus believers' attention on the lives of those who have passed into a dimension beyond time."[19] Catholicism places eternity beyond the limit of human mortality, beyond time. The structuring of the novel around the church calendar infuses the narrative with two levels of temporality: one inside of time and one outside of it. The occasion of the Eve of All Saints allows the dead to return to earth, thus placing those individuals who have passed beyond time, but who have not yet entered heaven, into the lives of those still living. At the same time, the characters in the novel seek to transcend the boundaries of time and their ordinary lives (signified by the ticking clock and church bells) through dreams and imaginings.

The opening lines of the novel make clear this concern with time and establish the fragility of the crepuscular world O'Brien depicts: "By eight o'clock the last day of October was about as well lighted as it would be." The setting of the novel on the last day of October, just as dawn breaks with its "tenuous sunshine" and "an air that moved elegiacally and carried a shroud of mist," suggests a world that, while still living, is slowly dying. This sense of time running out contributes to the novel's somber mood. While the thoughts of the various characters are disparate, the church bells summon them back to reality, bringing them together by creating a shared sense of time. Yet there is a sense that these characters' lives have lost their meaning and that their desires are impossible to realize. In this environment reminders of time serve only to aggravate Teresa's suffering. Thinking of her mother's anguish, Agnes remembers, "Once, when every whisper in the house had seemed to aggravate her mother's suffering, she had suggested silencing that clock. But Teresa would not have it. 'When I can't hear it any more,' she said, 'I'll know I'm at the Judgment Seat.'"[20] Teresa's conflicting emotions about the clock highlight the beneficial as well as the detrimental effects of Catholicism. While the restraints Catholicism imposes on human life can cause suffering, religious faith also has the power to alleviate this suffering with the promise of eternal life.

Unlike Teresa, who wholly believes in the Catholic promise of eternal life, Agnes questions its focus on sacrifice. For Agnes, the physical world is linked with suffering, as she expresses in her description of being awakened by the Mass bells. Agnes sleeps with the curtains open so that at eight o'clock, "she was aware of movement and light," again suggesting that the clock draws her back to the movement of life. For Agnes, the "bells and clocks and thin autumnal light" that wake her are not necessarily positive but are "calling her back to things she did not wish to face."[21] Presumably, the reality that Agnes does not want to face is her mother's death. The bells serve as both keepers of time and a call to prayer; the clock and thin autumnal light are reminders of the season (autumn's melancholy associations with the coming of winter) and of the fleeting nature of human life. The tolling Mass bells also remind Agnes of her Catholic faith and her communal responsibilities, separating her dreams from the world of everyday existence.

While the Mass bells remind Agnes of the reality she does not want to face, they affirm Teresa's life and the devout Catholicism she represents. Teresa reflects, "So well did she know those sounds that often now, when in pain or in a morphia half-dream, she was uncertain whether she heard or only remembered them. But this morning, after a night which she must not let herself think about, there had suddenly been some real sleep and a lull. She was awake, and the pain was vague, hardly there at all, you might say."[22] Teresa has a difficult time discerning the difference between the dreams induced by morphine and her waking reality. Her proximity to death has caused this line to be blurred, whereas for Agnes the two remain incompatible. This contrast in perception indicates the differences between their views of Catholicism: Teresa unthinkingly adheres to Catholic teachings, whereas Agnes, though devout, questions the ability of Catholic rituals to control passion or to ease suffering.

O'Brien juxtaposes these two devoutly Catholic yet distinctly different views in order to highlight the division between the present—filled with limitations—and the possibilities of the future. The setting of the Eve of All Saints offers a glimpse of that future possibility, as it encourages a bridging of the divide between mortal existence and the promise of everlasting life in heaven. According to Frederick Hoffman, "One of the most important of all elements in the literary view of mortality is the time-space relationship that at any moment helps to define human nature. This relationship is indispensably associated with eternity and its effect upon the measurement or the sensing of time."[23] A secular sense of time can be constricted to the life span of the individual or stretched to encompass the longer life of the nation or even of the species. But religions (including Catholicism) fold it into an even wider sense of time before the world (before creation) and an eternity, which is essentially a cancellation of time. On the Eve of All Saints, this division of space is mended, temporarily freeing the characters from their obligations to the living and allowing them to mingle with the dead.

Teresa in particular feels the effect of eternity on her experience of time. As she lies in her sickbed, Teresa's prayers and thoughts of eternity are interrupted by her earthly concerns about her family. Despite any delirium brought on by her illness or medication, Teresa remains aware of the feast day; when she inquires of Nurse Cunningham what feast it is, she is reminded that it is the thirty-first of October. The nurse does not appear to recognize the significance of the date, but

Teresa immediately identifies it as the Eve of All Saints. She begins her prayers: "She shut her eyes and let the brown beads slip through her worn-out fingers. 'First Glorious Mystery, the Resurrection. Our Father who art in Heaven—there had always been great fun in this house on the Eve of all Saints.'"[24] The loosening of the beads around Teresa's fingers is suggestive of a slackening of Catholic restrictions. The formal prayer of the "Our Father" is contrasted with the more secular sense of "fun" associated with Halloween, as Teresa's prayers are interrupted by memories of the parties her family used to have on All Saints' Eve. But this memory too is spoiled, as Teresa remembers that a specialist doctor is coming from Dublin the next day. The thought of the doctor's visit makes her anxious, as it reminds her of how unprepared her family—particularly Reggie—is to live life without her. Thus, the fate of Teresa's soul is contingent on the ordering of her family's life. The only way that she can reconcile mortal and eternal time is by correlating her death with the fulfillment of her desire that Reggie find someone to care for him.

A further breakdown of the boundaries separating past from present occurs when Agnes receives news that her sister, Marie-Rose, is arriving at Roseholm that day. Despite the fact that Marie-Rose's letter says that her husband, Vincent, will not accompany her, Agnes suspects that he will. Agnes is reminded of her infatuation with Vincent and begins to see his ghost everywhere: "She glanced at the place at her right hand, at the empty chair which he would fill—and saw him in it, more clearly than to-night she would allow herself to do."[25] Vincent is not an actual ghost, but throughout the novel he is presented as a shadow of himself, as a living-dead figure who represents the ghost of Agnes's suppressed desires. The use of "ghost" here is best understood in the way Luke Gibbons employs the term as a "spectre" that "emanates from an incomplete project of self-formation, as in the failure to internalize memory itself in a colonial culture," rather than in the more Freudian sense of a projection of inner life.[26] Vincent, then, can be seen as an undeveloped character, one whose unfulfilled potential and failure to achieve a fully formed sense of self permeate the claustrophobic air at Roseholm. When Agnes thinks of the change in Vincent's personality that has occurred since he married Marie-Rose—he has changed from gay to sulky and intelligent to bored—she begins to feel sorry for him. She notes that he has transformed from "heavenly beautiful to mortally, so that time and pain could scar him."[27] Agnes's role as narrator is critical here as Vincent is presented from her point of view. The bounds of marriage have wounded Vincent, made him vulnerable, and, most of all, made him mortal. Now he is subject to the ravages of both time and pain.

Yet Agnes's love has a redemptive quality as Vincent is transformed in her mind, allowing the old godlike Vincent to return, albeit in spectral form. Her feelings for Vincent are so strong that she does not simply imagine him but feels compelled to reach out and touch him, reinforcing the idea of the spectre as something that is both imagined and a physical manifestation of unlived futures. This scene echoes an earlier one in which Agnes "stared at the empty chair and saw its ghost with pity, so that involuntarily her hand ran along the edge of the table as if to touch his lying there. Then, chilled with fear by such an odd impulse, she drew it back and shivered."[28] This description of Agnes's behavior is indicative of the level of restraint in her daily life; her impulse to run her hand along the edge of the table frightens her. At the same time, her urge is to touch an imagined hand rather than an actual one, indicating the hold that the past has over the present.

In an effort to banish her desire for Vincent, Agnes attempts to pray, hoping that confessing her sins will work to keep temptations at bay. Although Agnes knows that her profession of faith will help relieve her suffering, she remains reluctant to pray: "At Mass and in her prayers Agnes sought to face her moral problem—but kept ashamedly turning back from its categorical demands. 'I'm doing no harm to anyone, and I have nothing else of my own to think about.'"[29] Agnes's beliefs are shaped by two incompatible worldviews: a Catholic ideology and a secular sense of personal fulfillment, and she has difficulty separating them from one another. In the religious society Agnes inhabits, she does not really have a choice between personal fulfillment and communal commitments; forsaking Catholicism would mean social death for her. Instead, she attempts to kill her feelings for Vincent through confession. It is during that confession that Catholicism's role in controlling human impulses becomes particularly apparent.

Sitting in the confession box, thinking of the impure thoughts about Vincent she must confess to the priest, Agnes warns herself not to be too dramatic: "Our absurdity must be more a wound to the Eternal, Agnes thought, than our guilt. To have sinned was only too nauseatingly ordinary; not to see that and to make a self-inflating drama of sin was not so ordinary, but more despicable."[30] Sin is an inevitable part of human existence, but to treat sin too seriously is to elevate humanity, since it suggests that one might even become sinless. In contrast, to dismiss sin as trivial is to dismiss humanity too much, suggesting it has no value—a nihilism that finds its extreme in murder or suicide. In her confession Agnes feels trapped between these contradictory impulses of avoiding melodrama or nihilistic absurdity. Agnes's dilemma can be connected to the style that O'Brien uses to portray it: *The Ante-Room* does not fit completely into the categories of either popular cultural melodrama or modernism.

Having listened to her confession, the priest tells Agnes that her love for Vincent will "die" as a result of prayer: "That is in any case the fate of earthly love, my child. Whereas in the search for God, in the idea of God there is matter for eternity."[31] The priest privileges the spiritual world that exists outside of time over both the psychological realm of desires and the mortal realm dominated by physical needs. The function of Catholicism here is to impose order on society, an order that forces the fulfillment of desires outside of mortal time. The drama of Agnes's struggle between individual and communal needs is self-contained in that, for most of the novel, the dramatic battle of emotions is fought inside her head. Conversely, Teresa's struggle with death is fought on the public level, and we are only occasionally given insight into her thoughts. O'Brien uses this contrast between Agnes and Teresa to highlight the ways in which even devout Catholics have been influenced by secular thought. In its attempts to control all aspects of social and religious life, the Catholic Church is at risk of losing its religious function and becoming associated solely with restriction.

O'Brien's desire to undo this association between religious and social functions is apparent in her narrative focus on the inner lives of her characters. The plot of *The Ante-Room* itself is driven by thought rather than action. As they await their mother's death, the children deal with their conflicting emotions not through dialogue but through private observations. The narrative focus on thoughts over action emphasizes the oppressive and predetermined nature of these characters who are unable to bring about major changes in their lives. Early in the novel, Agnes notes that her "final fear was of words. When she was a schoolgirl once or twice she had had to accuse herself of vague curiosities and stirrings of her sensual imagination—matters which she had not understood, but which she knew to wear the looks of sins against the sixth commandment."[32] Agnes fears words because they give shape to her thoughts; speech and writing become associates of action. However, these forms of expression do not accurately convey meaning, and the novel often depicts conflicts between what is said and what is meant. Words are dangerous because they can provoke action and inflict suffering, while their meanings are often ambiguous. O'Brien's narrative mediates between thought and action, depicting the moral and religious conflicts that define life and, in turn, shape conceptions of death.

The link between the spiritual world and earthly existence is maintained in Christianity through symbols such as the crucifix that is a reminder of Christ's suffering, the wine that represents his blood, and the bread that represents his body.[33] These images serve as reminders of the sacrifices necessary to attain eternal life. The social environment depicted in *The Ante-Room* is so suffused with religious imagery that it permeates the consciousness of characters such as Agnes, who turns to prayer to rid herself of her emergent sense of selfhood. As she attends Mass before her confession, Agnes realizes that she must suppress what she most desires in order to live: she must rid herself of her feelings for Vincent. As she sits through the Benediction, she thinks, "She was not herself. She was, much more fortunately, part of a formula. What was required of her was to be accurate in moving with that formula."[34] The thought that she is *not* herself comforts Agnes. She is much more comfortable living according to a formula dictated by her family and the Catholic Church than she is attending to her own needs. While Agnes wants to conform to society's expectations of her, her emotions get in the way and compel her to do things that she should not do.

As Agnes struggles to overcome her feelings for Vincent, she makes a distinction between rational knowledge and felt emotion: "She only wanted to know this—that God blessed her. Not to feel it. Feelings, amorphous things, pressed on each other, merged, disturbed—were of their very nature stained by human life."[35] By describing these ever-shifting emotions as somehow soiled by human life, Agnes suggests that intentions are contaminated by action. Knowledge, then, is an untainted spiritual thing rather than something attained through experience. Paradoxically, Agnes consistently puts her trust in emotions over rationality, in bodily experience over celestial wisdom. Despite her desire simply to know that God blesses her, she seeks proof of his blessing in her life and experience.

In particular, Agnes focuses on her memories to bring her knowledge and clarity or to redeem the present. Her memories, however, often fail to bring her the enlightenment she seeks. When Agnes returns from confession, she finds that Vincent has indeed accompanied Marie-Rose to Roseholm. At the dinner table, Agnes witnesses Vincent's "mood of radiance" with "a hint of madness in it" that she interprets as unhappiness in his marriage and thinks that it must be a "test of heaven" that he is treating her so kindly. Vincent's kindness toward her reminds Agnes of the feelings she has repressed in order to live. After some thought, Agnes decides, "Even Heaven, it seemed, could not quite do that, could not quite bring back the demigod of that far time. Her memory was a better re-creator, and this charmer who was carrying off his part so well was no more than a tired, unhappy man, impelled to give a superb impersonation of the dead."[36] By describing Vincent in this way, Agnes suggests that the person she fell in love with has died and that any feelings she retains for him are linked with the past.

Yet Agnes cannot banish her feelings for Vincent; they are greater than her religious constraints. The image of Vincent as an impersonator of the dead resonates deeply with the end of the novel when he takes his own life. There is an inverse logic in Agnes's description—Vincent's old self, the one that has been killed through his marriage to Marie-Rose, arises in Agnes's memory as a "ghost" that he must impersonate in order to live. Living here is equated with assuming the identity of the dead. However, Vincent's assumption of "dead" desires and his embrace of the ghostly ultimately prove dangerously incompatible with his social reality.

Although the novel is organized around Teresa's dying body, the predominant narrative focuses on the death of the souls whose bodies are still living (namely, Agnes and Vincent). The Eve of All Saints section brings together characters who are trapped in purgatory. As the evening comes to an end, it becomes clear that while Catholicism offers some hope for resolving the conflicts between body and soul, it does not solve the problem of desire itself, which persists even when repressed.[37] This first section, the longest section of the novel, highlights the tensions between religious and secular worldviews, weighing the pros and cons of Catholic belief. The benefits are made clear in the narrative of Dr. Curran, Teresa's doctor, as he observes the Mulqueen family's devotion.

As a "hereditary Catholic," Curran takes prayer only as a "matter of human impulse." He reflects, "The pros and cons of religion never stayed his thought, life as he found it being the field of his concern. And in that field it seemed to him that the Catholic Church provided as good a system as might be found for keeping the human animal in order—a necessity which he emphatically accepted. A good system, because through thick and thin, it exacted a soul of every man and instilled in the very lowest of its creatures an innocent familiarity with things not apprehended of the flesh."[38] Curran's description again calls to mind Freud's claim that Christianity is useful in keeping human desires in check by offering redemption from the sense of guilt created by the contradictory desires of *Eros* and *Thanatos*.

O'Brien sees control over human instincts as one of the benefits of religion but is also skeptical of this view as it closely aligns Catholicism's religious function with its social one, ignoring its spiritual benefits and highlighting its power to punish. For Dr. Curran, humans are simply bundles of instincts, which must be controlled externally by the church. Death, as that which cannot be fully apprehended by science, lies in the realm of religion and is at once the limit of the church's regulation and also its final goal. As the dead return on the Eve of All Saints, so too do all the impulses Catholicism attempts to keep at bay. In this section, prayers are offered in vain, as the overwhelming powers of human emotion threaten to overcome the narrative, illustrating the weakness in the church's domination over these compulsions as well as the futility of its attempts to control death.

The feast day that lends its name to the novel's second section, "The Feast of All Saints," marks the beginning of winter according to the ancient Celtic calendar as well as the Catholic feast of celebration for the souls that have reached heaven.[39] Again, O'Brien skillfully combines both the Catholic and the pagan meanings of the feast day, using them to inform the mood of the chapter and to lend added significance to its events. This section is characterized by an increasing sense of approaching death, as dying is extended beyond Teresa Mulqueen to the landscape, which is described as freezing and icy, descriptions consistent with the approach of winter. There is also a strong sense of martyrdom, reinforcing the feast day's association with the Catholic celebration of all the saints who died for the sins of mankind. Although Teresa's unwavering faith in God and her endurance of physical pain cast her as a martyr figure from the beginning of the novel, it is Agnes who is martyred in the end, as she must sacrifice her own happiness for the good of her family. Contrary to Dr. Curran's view, O'Brien's portrayal of Agnes implies that Catholicism does not simply keep human desires in check but gives human life a higher purpose.

"The Feast of All Saints" begins with Teresa's dressing room being transformed into the sanctuary of a chapel where the mystery of the transubstantiation will occur. According to the doctrine of transubstantiation, during the Mass bread and wine become the body and blood of Christ. This notion of Christ's sacrifice being made real is essential to this section of the novel in which fantasy is actualized. The power of O'Brien's omniscient narrative is apparent in the description of the Mass scene: "After the Offertory, the room, the chapel, became profoundly quiet. A stillness which seemed of vast but undefined significance and as if exacted by some unknown, external will, which unified while it subjugated this assemblage of isolated hearts." The power of Catholic ritual to unify is particularly apparent in this passage in which human life is given a distinct, if unknown, meaning and the isolated hearts of those individuals in the room are brought together. Despite the advantages apparent in the uniting power of ritual, the negative aspects of Catholicism are present here in the word "subjugate," implying that the ritual is conquering their individual wills. The failure of religious ritual to vanquish individual human suffering is apparent in Teresa's physical pain, and she is described as being "disappointed that she should be in pain through this blessed Mass in her room, and now when Our Lord Himself was in her heart. If only she could pray, if only she could pray properly!"[40] Teresa cannot pray properly because her concerns over Reggie's fate distract her from fully surrendering herself to prayer.

By contrasting Teresa's deathbed prayers for Reggie's happiness with Agnes's longings for Vincent, O'Brien interrogates the power that religious faith has to shape human actions and to change social reality. In this section dreams appear to come true, but reality can never match imagination. Vincent and Agnes finally express their feelings for each other verbally, even if they remain unable to be together. Vincent tells Agnes, "'When I'm in Dublin, I manage most of the time to live a fantasy life,' he said, 'but here, when I see you, how real you are, with activities and plans that have nothing to do with me—that goes. And then there is nothing.'"[41] Vincent's fantasy of Agnes has been destroyed by the reality of her appearance in front of him, yet she remains unattainable, resulting in a situation in which he is able to live neither in fantasy nor in reality.

Agnes similarly thinks of the fantasies that make life bearable. She considers how Marie-Rose hates realities and Vincent lives a fantasy life; her father maintains his cheerfulness in the face of his wife's death, and her mother's morphine-induced dreams keep her from despair, but Agnes questions what her own delusions might be: "Was her present foolery the pharisaical one that she had, by one confession, one repentance, killed desire?" In this recognition that she cannot kill desire, Agnes confronts the reality that Catholicism lacks the power to relieve her of her problems. She thinks of Vincent's reference to a fantasy life and of how she knows what he means: "He thought it was an escape, apparently, but it had been her prison. To her it had lately seemed, in its sweetness, its uncertainty, its truthfulness, to be taking on the very bulk and texture of reality. It had made fantasy of every day and what she saw and touched."[42] For Agnes, fantasy is not an escape but a prison, as it has begun to solidify into reality, trapping her in an impossible situation. This dangerous conflation transforms Agnes's world irrevocably, and she realizes that she cannot go back to living as she did before, her life dictated by the church and by her family. At the same time, she also realizes that she cannot escape these constraints.

When Vincent and Marie-Rose have a disagreement, Agnes is left to comfort her sister. As she listens to Marie-Rose, Agnes feels guilty about her own feelings for Vincent. She remembers what the priest told her at confession and compares human love with divine love: "How sordid a private love became, and how extremely embarrassing! '. . . whereas in the idea of God there is matter for eternity.' Yes, holy Jesuit, that's all very fine. But we aren't made in the most convenient form in which to pursue ideas, and we have no notion at all of how to front eternity."[43] Agnes's inner questioning of the Jesuit and his suggestion that she cure the basic human problems of lust by thinking of God reveals the absurdity of such a suggestion. Through her portrayal of Agnes, O'Brien highlights the rift between Catholic doctrines and the reality of trying to live by them. Additionally, she points to the plight of women in Ireland at the end of the nineteenth century who found themselves relegated to domestic spaces in a land dominated by male values.[44]

Agnes's moral conflict is heightened by her mother's final illness. She must witness the deterioration of Teresa's bodily form, with little knowledge of what will happen to her soul. As she makes her daily visit to her mother's deathbed, Agnes imagines her mother's corpse: "In this light, which was no light at all but only an irregular lifting here and there of darkness, Teresa seemed a stranger. . . . A corpse, a shadow of a corpse, breathing in heaviness and fear, a corpse made dreadful to the senses, groaning in its half-dream, half-pang—a corpse, unrecognizable were it not for the little sobbing familiar man who knelt beside it, and whose woe identified its story."[45] The corpse is not here an aesthetic object but a body "made dreadful to the senses" because it is caught between dreams and the reality of illness. As Teresa approaches death, Agnes must project herself into the future, imagining her father's grief. It is this grief that distinguishes her mother's corpse from any other corpse. Death has the transformative ability to turn a loved one into a stranger, enhancing the mystery surrounding Catholic conceptions of eternity. At the same time, Agnes finds relief in envisioning her mother as a corpse, as it alleviates the pain of waiting for her mother's death.

This sense of waiting for a death permeates the atmosphere of the novel, and the end of this section, "The Feast of All Saints," sees a culmination of textual energies as the time of Teresa's death approaches. O'Brien's narrative shifts away from Agnes as Vincent's mental state begins to unravel. He thinks to himself, "'To-day is an ante-room,' you said. Admit your meaning. Or are you trapped now by the inexorability of time? What was your meaning then?" Here, Vincent's conception of time as unyielding conflicts with Catholic notions of redemption for sin. He awaits an inevitable end rather than a new beginning. Vincent's comment about the day being an ante-room is one that he made in front of Agnes, Marie-Rose, and Dr. Curran, among others. Yet no one questioned what he meant. Rather, Vincent must question himself to establish his own meaning: "An ante-room—well, perhaps to truth, to fate, or any of these useful abstracts. And she was all of them, entangled in their moonshine, making both sense and nonsense of their echoes."[46] The ante-room not only does not lead Vincent to reality but plunges him further into abstraction. In his mind, Agnes is tangled in this unreality, this "moonshine" or illumination in the darkness, which serves to reveal the rift between the truth of emotion and the social reality that keeps them apart.

Just prior to his thoughts about the day being an ante-room, Vincent was thinking about Teresa's imminent death as a "savagery which it seemed no Christian could help to keep her living—but the eternal Church, making so little of the visible woe to the flesh, and so much of the soul's elected stay within that woe, did ring a harsh peal which the imagination answered. The horrible death-bed had its point then, would he say?"[47] The point of the deathbed is supposedly to illustrate one of the precepts of Christianity: for the soul to transcend the human flesh and thereby achieve immortality. In Vincent's understanding of the deathbed scene, imagination has more power than Christian faith. Christian rituals cannot tame death, but the pain of dying can provoke the human mind to dream.

In literature of the nineteenth century, the deathbed scene functions, as Peter Brooks notes, as "a key moment of summing-up and transmission" that endows death with a retrospective quality.[48] Yet this summing up is also performed in anticipation of an ending that will allow the story to become transmissible. Teresa's deathbed scene essentially occupies the entirety of *The Ante-Room* and reveals Agnes's moral conflicts and the forces that restrict both the development of the characters and the fulfillment of the novel's competing plot lines. O'Brien uses the deathbed scene to force the characters to consider the future rather than to order the past. As Vincent's narrative indicates, Christianity provides little relief from deathbed suffering and instead stresses the importance of pain as a reminder of the sacrifice necessary to attain eternal life.

"The Feast of All Saints" ends with the relief of Teresa's worries about Reggie's fate as Nurse Cunningham agrees to marry him, but this resolution fails to quell the reader's increasing anxiety as Agnes and Vincent's situation intensifies. As he waits for Agnes to meet him, Vincent thinks, "Midnight was striking in the town. A jumble of the reminder—there were so many spires—but at last it was no longer midnight. It was All Saints' Day, he thought irrelevantly. And as he savored again the quiet which the subsided clocks enhanced, he heard footsteps coming from the east, from beyond the fir trees."⁴⁹ The chiming bells sound from church spires, reminding Vincent of the communal and religious commitments that prevent him from being with Agnes. The bells also signal the end of All Saints' Day (a time to celebrate those who have reached heaven) and the beginning of the Feast of All Souls (a time to remember the souls that remain in purgatory). There is an ominous sense that the tolling of the bells indicates that Vincent must abandon hope of heaven and join those souls in purgatory.

This purgatorial sense of being trapped between worlds deepens when the narrative shifts to Agnes's perspective. On her way to meet Vincent, Agnes approaches the threshold of the house and notices, "The bells and clocks of Mellick were withdrawing one by one from their discussion of midnight. The stars were clear. The freezing air had danger in it."⁵⁰ Like Vincent, Agnes is hyperaware of the chiming bells that mark midnight, but it is not only church bells that Agnes notices but also the secular clocks of Mellick, signifying the degree to which Agnes is caught between religious and secular worlds. That the clocks and bells are "discussing" midnight indicates a conflict between these two different conceptions of time. As the tolling bells and clocks subside, Agnes is left in silence, suggesting that time has been paused. She is under the clarity of the stars, linking this in-between world she is about to enter with heaven. However, the freezing air has danger in it, suggesting that her meeting with Vincent cannot end well. The section concludes not only with a sense of foreboding but also with a sense of death—the freezing air can pause time, but it cannot sustain life. On the brink of a dying world, these characters are burdened with a sense of guilt and are unable to realize their love, bringing to the fore the destructive death instinct that promises the release from the torment of desire and the end of human suffering.

꧁꧂

"The Feast of All Souls" marks the last episode of the novel and is also the feast day on which those souls who have failed to attain the beatific vision of heaven are remembered. These souls have not yet been cleansed of their mortal sins and must rely on the prayers of others to save them. In spite of their Catholic devotion, the characters in *The Ante-Room* all fit this description of souls who have not yet attained heaven. Teresa's death is the novel's anticipated end, but her final moments are not described, nor does the narrative clearly state that her death has occurred. Instead, her demise is overshadowed by Vincent's suicide. Rather than ending the novel with a point of closure—the death of Teresa—O'Brien's narrative ends on a disorienting note that not only leaves the characters' futures in jeopardy but also calls into question Catholic attitudes toward suicide. By ending the novel in this unsettling way, O'Brien leaves her readers dissatisfied, forcing them to reconsider the Catholic Church's control over social, religious, and spiritual life and its attempted monopoly over the afterlife.

The beginning of this section presents a hauntingly beautiful image of Vincent and Agnes's first and final embrace. Time seems to have stopped, and the surrounding world appears muted, in order for them to be together for a brief moment. O'Brien describes how "line for line, bone for bone, they seemed to fit together as if by heaven grooved to take each other, as if the platonic split was mended here, and a completed creature stood united to itself at last."[51] This image of unity presents Vincent and Agnes's love as not only natural but also heavenly. Any sense of divided worlds is mended in their embrace. The use of "seems" and the qualifying "as if" suggests that this appearance is an effect of heightened emotion rather than something that has actually occurred. This description enhances the reader's sense of injustice that these characters cannot be together. It also offers a criticism of society. Heaven has fitted these lovers together; it is the world that has divided them.

Agnes's love for Vincent is associated with the celestial, but it cannot be reconciled with her daily existence, no matter how holy. When her mother's condition grows worse, Agnes is reminded that to continue her life, she must sacrifice her love for Vincent. Agnes thinks of the "idiotic unrealities" she has dreamed of with Vincent and how these feelings "cannot be trusted to keep their character, but from hour to hour assume and abdicate a senseless power!" Agnes remarks on this discontinuity in her life: "Meantime there was this family reality of her mother's ending life; contemplating that grey fact in her uncle's eyes, in Reggie's and her sister's. Agnes felt almost relieved that there was something that did not recede from her, something that defied her relativity."[52] Death reminds Agnes of the stability provided by familial love, but it also represents something final. In this sense, Agnes's conception of death is secular and distinctly modern as she finds relief in its finality.

As Teresa's death approaches, there is an increasing urgency for her to find peace before she dies. Nurse Cunningham observes Teresa's body: "She looked like the corpse of someone who had been overmuch beaten and driven to this belated peace. But even the nurse knew that life was still rampant there—and even happy." The dying and battered body of Teresa Mulqueen is contrasted with her living and happy soul. As Agnes bends over her dying mother, she is startled by the expression of happiness on Teresa's face: "This is happiness, she thought, and wondered if even here she did not grudge it."[53] Teresa's happiness overwhelms her dying body, and she approaches the end of her life looking more alive than dead. Although Teresa seems to have achieved some kind of earthly heaven even before her actual death, the reader remains aware that Nurse Cunningham is marrying Reggie only for his fortune and that Reggie's disease will eventually end in madness. Thus, O'Brien presents Teresa's belief that she has reached heaven as a kind of delusion, again highlighting the disparity between the consolation provided by Catholicism and the reality of death.

As Agnes realizes the happiness that the news of Reggie's engagement has brought her mother, her thoughts turn to her own fate: "They are all alive, even Mother. But I'm dying. Vincent, if only I could die—oh Vincent, darling."[54] This is the last time that Agnes appears in the novel. Although she has no way of knowing that Vincent is about to take his own life, Agnes professes an urge to die herself. Thus, the novel ends with Teresa dying, yet happy, believing that God is good and has never failed her. Agnes chooses to sacrifice her own happiness in order to uphold her loyalty to her family. This choice results in a kind of liberal-secular death, as Agnes is left with no way of achieving personal fulfillment. Finally, there is Vincent's suicide, which is a destruction of self, a sin against the church as well as against his wife and family. The novel ends in a stalemate, as neither religious nor liberal-secular worldviews have triumphed and both have resulted in death. O'Brien's failure to endorse either worldview indicates her advocacy for a freeing of Catholic restrictions rather than an embrace of a purely secular society.

Vincent's suicide is striking because he sees the act not as a mortal sin but as a means of being reunited with his mother in heaven. Suicide goes against all Catholic teaching, which condemns it as a selfish and therefore sinful act. Yet Vincent views his self-destruction as the supreme sacrifice to save Agnes and her family from suffering. While Vincent is rationally aware that he is committing a sin, he sees it as a venial sin that is easily forgiven by the church. He believes that he is going to heaven, where he will "find [his mother] soon—in spite of the sin he was going to commit. Yes, it was a sin—but would God show him an alternative? To end things in one crime or live in an unending vulgar guilt?"[55] The sense of guilt Vincent feels does not guard against his destructive impulse but fosters it. Death is a solution to Vincent's problems, the only way of bridging the gap between his love for Agnes—associated with the eternal—and the reality that prevents them from being together.

Vincent's choice of suicide represents a dangerous collusion of religious and secular worldviews that results in his belief that he can realize his desires by sacrificing his own life. Vincent's fantasy of Agnes has collided with his reality—tempting him with the possibility of achieving happiness in his lifetime. However, Catholicism asserts that living out this fantasy would be a sin, forcing him to sacrifice that possibility. While in liberal-secular terms suicide would be the ultimate failure—a destruction of the self—Vincent justifies his action by viewing it as the ultimate sacrifice for the greater good of the community. Here, the guilt stemming from the tension between *Eros* and the death drive does not work to promote life but proves overpowering for the individual. This overwhelming sense of guilt can be attributed to the fusion of Catholic morality with social constraints that combine to devastating effect, making life impossible and leaving death as the only option. Perhaps most crucially of all, Vincent ends the novel believing that he will be reunited with his mother, suggesting a return to the primeval state that Freud describes as the end of the death instinct.[56] This ending both defies the reader's expectations and fails to provide a sense of resolution. The future of the other characters, such as Agnes and Marie-Rose, whose lives will be dramatically altered by this death, is left unexplained. In this sense, the narrative does not end, although the narrative time of the novel is over, as the reader has reached the final pages. In the concluding sentence of the novel, Vincent's thoughts return to boyhood, indicating an emotional regression. Rather than ending in a culmination and release of textual energies, the plot of the narrative loses all sense of forward motion and bends back to the past, leaving the reader with a sense that all this struggle has been futile. O'Brien uses death in *The Ante-Room* to highlight the dangers inherent in the complete repression of desire and to advocate for a more liberal Catholicism that allows for human weakness and incorporates secular ideas of self-fulfillment.

Structured around the three consecutive Catholic feast days commemorating the dead, Kate O'Brien's *The Ante-Room* is a novel concerned with the boundaries between life and death and between mortal and eternal time. Writing in the style of a popular romance novel, O'Brien combines death and marriage plots to highlight the tensions between *Eros* and the death instinct that constitute human life. This tension is further complicated by the conflicting Catholic and secular worldviews that influence these characters' sense of morality that manifests itself in a sense of guilt. While such guilt may be useful in keeping human impulses in check, it threatens to overwhelm the individual who has no way of fulfilling his own needs. The plot of *The Ante-Room* is initially compelled by the reader's desire for Teresa's death that offers the hope of a conclusive ending. This desire is further complicated by a related, though conflicting, desire for Vincent and Agnes to realize their love. The ending of the novel ultimately thwarts both these readerly desires by reversing these two plots. Teresa remains alive at the end of the novel, while Vincent dies.

This reversal reveals O'Brien's unconventional way of employing the form of the popular romance to critique Catholicism and its focus on guilt and suffering. Vincent's suicide in the final pages of the novel works as a fragmenting force, which illustrates the problems associated with Catholic control over both religious and social life in Ireland. When Catholicism functions mostly as a social force intent on controlling human impulses, it puts the religious power of hope at risk. The yoking together of these two functions produces an overly restrictive environment that attempts to control mortal time as well as eternal. The ending of the novel, which leaves the characters with little hope for the future, also calls into question liberal-secular worldviews that privilege the fulfillment of self within mortal time. In her refusal to endorse either view, O'Brien highlights the benefits of Catholic consolation, while at the same time arguing for a more liberal version of Catholicism that is more sympathetic to human failings. Thus, the author uses death and dying to force a reexamination of the social function of Catholicism in Ireland and to question how closely it is allied with its religious purpose.

This need to examine the social function of religion in keeping human desires in check and particularly in regulating the transition between life and death finds further elaboration in Samuel Beckett's *Malone Dies*. Beckett's novel, like O'Brien's, ends with its character's future uncertain, but whereas O'Brien argues for a humane relaxation of Catholic restrictions, Beckett experiments with what happens when religious structures are removed entirely. In *The Ante-Room* the imminent death of Teresa Mulqueen arouses conflicting impulses within her children, who seek to fulfill their own earthly desires but also feel constrained by their Catholic faith. These contradictory impulses cannot be made to cohere, resulting in death. Death, for both Agnes and Vincent, is a choice: while Agnes sacrifices her soul in order to live, Vincent sacrifices his life in order to free himself from his desires.

By employing a realist style and utilizing the tropes of popular romance novels to describe various kinds of death, both real and symbolic, O'Brien brings to the fore the underdevelopment of the Irish novel as a form. According to Kiberd, *The Ante-Room*'s title "may also indicate [O'Brien's] conviction that the novel of personal relations in Ireland has yet to be fully made, the house of fiction has yet to be built and entered."[57] Kiberd is right to point out O'Brien's efforts to highlight the Irish novel as a form that is not yet fully realized and remains caught between the secular demands of literary realism and the nonempirical, spiritual needs attended to by religion. In *The Ante-Room* O'Brien suggests that the Irish novel must mend this divide between realism and popular romance and address not only the reality of death but also the spiritual concerns it raises. Beckett's experimentation with the novel form in *Malone Dies* addresses these concerns by imagining a character who is caught between reality and fiction and attempts to engineer his own death by fictionally narrating it. In both O'Brien and Beckett, death holds the possibility of release from the boundaries and constraints of reality. While Beckett's fictional depictions of death collapse the boundaries of form and structure, O'Brien's novel remains informed by these boundaries, failing to make the secular and the religious cohere or to imagine a world in which such a reconciliation is possible.

3

Deathbed Confessions and Unraveling Narration

Samuel Beckett's *Malone Dies*

Samuel Beckett's *Malone Dies* (first published in English in 1955), the middle novel of the trilogy, is one of the twentieth century's most memorable and comic novelistic portrayals of the process of dying. Beckett's intention to explore the themes of death and dying is apparent in the novel's title itself, which declares the death of the narrator, Malone, even before the novel has begun. Within the trilogy, *Malone Dies* is a transitional text, situated between *Molloy*, which depicts the process of establishing an "I" and the emergence of self and author, and *The Unnamable*, which can be read as the realization of Beckett's desire to abolish the subjective "I" so that narrator, author, and character all become fused. *Malone Dies* is balanced between these two extremes of narrative subject and object, of death and the afterlife. Unlike *Ulysses* or *The Ante-Room*, which depict the effect that the dead or dying have on the living, Beckett's novel is focused on the process of dying itself and on the role that narrative has in keeping death at bay.

Malone Dies stands out in this study as the novel most concentrated on death. In the other novels discussed here, death and dying provoke new thoughts or actions in the characters. In *Ulysses*, for instance, memories of deceased family members and thoughts about mortality shape the characters' actions. Beckett's novel is different in that it is a text *about dying*. For Beckett's narrator, Malone, writing is both a compulsion and a tool with which to engineer his own demise.

Malone wishes to commit a kind of textual suicide, correlating the end of his narrative with his bodily expiration. Yet he finds that despite his attempts to pare down his language, he cannot fully attain his narrative goals but approach them only discursively, ultimately failing to formulate an identity through the convergence of his fictional creations. Therefore, his narrative cannot properly end; it can only trail off inconclusively.

The process of dying depicted in *Malone Dies* ramifies in powerful and interesting ways both outward, toward literary theory and philosophical thought, and inward, in the sense that it seeks to annihilate itself. In his portrayal of a narrator who is attempting to end himself, Beckett is engaging with major literary and philosophical movements concerned with the "death of the author," "the end of the novel," "the end of man." As much as Malone's desire to narrate his own death and failure to do so evoke these wider themes on the death of the subject in Western thought, the use of Catholic religious materials and the subversion of the *ars moriendi* tradition of religious writing on death, as well as the hints of Irish references in the text, situate Beckett's novel in an Irish novelistic context even while it seeks to eviscerate this relation. *Malone Dies* is a text that implodes the form and structure of the Irish novel where *Ulysses* explodes it; it produces a set of unresolvable aporia, as against the ideological contradictions of *The Ante-Room*. In its portrayal of the entropic running down of textual energies, *Malone Dies* succeeds in stripping novelistic narrative to its barest form. Yet rather than simply depicting the "death" of the novel or the end of life, Beckett's novel ends inconclusively, leaving Malone still poised between life and death. Malone's failure to narrate his own demise is comic in a macabre way, revealing the absurd nature of human desires to control death. The conflict between the desire to die and the desire to create impels the plot of the novel, highlighting the implicit connection between death and novelistic narrative. Even after narrative and religious structures for understanding human experience have been dismantled, there still remains a human need for narrative, which at once offers distraction from the terror of death while also demanding a confrontation with mortality.

Beckett wrote *Malone Dies* just after World War II, during the most prolific period of his writing career, between May 1947 and January 1950. This postwar context is significant because, as David Weisberg rightly argues, the war provided both the catalyst and the grounding for the trilogy in which Beckett sought to "reimagine a communicative literature beyond the choices of autonomy of commitment."[1] Though he began work on *Malone Dies* directly after finishing *Molloy*, he soon found his writing blocked and decided to go to visit his mother, bringing a major work back home to Ireland with him for the first time in his career.[2] Beckett returned to Paris soon after completing the novel and went on to write one of his most highly acclaimed plays, *Waiting for Godot*.[3] This period also coincided with Beckett's decision to write in French rather than his native English. Many explanations have been offered for this choice of French, but one of the most convincing reasons is the one offered by Beckett himself when he claimed that, for him, English was too burdened with allusions and association and what he called "Anglo-Irish exuberance and automatisms." He found that in French, it was easier to write "without style" or to write in a sparer style.[4] This need to distance himself from his native language and to reinvigorate his fiction by making the process of writing strange has important implications for his depictions of death and dying in *Malone Dies*. Indeed, this method of writing in a pared-down style is related to his project of dismantling the narrative and religious structures that make sense of death and hold meaning in place. In *Malone Dies*, Beckett forces his readers to see the process of dying anew and challenges them to arrive at a different understanding of death than the ones offered by the religious promise of paradise or secular notion of oblivion.

Early critics and readers of Beckett's work have tended to interpret his decision to write in French as an attempt to distance himself from his Irish background. However, beginning in the 1980s there has been significant critical interest in situating Beckett in an Irish context. Since then critics such as Seamus Deane, Declan Kiberd, David Lloyd, and, more recently, Seán Kennedy, Emilie Morin, and Patrick Bixby have read Beckett's work not only in an Irish context but in a postcolonial one as well.[5] Deane argues that Ireland functions as a "mode of absence" in Beckett's writing, suggesting that the lack of Irish referents in Beckett's texts becomes a way of representing Ireland. Building on these arguments, Morin further maintains that Beckett's Irish background contributes to his development as an artist, arguing that he is an avant-garde writer because of the way that he engages the Irish context by "deflecting it." Kiberd observes that the landscape of South County Dublin is celebrated in the trilogy and that, for Beckett, "the Gaelic tradition seemed posited on void, every poem an utterance in the face of imminent annihilation, every list an inventory of shreds from a culture verging on extinction," thus reinforcing the association of the trilogy's evacuation of consciousness with Ireland's devastating colonial history.[6] But if Beckett's work can be linked to Irishness in these ways, it can also be linked to it by virtue of its tendencies to subvert received forms of novelistic narration, a propensity to write parodic antinovels evident in Irish writing from Laurence Sterne to James Joyce or Flann O'Brien.

Like other Irish writers, Beckett is obsessed with religion, even if that obsession most commonly takes comic or parodic form. "To die or not to die" is the question that plagues Malone, as it does many of Beckett's other characters. The answer that Malone arrives at is that in order to die, he would first have to have lived, and in order to live he must first escape the terror of death, even though in the end doing so is impossible. For Beckett, these paradoxes are the source of much agony but also of comedy, provoking in the reader a mirthless laughter. While this humor cannot ease the pain of death, it does serve to make it slightly less terrifying. Malone eagerly anticipates the end of his life because he believes it will mark the end of his suffering. At the same time, he dreads death and fears it will increase his pain. The act of telling stories serves to ease Malone's anxieties, even while the forward motion of plot draws him closer to the end.

Malone Dies is not a comic novel in the traditional sense of the term, as the novel does not depict a rise in Malone's fortunes, nor does it end happily. However, Beckett's novel does succeed in a macabre humor that stems from Malone's failure to die properly according to any of the rules he sets for himself. According to Vivian Mercier, the Irish have a propensity for macabre humor, which inspires "laughter tinged with terror" and serves as a "defense mechanism against the fear of death." This is a particularly apt way to characterize Malone's use of humor throughout the narrative, as his jokes serve to deflect his fear, just as writing postpones his death. What makes *Malone Dies* humorous is Malone's attempt and failure to narrate his own demise. The cause of this failure is his inability to stop imagining. As Christopher Ricks notes, Beckett's portrayals of the imagination's failure to imagine its own death reflect his desire to fail as no one else has failed.[7] What Beckett succeeds in doing is portraying the writer's inability to narrate death while also illustrating the importance of narrative as a way of coping with the end of life. By dismantling the novel form, Beckett forces his readers to confront the inevitability of death but also, through his use of macabre humor, makes this realization bearable.

Narrated in the first person, *Malone Dies* is an account of Malone's attempt to record his own demise. All that is known about Malone's surroundings is that he is lying in a bed in a room that is neither an insane asylum nor a hospital and that someone brings him food and takes away his waste. His most treasured possessions are his pencil and exercise book. Though Malone is certain that he will die, he remains unsure of when or how, and he occupies his time by creating an inventory of his possessions and inventing stories about Macmann and Lemuel, who can be read as alter egos of Malone himself.[8] These stories function as subplots meant to distract the reader, and Malone himself, from his own imminent demise. From this setting and plot description, it is difficult to place Beckett in a distinctly Irish locale, or any locale for that matter.

However, the vehemence of Malone's categorical rejection of the religious structures and rituals that surround dying, the confessional aspect to his writing, the persistence of the trope of the dead mother, and his purgatorial state are all in line with Joyce's and O'Brien's depictions of death and dying, situating him in a similar trajectory of Irish writing about death.[9] Moreover, one of the most productive strands of criticism to emerge out of the intersection of Beckett studies and Irish studies has been, as Rónán McDonald notes, the view of Beckett as a Protestant writer.[10] While Beckett's Protestant heritage appears on the surface to separate him from the Catholic authors in this study, the theme of death and dying serves as a useful point of intersection where these various conceptions of Beckett as an Irish writer and a religious writer come together. As a member of the Anglo-Irish minority in a country dominated by Catholicism, Beckett and his work were therefore influenced by both the Catholic and the Protestant traditions. A novel such as *Malone Dies* reveals this dual influence, weaving together Catholic concepts of confession and purgatory with Protestant concerns with self-reliance and self-scrutiny.[11]

Criticism on Beckett and death, and particularly on *Malone Dies*, has focused on the relationship between writing and existence, Beckett's depictions of death as oblivion, the religious elements present in the text, and on death as a philosophical question. The collection *Beckett and Death*, edited by Steven Barfield, Matthew Feldman, and Phillip Tew, offers a variety of critical approaches to Beckett's representation of dying. This volume argues that the "juxtaposition between birth and death remains one of Beckett's favorite comic tropes," and it further proposes that while Beckett's fiction is characterized by a drive for oblivion, it also "seems just as determined to never grasp death as an exact finitude or boundary."[12] The most important essays on death and the trilogy in this collection—Erik Tonning's "Beckett's Unholy Dying: From *Malone Dies* to *The Unnamable*" and Elizabeth Barry's "Beckett, Augustine, and the Rhetoric of Dying"—discuss Beckett's fictional portrayals of dying and their connection to religious ways of making sense of the end of life. Though Malone rejects these religious conceptions of a "good death," they continue to inform his narrative, hinting at a persistent human need for meaning even while acknowledging that there is none. This chapter shares many of the same concerns as the essays in *Beckett and Death*, particularly the relationship between death and religion in Beckett's fiction, but differs from the arguments of Tonning and Barry because it seeks to situate *Malone Dies* in the specific literary-historical trajectory of the Irish novel and its treatments of death and dying, arguing that *Malone Dies* not only expresses the absurdities of a post–world war society that has lost its ability to make sense of death, but also proposes a distinctly Irish solution to coping with these problems: through storytelling and humor.

At the beginning of *Malone Dies*, Malone initially presents his death as inevitable, but it turns out to be indeterminate. Death, then, is not simply a boundary but an imagined end, the knowledge of which drives the need for narrative creation. In his struggle to reconcile himself to death, Malone is determined to correlate his death moment with the end of his text, a goal he largely fails to accomplish.[13] The exceptional nature of Beckett's novel stems from its experimentation with narrative form, structure, and voice. *Malone Dies* reveals the structure of narrative only to dismantle it. Yet no matter how hard Malone tries, he cannot quite bring his narrative to a satisfactory ending or reach the state of oblivion he seeks. It is fair to say, then, that Malone fails in his project of dying. Yet as Thomas Cousineau argues, Beckett's work does far more than fail to offer a solution to the human condition: instead, it liberates its characters from outmoded literary structures through the expression of failure and nothingness.[14] Similarly, though Malone does not accomplish the task he has set for himself, he succeeds in portraying the process of dying through his narrative. Malone strips his narrative down by killing characters and losing objects, so that by the end of the novel he has only reached an impasse, a pause in his narration before the voice of the Unnamable begins, this time with no characters or objects to manipulate.

While Beckett's outlook can hardly be called a humanist one—his work often questions long-held assumptions about man and his relationship with the world—*Malone Dies* does reveal the functions of human desire and suffering.[15] The reader is left with no sense of closure, but what remains after the layers of narrative structure have been pared away are the fears and desires that drive the human need for order and meaning. The compulsion to reach what Peter Brooks would call the "unnamed meaning" of the text, a meaning that can never fully be known or articulated, is revealed through Malone's narrative and continued into *The Unnamable*.[16]

In *Malone Dies*, writing becomes a way of evacuating consciousness but also in its proliferation of stories serves as an act of creation. Assuming the characteristics of a religious confessional, Malone's narrative functions as a purging of sin or an expunging of past experiences, but it also has life-giving properties in that it features the creation of characters such as Lemuel and Macmann. Yet as much as the act of writing may first appear to function as a substitute for more traditional forms of worship for Malone, at the end the reader is left with nothing but the ability to narrate nothing as the last of his lead pencil dwindles away and he loses the ability to write. Beckett's text leaves his readers at the end of his novel without the tools to construct narrative but with a voice that is, nonetheless, compelled to narrate. Brooks argues that narrative provides a way for us to think about the past, illustrating our refusal to "allow temporality to be meaningless, our stubborn insistence on making meaning in the world and in our lives."[17] While Beckett acknowledges that this need for meaning is achieved through narrative, he also denies his reader that meaning. In fact, Beckett's texts could be read as exercises in meaninglessness. Yet such a conclusion offers a much too simplistic reading of his novel.[18] Writing with an awareness of the persistent human need for meaning and order, Beckett deliberately denies these demands in order to emulate, as closely as possible, the experience of dying. Acknowledging the impossibility of accurately representing death, Beckett instead narrates the experience of dying, both textual and physical. In this sense he uses the breakdown of the novel form to force his readers to face the reality of death, while also employing macabre humor to emphasize the human need for novelistic narrative as a way of distracting from the horrors of dying.

Malone Dies stands out in the novel tradition in the way that it employs a metafictional narrative technique to reveal the forces driving narrative creation. Malone is not simply a character in Beckett's novel; he is the creator of the novel itself, blurring the lines between author and character, creator and created.[19] Malone's need to narrate conflicts with his desire to die or to reach the end of the text. Yet these two desires are not as contradictory as they may first appear. In fact, according to Freud, it is the conflicting urges to live and procreate (*Eros*) and to die and achieve stasis (*Thanatos*) that constitute human life.[20] Malone's process of dying, then, is not completely original or entirely unstructured. Even the metafictional narrative technique that Malone takes on is evident in the novel tradition as far back as Laurence Sterne's *Tristram Shandy*, and Malone's mode of first-person narrative is closely related to, and at points even parodies, religious manuals on an ideal death that offer advice on how to die properly.[21] Additionally, as Kiberd observes, *Malone Dies* fits into a long history of Irish writing about death, particularly one's own, that dates back to the bardic tradition in which bards not only wrote laments about kings and queens but were often forced to write laments for themselves. This kind of self-elegizing, Kiberd argues, "has persisted ever since in Irish culture, in the diaries of hunger strikers and the poems of condemned rebels on the eve of execution" and also strongly influences Beckett's novel.[22] What distinguishes Malone's project of dying is the unique way that he seeks to both employ and dismantle the religious structures and narrative techniques that attend death.

The concept of the *ars moriendi*, or the "art of dying," arose out of two related Latin texts: The *Tractatus*, a six-chapter treatise on the rituals and practices of death, and the other, known simply as *Ars Moriendi*, which featured illustrations of the dying surrounded by temptation. These texts were published anonymously, and both enjoyed popularity during the fifteenth and early sixteenth centuries and influenced later literary traditions concerning death and dying.[23] While the *ars moriendi* of the early Middle Ages emphasized collective judgment, beginning in the fifteenth century the focus shifted from communal to individual judgment. Such texts, which instructed the living on how to die a "good death," multiplied as printed texts became more widely available, ultimately resulting in what is considered one of the genre's best texts, Jeremy Taylor's *The Rule and Exercises of Holy Dying*, published in London in 1651. What is notable about Taylor's text is that it revises the originally Catholic *ars moriendi* and establishes it as a genre within Protestantism.[24] As is evident from this example, the tradition of the *ars moriendi* itself spans both Catholic and Protestant belief systems and for this reason appealed to Beckett. In fact, Beckett read Taylor's book after the publication of *More Pricks than Kicks*, and its influence is evident from the unfinished manuscript of his play "Human Wishes," based on Samuel Johnson's life, which features a character who reads a passage from Taylor's book (the passage itself a favorite of Dr. Johnson's).[25] While references to Taylor are not as explicitly evident in *Malone Dies*, Beckett undoubtedly drew on this text heavily while writing his novel.[26] The influence of Taylor's book is apparent in Malone's decision to set himself against the ways of organizing one's life in preparation for death laid out by such texts.

Malone's rejection of the *ars moriendi* is most apparent in his "ostentatious and otherwise unmotivated refusal to forgive his enemies—a staple instruction of every *Ars Moriendi* manual since medieval times." Tonning's contention that Malone rejects holy dying because he sees it as conflicting with his own project, which is "birth unto death," or oblivion, is extremely useful here, as is his observation that Malone views reliance on God or an "external divinity" as an interference in his project of self-knowledge.[27] For Malone, Christianity offers hope that individual existence will continue in another dimension and thus refuses the idea of death as a descent into nothingness. Tonning attempts to explain the seemingly casual Christian references in Beckett's novel as Malone's desire to find an alternative form of salvation. Rather than trying to die a "holy" death, Malone desires complete annihilation. However, the persistence of religious references and Malone's last prayer at the end are suggestive, Tonning argues, of his realization that his project has failed. Malone's "programme," through which he seeks to vanquish himself by creating fictional characters to confess for him, succeeds only in creating a further fiction, an extension of his own life. Essentially, Malone fails to die properly, even according to his own plan, and therefore the novel itself fails to offer an alternative *ars moriendi* but succeeds in challenging the notions of a "good death" laid out by such manuals.

Beckett's inversion of the *ars moriendi*, the religious confessional, and the persistence of Christian references throughout his text, alongside modern notions of death as absence, highlight the conflicts troubling modern men and women in the wake of the Second World War. Without the comfort offered by the knowledge that a loved one died a "good death" and has attained eternal life in heaven, humans have few ways of achieving consolation. Beckett explores the beliefs underlying humans' understanding of life and death by dismantling the religious structures that inform these beliefs and studying what remains when these structures are gone. Nonetheless, traces of religious references remain in Beckett's texts, even if his ultimate goal is to eradicate them. In his failure to completely erase the Christian elements of his text, Beckett suggests that while religious ways of making sense of death have some value, they are in need of reinvention.

Malone Dies opens with Malone announcing, "I shall soon be quite dead at last in spite of it all." But this assertion is called into question a few sentences later, when Malone contradicts himself: "Indeed, I would not put it past me to pant on to the Transfiguration, not to speak of the Assumption. But I do not think I am wrong in saying that these rejoicings will take place in my absence, this year."[28] The Transfiguration, a Christian feast day, celebrates Christ's revelation of himself as God in the form of man. Malone places himself in a godlike position in this text, as creator and master of the fictional lives of Sapo, Macmann, and Lemuel. His reference to panting on past the Transfiguration could suggest an ability to endure beyond a Christian heaven, seeing death not as a beginning or an end but as a state in between the two. The celebrations of the liturgical calendar that Malone attempts to use as structural marking points for his existence instead serve merely as reminders of the absence of order. The Assumption celebrates Mary's departure from earth and ascent into heaven. Catholic teachings about the day, year, and manner of Mary's death are all uncertain; it is also unclear as to whether Mary was assumed to heaven before or after her bodily death. The fact that Beckett includes these religious references here attests to the human need for religion to structure temporal experience, while underscoring the arbitrary nature of such conventions.

It is evident from the first few sentences of Beckett's novel that Malone cannot quite accept his own death, despite his attempts to do so. Anticipating his death, he says that he will soon be "quite dead at last in spite of it all," suggesting that any efforts to hasten his death will be in vain. There is a darkly comic aspect to Malone's statement: he states that he shall soon be quite dead and then proceeds to defer his death by listing the holidays that will take place in his absence. Malone's playful approach to death as something he has long desired but has up until now failed to attain reduces the seriousness attached to the question of death without making it any less real.

The reader's interest in Malone's narrative is compelled by two questions: Will he actually die? And if he succeeds in rejecting a religious death, what will follow life? Tonning argues that Malone's project of rejecting divinity may indeed have proved impossible, concluding as it does on an unanswered prayer for light through the darkness while the life beyond Malone's text continues to exist. The line Tonning is referring to comes at the end of the text when Malone is describing how Lemuel will never hit anyone anymore with his hammer or stick, "or with his pencil or with his stick or or light light I mean never there he will never never anything there any more."[29] Despite the fact that Malone's narration is focused on Lemuel, his own emotions begin to interfere with his story, as is most evident in the reference to light as he breaks in with a corrective tic, "I mean," to suggest that it is in fact *he* who desires light. While death is often associated with darkness, Malone sees his life as darkness, and he imagines the oblivion he seeks as light and blank. The references to the stick and pencil—Malone has lost the former, and the latter is quickly dwindling—suggest that Malone is referring to his own lack of ability to manipulate either the external world or the world of his fiction. Malone's prayer for oblivion is ultimately denied because of the strong bond between himself and his text, yet the very process of his dying is linked with the process of writing. His attempt to dissolve his fictions and insist that nothing will exist anymore is at once a final attempt at control and an example of his complete lack of control over his text. Even as Malone acknowledges a lack of meaning to human existence, he is still compelled to seek illumination.

Malone's stories of Sapo, the boy who becomes Macmann, and then Lemuel provide an escape from the confines of his own mind but cannot provide relief from bodily suffering. This pain reminds him of his own mortality and also reveals the boundaries that order human experience. Malone finds a way of ordering his life by inventing these fictional characters, but writing their stories also serves as a painful reminder of his own failures. Malone's inventory of his possessions connects him to the outside world, even as his relationship to that world slowly deteriorates.[30] This inventory becomes increasingly important to him as the novel progresses, revealing the anxiety that death will divorce him from the world of objects. Malone's collection of objects mocks manuals of dying such as Taylor's that instruct the dying to order their lives by writing wills and inventorying possessions. It is in the sections that discuss Malone's possessions that his narrative's resemblance to both the *ars moriendi* and the closely related deathbed confessional becomes most apparent.

After deciding that his inventory must come after his stories, Malone questions whether he can resign himself to dying without leaving an inventory behind and concludes, "Presumably I can, since I intend to take that risk. All my life long I have put off this reckoning, saying, Too soon, too soon. Well it is still too soon. . . . This moment seems now at hand." Here, Malone's language takes on an evangelical tone with the word "reckoning" and the phrase describing the moment "now at hand" mimicking sacred language designed to encourage believers to redeem themselves of their sins so they can attain the kingdom of heaven at the hour of judgment. The need to produce an inventory that will supposedly order Malone's life is futile, as the project of establishing which objects belong to him proves problematic: "For only those things are mine the whereabouts of which I know well enough to be able to lay hold of them, if necessary, that is the definition I have adopted, to define my possessions. For otherwise there would be no end of it. But in any case there will be no end to it."[31]

Here, endlessness becomes a characteristic even of physical objects whose reality is supposed to be finite. The only thing that counters the infinite is a definition that has been "adopted" in an effort to reach an ending. Beckett indicates here that the sense of an ending that Malone is experiencing is in fact a construct that has been created in order to arbitrarily form a boundary between this world and another, less determinate, reality. Malone recognizes that he cannot reach the ending that he desires without first establishing the boundaries that define his reality, while acknowledging that these boundaries are not as stable as they might first appear.

While Malone's body should provide a reminder of his own mortality, it is so useless in manipulating the objects in his room that it fails to serve as an indicator of whether he is living or dead. By employing the structure of the *ars moriendi* and Taylor's rules of holy dying, Beckett points out the arbitrary nature of such deathbed conventions. *Malone Dies* attempts to create an alternate model of how to die, free from the strictures and structures of organized religion with its ideas of sacrifice and redemption. Malone's project succeeds in destroying the structures circumscribed by religious deathbed confessionals, but the destruction of these conventions serves, more than anything, to reveal the human need for structure and divinity. Without the boundaries between this world and the next imposed by Christian notions of the afterlife, a definitive ending becomes difficult to achieve.

Malone's world lacks meaning, and its objects lack any sense of the sacred. Nevertheless, physical objects are important to him, illustrating Malone's desire to collect goods in an effort to establish his identity. In the end, these objects prove meaningless. Malone has no time for manuals of dying; even after he plans his own narrative "programme," he cannot adhere to this form and must deviate from it in his "hurry to be done." Yet Malone contradicts himself, saying that he is in no hurry, thus emphasizing the conflicting pulls of his desire to reach the end and his fear of the end. Alan Warren Friedman blames this lack of time for death on modern technologies, largely in the form of medical advancements that have "removed death from the home and rendered it artificial, arranged, civilization's chief product."[32] This artificial arrangement is the very structure that Malone is attempting to disarrange. In his efforts to strip away the constructs surrounding death, Malone returns again and again to historical events or feast days on the liturgical calendar in order to structure his experience. Malone's struggle to maintain his narrative after it has been freed from its constraints not only reveals the conventions of narrative itself but also exposes the drives behind the need to narrate.

Malone's attempts to undo the Christian notion of a "good death" result in a breakdown of the distinction between self and other, living and dying, beginning and end, plunging him into a purgatorial state of nonexistence. This purgatorial state is the result of Malone's rejection of Christian conceptions of the afterlife, but also reveals the influence of Catholic ideas of salvation and functions as a reminder of Ireland.[33] Beckett's depiction of Malone in a purgatorial state indicates Beckett's own familiarity with Catholicism. While Protestants believe that upon death the faithful are delivered directly to heaven, the sinners directly to hell, Catholics believe in a state after death where souls remain stranded between two extremes. Despite its religious associations, the trope of purgatory has a distinct tradition in literature as well, perhaps most important in Dante's *Divine Comedy*, an epic poem that had a profound influence on both Joyce and Beckett.

Beginning in the twelfth century, purgatory was believed to be located in Ireland, on Station Island, near Lough Derg.[34] This site is thought to be the place where Saint Patrick sent penitents down a dark hole to repent for their sins. This association between Ireland and purgatory provides an important link between Beckett's work and a prominent theme in twentieth-century Irish culture. Pascale Casanova argues that Beckett puts Ireland at the center of his texts by linking it with purgatory, calling purgatory one of Western society's greatest religious and literary mythologies. Purgatory is indeed a prominent feature in the work of many major Irish writers and poets of the twentieth century, including W. B. Yeats and Seamus Heaney.[35] It is significant that one of Yeats's best plays should be called

Purgatory and that Beckett should also capitalize on this theme. This preoccupation with purgatory indicates a larger anxiety concerning death in twentieth-century Irish literature. As with the in-between state that Malone inhabits, the characters in Yeats's *Purgatory* occupy a hollowed-out landscape, observing ghosts of the past in the ruins of an old home. After narrating the story of his parents' unhappy marriage and detailing how he murdered his own father, the Old Man kills the Boy in an attempt to end the cycle of repetition and free his mother's ghost from its torturous repetition of the past. Both Yeats's play and Beckett's novel feature characters who must narrate the past in order to make peace with it, and both end with murder—Lemuel murders the inmates in his care, and the Old Man murders the Boy in Yeats's play. For Yeats and Beckett, violence is necessary to end life's vicious cycle of repetition, but Yeats's play ends on a more final note than Beckett's, with the Old Man asking God to release his mother's soul from its suffering. For Yeats, then, narrating death carries with it the possibility of redemption through violence. In Beckett's fiction even the narration of violence only perpetuates the story: Lemuel's act of murder continues Malone's narrative rather than ending it. For Malone, the Christian promise of eternal life is not a reward but an agonizing continuation of life.

In his systematic rejection of Christian death rituals, Malone is attempting to free himself from the suffering attached to penance and to escape the fate of choosing between heaven and hell. However, in the absence of Christian notions of sin and redemption, there is no end to suffering, only a perpetual purgatorial state of unbeing. Beckett is experimenting with the modern idea of a godless world, a place where salvation is not only questionable but virtually impossible to attain. Malone's own purgatorial state is significant because it is at once an erasure of self and a reaffirmation of it. The ritual of purgatory performed at Lough Derg, where penitents descend into a dark hole, was, as Peggy O'Brien notes, a "submission to total self-effacement," while also resulting in "an increased sense of both new-found isolation and reaffirmed selfhood."[36] These two contradictory effects of purgatory are apparent in Malone's narrative in which he attempts to efface his own selfhood while also struggling to determine his identity.

Malone confirms his purgatorial state: "Yes I shall be natural at last, I shall suffer more, then less, without drawing any conclusions, I shall pay less heed to myself, I shall be neither hot nor cold any more. I shall be tepid, I shall die tepid, without enthusiasm." This description of his own process of dying deliberately sets Malone against Taylor's *Rule and Exercises of Holy Dying.* Taylor asserts that "scrupulous persons are always the most religious; and that to feel nothing is not *of life* but *of death.* . . . [A] lukewarm person is only secured in his own thoughts but very unsafe in the event, and despised by God."[37] Malone's project, to die "lukewarm," purposely defies the rules laid out by Taylor. Malone's goal is to die while feeling nothing, which suggests that his being saved in his own mind is more important than proving anything to God.

The state of suffering that Malone finds himself in can be attributed to his inability to remember his past or establish his own identity. He manages to relieve some of his mental anguish by creating stories, dissolving the boundaries between himself and his inventions, but he cannot escape his physical pain. This point is where the influence of Johnson's "Sick Man's Journal" on Beckett becomes most evident, serving to illuminate Malone's problematic position. Tonning notes that Malone's position at the end of the text becomes a "Johnsonian" one, in that Malone's inability to escape suffering contrasts with Johnson's commitment to Christian salvation through which his suffering is relieved.[38] Despite his efforts to expel all needs, Malone fails to attain oblivion as he is compelled to narrate, even though he lacks a subject or object of narration. The process of narrating therefore becomes that which constitutes identity as well as an expression of its dissolution.

Malone's purgatorial state allows him to put off death, to continue to exist between the extremes of life and death. In this middle novel of the trilogy, Malone admits, "This exercise book is my life, it has taken me a long time to resign myself to that. . . . And yet I shall not throw it away. For I want to put down in it, those I have called to my help, but ill, so that they did not understand, so that they may cease with me. Now rest," thus linking the purgatorial state of writing to his life.[39] This state of being tied to his narrative is painful, but it also gives Malone power. Malone does not face any real decisions, as everything is deferred to another time, yet he exists in a continual state of desire to know the end, to finish, goals that he cannot quite achieve.

Malone's darkly comic approach to his situation serves to make the question of death more approachable. Malone is strikingly aware of his state of unbeing in all its complexity. He expresses a longing for closure that manifests itself in his desire for death. Garrett Stewart points out that while the deathbed scenes of modernists like Hardy and Conrad express a "repressed yearning for the spiritual sureties" of the Victorian deathbed, *Malone Dies* expresses a "sardonic nostalgia" and a "vain craving" for "closural satisfaction" that takes the "inverted form of a metaphysical send-up expelling from the confines of narrative all the familiar prescriptions for dramatized demise in literature."[40] This notion of ending as a way of encapsulating life is confounded by the figure of Malone, who has no clear sense of beginning or ending and therefore cannot establish whether he is living or dead.

Malone's narrative is driven by his paradoxical desires both to die and to establish his origins. By writing invented stories, Malone attempts to understand his past. It is by achieving an understanding of who he is and where he came from that Malone hopes to escape his purgatorial state of indeterminacy. However, as both author and narrator of his own story, Malone has difficulty establishing his origins and dividing himself from his stories. As Abbott notes, while Beckett's text "invites us to think of autobiography," it also goes against this urge and "repeatedly sabotages both the narrative character and historical authority of autobiography, and . . . the 'figments' and 'imaginings' that emerge in the text are, as it were, unborn." While his position as author gives Malone, and earlier Molloy, authority over his narrative, it deprives both of a sense of identity. Malone notes that he "could die today, if I wished, merely by making a little effort. But it is just as well to let myself die, quietly, without rushing things. Something must have changed." As author, Malone possesses the power to end his text. Yet as soon as he articulates this ability, he immediately backs down, saying that it is better to let himself go without rushing to the end. The statement that "something must have changed" could suggest that Malone is looking for a retrospective view of his life, which will give it significance. In the next sentence he resolves, "I will not weigh upon the balance anymore, one way or the other," suggesting that what has changed is that he has decided to give up balancing between author and character.[41] This decision has profound implications for Malone's narrative, as without this distinction Malone also loses the power of understanding death through the narrative of someone else's life. Without the retrospective understanding of life achieved in the deathbed scene, Malone has no way of making sense of his own life.

As is evident from the other novels in this study, the Irish novelistic deathbed scene is linked to Catholic guilt through the figure of the mother. Beckett's novel challenges this trope of the dying or dead mother with Malone unable to determine who his mother is or, indeed, to separate himself from her. The trope of the dying or dead mother appears in both Joyce's *Ulysses*, in which Stephen's mother urges him to pray for her on her deathbed, and in O'Brien's *The Ante-Room*, in which Teresa, the dying mother, seeks to mend relations between her children before she dies, while the threat of her death provokes religious devotions from her family. Beckett, like Joyce and O'Brien, associates the mother with both birth and death. In *Molloy* the title character searches for his mother and attempts, in vain, to determine whether she is dead.[42] Rather than trying to find his mother, Malone assumes the role of author and creator, and in so doing he becomes his own mother.

Malone hopes that by narrating the lives of others, he can both distract himself from his own death and understand his life. Brooks argues that narrative is a way of understanding human temporality, or "man's time-bound-edness, his consciousness of existence within the limits of mortality."[43] Malone's narrative, then, can be best understood as an attempt to comprehend his own existence. However, Malone's experiences as character cannot be divided from his experiences as author; therefore, his narrative cannot achieve the retrospective quality that will enable him to better understand life. The threat of death compels Malone's need to narrate and invent, but with no way of separating himself from these creations, Malone cannot truly die.

Freud's theory of the death drive, as outlined in "Beyond the Pleasure Principle," is of great relevance here, particularly his argument that all humans possess the contradictory impulses toward life and procreation or toward death and self-destruction. In "Civilization and Its Discontents," Freud elaborates this theory further, arguing that the contradictory impulses of *Eros* and *Thanatos* manifest themselves in a sense of guilt and that Christianity capitalizes on this sense of guilt and offers relief from it in the form of redemption, achieved through a sacrificial death.[44] Malone's rejection of the religious structures informing the process of dying, then, has profound implications for how death functions in his narrative. Without the idea of redemption and belief in the sacrificial death of Christ, Malone has no sense of guilt to prevent him from taking his own life, but he also cannot attain the bliss offered by heaven. Malone's repetition compulsion, his desire for death, his dismantling of narrative form, as well as his obsession with bodily disintegration conform to Freud's theory of the death drive. However, as Malone cannot establish who his mother is, or what his origins are, his drive toward death is hardly motivated by his desire to return to a primordial state; in fact, Malone seems already to exist in this state.

Malone concludes that he is an old fetus. He confirms, "Yes an old foetus, that's what I am now, hoar and impotent, mother is done for, I've rotted her, she'll drop me with the help of gangrene, perhaps papa is at the party too, I'll land head-foremost mewling in the charnel-house, not that I'll mewl, not worth it."[45] Malone here envisions his death as a reverse birth. The image of Malone as an "old foetus" is a darkly comic one, conjuring images of a baby with a wrinkled complexion and gray hair, and serves to bring together the two chief mysteries of human existence, birth and death. Death here is figured not as ending but as beginning. Malone has "rotted" his mother, yet his reference to gangrene (death in a bodily tissue) suggests that he is still attached to her and, as part of the same body, can be freed of her only by death. After being freed from the rotted-out corpse of his mother (and possibly his father), Malone envisions himself landing in the charnel house, suggesting that he not only will be dead but will also be a skeleton, devoid of flesh. His location in the charnel house, a place where bones are interred after their flesh has rotted away, implies that his separation from his mother can be achieved only through their shared bodily decay, not through a death of consciousness. Malone is his own mother and creator, and rather than leading back to his prebirth state, as Freud's theory of the death drive suggests, he will instead achieve birth only through death. Thus, Malone's death is not a return to the mother but a further separation from her. Malone's description of landing headfirst and mewling into the charnel house mimics the language used to describe births, with the babies crying as they are delivered. The birth-unto-death described here differs from ordinary birth or death; it is a condition that exists between the two states, as birth implies an emergence into life as a physically separate being. Malone's desire for death, then, is driven by a desire for a separate existence, divided from the body of his mother and father, separated from his past.

The notion that Malone is his own mother and also his own father can be linked to the question of the relationship between author and narrator and Malone's inability to separate the two. In order to divide himself from his fictions, Malone must either kill them off or die himself; he must relinquish his need to narrate. Yet Malone's narration is impelled not only by his desire to reach the end but also by his fear of absence. Malone illustrates Freud's repetition compulsion by varying his original statement that he shall "soon be quite dead in spite of it all." After much inner debate about when he wrote that he shall soon be quite dead, Malone concludes that he wrote it when he was unaware that he was repeating himself, at the point when he decided that he would live and "die alive." He describes how he found the exercise book just when he needed it. On the first page he writes, "Soon I shall be quite dead at last, and so on, without even going on to the next page, which was blank."⁴⁶ The certainty of his own death becomes a mantra for Malone as he attempts to write himself out of existence through repetition. Writing, however, serves not as a destructive force; rather, it becomes a way of representing absence or making inexistence present within the text. Malone knows that if he fills the entire exercise book, his narrative will come to an end. Yet the unfulfilled meaning that the blank pages represent are also what propel Malone's narrative forward. Malone is compelled to perform the act of writing, to fill the blank pages, to complete his life. His writing also serves, paradoxically, as an evacuation of consciousness, a purging of sin. Malone has usurped his mother and assumed her role as creator, thus encompassing within his own being both the beginning and the end of life, making it impossible for him to die. Instead, Malone is forced to write in an effort to purge his consciousness of thought and to end his life. His narrative then, takes on a confessional form that serves to lay bare the desires and drives that compel narration.

The confessional form gives Malone's narrative a shape and purpose in theory but does not provide him with a better understanding of his motivations. Nor does it serve to organize his life in preparation for the life to come. The sins that Malone is confessing are not his own but those of the fictional characters he creates. Even as Beckett's characters express a human desire to reach the end, to know death, it remains outside of their grasp, even in an imagined fictionalized form. While seeking in some sense to emulate the religious deathbed confessional, Malone's text shifts the focus from a self's confession to another, to a self confessing to himself. The hermeneutic mode described here does not reveal hidden secrets; rather, it indicates that there is nothing to confess. While the point of the confessional in religious texts is to repent for sins and thereby achieve salvation and eternal life, Malone himself does not admit to any sins. The fictional characters that Malone invents become a way of ridding himself of his past transgressions and, in essence, escaping himself. By fleeing the agonizing confines of his own mind, Malone hopes to achieve oblivion.

Malone's goal of ridding himself of sin through fictional characters is an effort to be less self-aware. The fictionalization of his past lives in the forms of Sapo, Macmann, and Lemuel distances him from the past rather than providing any meaningful retrospection. According to Stewart, "Malone forges other selves so as to become the author, not just the victim, of his own effacement. If he can utter it, maybe he can suffer it without inordinate pain." Malone's separation from his past in the form of writing gives him a sense of control over his life while also providing an escape from the pain of memory. Malone describes how, when he first started writing, his characters came to him, "pleased that someone would want to play with them," but that "it was not long before I found myself alone, in the dark." In an effort to save himself from the darkness, he gives up trying to "play" and describes how he "took to [himself] for ever shapelessness and speechlessness, incurious wondering, darkness, long stumbling with outstretched arms, hiding." Malone gives up writing or "playing" for a time, which he sees as a period of darkness during which he lacked a means of expression. Trapped in "earnestness," Malone has spent "nearly a century trying to escape."[47] The state of "play" that Malone has now given himself over to is essentially a state where boundaries do not exist; objective truth therefore proves elusive. Malone's efforts to separate himself from himself succeed only in further blurring his identity, as the line between author and character becomes less determinate. Malone's project of dying reveals the inexpressible nature of death but also emphasizes his state of indeterminacy, caught between the desire to narrate and the desire for silence.

The religious confessional becomes, in the novel form, a way of expressing a character's motivations to a reader. Beckett plays with this relationship between the character and the reader by presenting the reader with a narrator who repeatedly contradicts himself and who cannot divide himself from his fictions, collapsing the distance between writer and character, author and narrator. The written word in Beckett's novel undermines the certainties of existence. The reader is plunged into Malone's inventing consciousness that makes truth indeterminable. The confessional form also has a metafictional aspect to it, as Malone comments on his current state, his writing, and his characters' actions. These metafictional aspects to Beckett's novel resemble those parts found in fellow Irishman Laurence Sterne's 1758 novel, *Tristram Shandy*. As Patrick Murray notes, all of Beckett's novels, aside from *Murphy*, lack recognizable plots; they "have no real beginning or end, breaking off when the inimitable flow of talk dries up."[48] The similarities between *Malone Dies* and *Tristram Shandy* are of particular note because they situate Beckett's work in a larger context of Irish writing that defies linear narrative temporality and plotting and disrupts narrative unity. The metafictional quality of these texts also makes them humorous, as the narrative comments on and even ridicules the narrator's own situation in the text. Whereas in *Tristram Shandy* the proliferation of stories becomes a kind of farce that mocks the exaggerated importance humans attach to their own lives, *Malone Dies* pares narrative down to its barest functioning and, in so doing, parodies human attempts to control death.

As Malone dies, he resolves to tell himself stories in order to relieve the tedium of waiting. He even plans a "programme" that he intends to follow in order to structure his narrative. After some deliberation, Malone decides that the program will involve five different parts: "Present state, three stories, inventory, there." He then remarks, "An occasional interlude is to be feared. A full programme. I shall not deviate from it any further than I must. So much for that. I feel I am making a great mistake. No matter." Even as Malone sets out a plan for himself, he immediately anticipates deviations from the plan and fears that it is a mistake to have made the plan at all. What becomes clear from Malone's resolutions about the shape, structure, and delivery of his narrative is that he is attempting to construct an ideal format for his story and thereby do things he has "always wanted to do" but never has. The need to fulfill these desires is driven by his proximity to death. Malone declares that his "desire is henceforward to be clear without being finical. I have always wanted that too. It is obvious I may suddenly expire, at any moment."[49] Malone's wish to know his own death is linked to his determination to make his writing as clear as possible. At the same time, Malone's inability to know the precise moment death will come makes him unsure of how exactly to shape his story.

Whether he succeeds in following it or not, Malone's "programme" can be read as a kind of plot. Eric Levy, however, makes a distinction between Malone's "programme" and a traditional novelistic plot: "But in narrating his own elapsation, Malone replaces the convention of plot (which concerns a temporal sequence of events tending toward some terminus or end) with the convention of 'programme' . . . whose function, unlike that of plot, is not causal but diversionary, 'While waiting I shall tell myself stories, if I can.'" The need for diversion is, Brooks would argue, a necessary aspect of plot, as it extends the desire for closure before reaching the end. Therefore, Malone's diversion becomes part of the plot structure itself, driven as it is by fear of death. Malone's stories can then be read as what Brooks would call "intentional deviance, in tension, which is the plot of narrative."[50] The stories of Sapo, Macmann, and Lemuel progress in a temporal sequence from adolescence to old age. While these stories do not function in the same way as a traditional plot since Malone repeatedly interrupts their narrative progression, they do serve as a retrospective of Malone's life, albeit a fictional one. In this sense Malone's narrative resembles more plot-driven novels that review a character's life leading up to his death, such as Tolstoy's *The Death of Ivan Ilych*, which begins with the death of the title character and then moves backward to review his life leading up to death. Though the novel begins from the perspective of the mourners, the focus then shifts to Ilych himself, hinting at the increasing privatization of the deathbed scene while also imposing a retrospective narrative that begins with the final judgment of a man's life before examining how his life was lived. Malone's narrative takes this privatization of the deathbed and the notion of individual salvation to a new extreme, as he must give both witness and testimony to his own demise.

Throughout his narrative, Malone struggles to adhere to his "programme," but he ultimately fails to achieve any sort of retrospection and is therefore unsuccessful in his project of dying. The lack of a final period as a grammatical signifier of closure indicates that Malone's narrative reaches no determinate meaning by the end. The lack of separation between the physical world and the world of his imagination has severe repercussions for his project of dying. Only Malone's bodily pain reminds him that he is still part of the physical world. He confesses, "The truth is, if I did not feel myself dying I could well believe myself dead, expiating my sins, or in one of heaven's mansions. But I feel at last that the sands are running out, which would be the case if I were in heaven or hell. Beyond the grave, the sensation of being beyond the grave was stronger with me six months ago."[51] The suffering implied here is a way of separating the earthly world of physical sensation from the spiritual realm. Yet this process of bodily suffering does not redeem Malone; he can still go to either heaven or hell. However, he does note that the sense that time is running out does not vanish with death but remains in both heaven and in hell. The idea that his sensation of "being beyond the grave" was stronger with him "six months ago" suggests that his sense of temporality is distorted and he has no clear idea of whether he is progressing or regressing.

This notion of being caught between moving forward and slipping backward, characterizes Malone's state and also highlights the relationship between dying and narrating. Stewart argues, "The paradox of death for Beckett, at once inner and outer, here and coming, inherent and unarrived, is at last and at large the paradox of narrative art as spatialized temporality. Story, a shape as well as a duration, is present to us as a defined whole even when it moves, or we through it, towards the completion of itself as a form." Malone's dying, then, is intrinsically linked with his writing. As we readers move through Malone's text, we are also moving closer to death and to the end of the novel. The comic aspects of the novel come from Malone's failure to accomplish his goal of writing himself to death. Malone thinks of how he remembers the last few days better than any other time: "When I have completed my inventory, if my death is not ready for me then, I shall write my memoirs. That's funny, I have made a joke. No matter."[52] Malone's contention that he will write his memoirs is a "joke" because it is an impossibility: he cannot write about what he cannot remember. This macabre humor serves to defend Malone against the terror of his own death. Malone realizes that even after all his preparation, death may not be "ready" for him. His narrative does not simply depict a progression toward death; it is also a move toward accepting mortality.

Malone assumes that, eventually, he will run out of lead and is concerned with correlating this loss of material objects with the death of his mind. The act of writing makes the interior thought become a material object, become exterior. By this process Malone is able to make some sense of his existence. He notes, "I have nothing to guide me. I did not want to write, but I had to resign myself to it in the end. It is in order to know where I have got to, where he has got to."[53] The ending slip between "I" and "he" makes clear that Malone cannot distinguish himself from his creations. In an effort to make sense of his life, Malone must establish a relationship between his mind and the external world. The difficulty of the task then becomes temporally complicated, as he has no way of establishing a time line for his life.

Malone's loss of temporality can be attributed in part to his inability to distinguish present from past: "It's vague, life and death. I must have had my little private idea on the subject when I began, otherwise I would not have begun, I would have held my peace, I would have gone on peacefully being bored to howls, having my little fun and games with the cones and cylinders . . . until someone was kind enough to come and coffin me."[54] The act of "beginning" (presumably to write) results in a clearer definition of self, but the more Malone writes, the more this distinction becomes confused. If he had not begun to write, he would have remained blissfully unaware of the separation between life and death until he was put into a coffin.

Anxieties over burial and coffins are characteristic of Beckett's fiction and also feature prominently in Beckett's play *Endgame*, in which Clov refuses to bury Hamm, Nell's death is unmarked by ceremony, and when Hamm asks to be put in his coffin, Clov tells him that there aren't any more coffins available. Being put in a coffin signals for Beckett's characters an end to suffering. The unavailability of coffins in

Endgame recalls, as Julieann Ulin notes, "one of the prominent horrors of the Famine continually remarked upon in the folklore," namely, the shortage of coffins for Famine victims and the large amounts of the dead that went unburied. Similarly, Malone's desire to be coffined can be read as a reference to the suffering endured during the Great Famine. However, there is a humorous aspect to the notion of someone being "kind" enough to "coffin" Malone that is evocative of the Irish wake tradition that featured games alongside mourning rituals. Indeed, Mercier links macabre humor to Irish wakes, "at which merriment alternates with or triumphs over mourning, in the very presence of the corpse."[55] Malone's alternation between death and play mirrors this process, situating him in an Irish tradition of using humor as a way of accommodating death. At the same time, Malone's reference to coffins alludes to the much-grimmer context of the Famine during which such ritualization was not possible, indicating a tension between the need for ritualization and an inability to ritualize.

This blurring of boundaries between life and death created by play is, then, problematic for Malone, as he cannot determine what is real and what is fiction. His sense that nothing exists or inexists can be read as an effort to destroy consciousness and therefore banish suffering. Levy argues, "But if, as Malone claims, 'Nothing is more real than nothing' . . . and the preeminent object of consciousness is therefore nothing, then consciousness itself cannot be distinguished from a vacuum." Levy's contention here is that consciousness cannot exist if nothing exists within it, if there is no sense of self and other. At first, this paring away of consciousness might appear a problematic assertion in a narrative that is itself so self-conscious. However, as Levy contends, it is in fact through Malone's attention to himself and his state of "inexisting within that attention" that Malone "progressively evacuates himself of all content." This self-emptying is linked by Levy to kenosis, or Christ's concession of his power when he reconciles himself to dying for the sins of man. In religious kenosis, the self is emptied of its human desires in order to exist for God. Malone is attempting a similar process of self-evacuation of desires, but unlike the process of religious kenosis, Malone is doing this to relieve himself from pain. Levy observes that Malone is caught between the two poles of "consciousness of nothing (or silence) and consciousness of distraction (or noise)" but that the play between these two extremes is complicated by the effort of consciousness to reestablish contact with the evacuated content, resulting in a struggle between what is recorded in Malone's exercise book and what goes unnarrated.[56] This state of indeterminacy between consciousness and content is not, however, merely a feature of what Levy calls "Beckettian mimesis," or the attempt to represent nothing, but can be read as a commentary on the state of modern men and women after World War II. Advances in modern medicine and warfare and the advent of psychoanalysis have created a pressure on humans both to know themselves and to escape themselves, to inflict harm but also to relieve suffering. Malone's efforts to escape his humanity prove impossible, as even after he has evacuated his consciousness, there still exists the need for narrative even if there is nothing to narrate, the need to understand death even if it cannot be understood.

In *Malone Dies* narrative highlights failure and the breakdown of temporal order. Elizabeth Barry observes a link between Beckett's and Augustine's conceptions of memory in that both conceive of it as a progress of imagined duration and both are intrigued by the relationship between memory and time. This relationship is highlighted in Malone's narration as he struggles to reconcile his memory of past events to his current state, always questioning his own thoughts. Through Malone's exclusion of slow moments from his narrative, Barry argues, Beckett "dismantles temporal experiences by emphasizing the discrepancy between textual and 'real' time," which slowly diminishes as the narrative progresses. In the end, Malone's attempt to correlate the time of his actual death with his textual death proves impossible. Even as Malone tries to conclude that "never there he will never never anything there any more" and thus end his character's fictional existence, these are just bits of fragmented sentences.[57] The reader is still left with the unsettling image of Lemuel, his hatchet raised and coated in blood that will never dry. Malone's pencil, his paper, and his ability to write run out before he gets the chance to narrate an end to Lemuel.

Malone Dies is Malone's attempt to purge himself of human desires in an effort to empty himself, creating a narrative with an absent center. However, Malone ultimately fails in his project of self-annihilation, as he cannot rid himself of the compulsion to fill the silence. Malone's self-emptying takes the form of words, which in turn begins a narrative, thus resulting in an act of creation rather than destruction. The problematic aspect to this process of creation is that Malone is compelled to expel words in an effort to express the experience of death, even though no accurate representation is possible.

Setting himself against religious and novelistic rules of dying, Malone seeks to narrate his dying process and to control the moment of his death. Yet as he soon realizes death itself is a state of formlessness, of silence, that which defies representation, Malone's project of self-annihilation is doomed to fail. Despite his best efforts, he cannot rid himself of the compulsion to narrate or the human need for meaning.

The persistence of religious references in *Malone Dies* alongside notions of death as oblivion suggests a disjuncture between the religious and the secular but also indicates that these two ways of making sense of death are not as disconnected as they may first appear. Even as Malone attempts to destroy religious structures of meaning, residual longings for the hope offered by Christian notions of heaven remain. In an effort to situate himself within a temporal sequence, Malone questions whether it could be Easter Week: "If it can, could this song I have just heard, and which quite frankly is not quite stilled within me, could this song have simply been to the honour and glory of him who was the first to rise from the dead, to him who saved me, twenty centuries in advance? Did I say the first? The final bawl lends colour to this view."[58] Malone's location on the brink of absence, between the speakable and the unspeakable, impels his narration, but it also reveals his need for meaning despite his knowledge that there is none.

In many ways, *Malone Dies* is the opposite of the bildungsroman, which depicts the moral and psychological development of a character from adolescence to adulthood, and instead depicts a process of unraveling or unmaking.[59] Beckett's novel is neither a manual on how to die nor a novel that describes a coming into being; rather, it is an exercise in representing the process of dying. Elaine Scarry discusses the problems involved in representing physical pain and death. She argues that any given subject resists representation, forcing the writer to alter sentence structure to accommodate this resistance, in essence shaping the writing around the resisting subject. In the case of Beckett's narratives, she argues, intentional objects are eliminated in order to draw attention to the universal human condition: "Given complexity and uncertainty, Beckett, in effect, clears the boards and begins again with those things about which we can be certain. Each of his works isolates and bestows visibility on modes of feeling, thinking, and acting that collectively constitute the central human experience."[60] The structure of *Malone Dies* is shaped around the unrepresentable subject of death. Malone's efforts to narrate this experience involve novelistic structures that have traditionally used death as a boundary to contain human experience and endow it with meaning. Malone's invocations of religious imagery reveal the human need for these devices to offer hope and at the same time emphasize how pointless these efforts are.

In the novel, death traditionally functions as a narrative limit, a way of revealing the boundaries that give meaning to life. As is evident from both *Ulysses* and *The Ante-Room*, Irish novels often reject this idea of death as a final boundary that provides closure. Instead, these novels connect death with the beginning of life. Like Joyce and O'Brien before him, Beckett uses the novel form to critique religious conceptions of death and the way that these attitudes limit life.

In *Malone Dies* Beckett reverses the notion of death as the final limit and uses it to destroy the rituals that hold meaning in place. What is revealed is that the need for narrative and for the consolation provided by Christianity persists, even when hope appears to be gone. In its portrayal of a man caught between religious notions of salvation and modern notions of godlessness, *Malone Dies* depicts the troubled state of modern humans following the horrors of World War II. At the same time, Beckett's use of macabre humor defends against a sense of utter hopelessness. Malone's very attempt to end himself through his writing is darkly humorous because it is impossible. Despite his efforts to construct a plot that he can follow, Malone's story cannot be told in a straightforward narrative, but functions in a discursive way.

While Irish novelists such as John McGahern attempt to piece the novel form back together, he retains Beckett's sense of hollowed-out subjectivity and meaningless rituals. Whereas Beckett portrays the excruciating state of inexistence and the inability to truly die as both comic and tragic, McGahern sees death as the only reality. *The Barracks* returns to the theme of the dying mother and depicts an Ireland in which the rituals of Catholicism dominate daily life but have become meaningless. Narrative offers the promise of expression and therefore relief from suffering, but it fails to alter society or to undo the constructs of reality. Beckett's darkly humorous tale of a man who cannot escape himself and therefore cannot die becomes, for McGahern, a grim reality where death threatens to destroy meaning and order but ultimately fails to provoke change.

4

Ritual and Denial in a World Stripped of Illusion

John McGahern's *The Barracks*

In his memoir, *All Will Be Well*, John McGahern wrote, "Those who are dying are marked not only by themselves but by the world they are losing. They have become the other people who die and threaten the illusion of endless continuity."[1] Written after his diagnosis with cancer, this quotation reveals McGahern's attitude toward dying; it also describes the way he depicts it in his fiction. The prospect of death endows the individual with a particular vision, an ability to appreciate the beauty of the world but also to view that world realistically—stripped of illusion. McGahern's first published novel, *The Barracks* (1963), tells the story of Elizabeth Reegan, a woman dying of breast cancer in the rural West of Ireland in the late 1940s. She lives in the police barracks with her husband, Reegan, a severe and emotionally distant police sergeant, and his children from his first marriage. The novel's depictions of Elizabeth's struggle to accept death and her process of dying are similar to other novels in this study in that they feature a conflict between Catholic notions of heaven and secular views of death as oblivion, a preoccupation with purgatory and with suffering, and a reliance on death to reveal the underlying structures of narrative. McGahern's novel, however, is unique in that it binds the concerns of the dying with those of the living, depicting a society that destroys and renews itself in a cycle of repetition. Read in the historical context of Ireland in the postwar decade, a period characterized by stagnation, crisis, and a lack of economic growth that resulted in mass emigration, *The Barracks* offers insight into the harsh realities that characterized Irish life at this time, particularly the constricted role of women, whose sense of self and agency were bound up in domestic life.[2] While rituals protect the illusion of continuity, McGahern's depictions of Elizabeth's physical pain establish death as the ultimate definer of a reality characterized by disjuncture.

In McGahern's fictions death becomes the ultimate manifestation of reality, a manifestation that when denied results in a traumatized sense of the past that continues to haunt the present. *The Barracks* returns to the theme of the dead or dying mother so apparent in the novels of Joyce, O'Brien, and Beckett and describes the process of dying from her point of view. In no earlier fiction do we experience the mother's death from so intimate a vantage point. Though Elizabeth has no children of her own, she features in McGahern's novel as a mother figure for Reegan's children from his first marriage. Rather than serving as a haunting reminder of the past, as in *Ulysses*, or as a symbol of a way of life that is dying, as in *The Ante-Room*, McGahern's Elizabeth is a strong and independent woman whose life has been equally influenced by the teachings of the Catholic Church and by existentialist notions of death as nothingness. As she faces the end of life, Elizabeth struggles to establish her own identity and to find meaning in her existence. In this sense, Elizabeth resembles Beckett's Malone as she attempts to define herself against physical objects and to establish a sense of self, while at the same time wanting to escape the self-enclosing confines of her own mind. The plot of *The Barracks* is driven by Elizabeth's imminent death and increasing urgency to make sense of her life before she dies. Elizabeth's memories of the past divert the novel's forward movement, sending it backward. Her memories enrich Elizabeth's present life and provide the novel's central conflict between existentialist notions of authenticity and freedom and the Catholic beliefs that bind her to her family and social world.

From the outset of the novel, Elizabeth is anxious and preoccupied by the lump in her breast, fearing the worst. Her diagnosis of cancer early in the novel confirms her fears and results in a narrative focus on her thoughts and memories as she recalls her time as a nurse during the Second World War, when she met and fell in love with a young doctor named Michael Halliday, who exposed her to existentialist ideas about the nature of life and death. McGahern's depiction of death and dying, as seen from Elizabeth's perspective, highlights a conflict between the human need for ritual and for meaning and the existential notion that life is ultimately meaningless. In *The Barracks* McGahern dramatically yokes together a naturalist depiction of the oppressive social conditions of Irish life in the 1940s and 1950s with Elizabeth's internalized, subjective narrative in order to highlight the rift between social reality and individual consciousness. Rituals may normalize death and make it bearable, but there is a danger associated with concealing death's traumatic impact. For McGahern, narrative holds the possibility of creating meaning through the expression of an individual vision, even if that vision cannot ultimately alter reality.

Throughout the novel, as Elizabeth gradually begins to accept death, her life becomes more meaningful, awakening within her a desire to express her perceptions of the world around her. The great tragedy of *The Barracks* is that Elizabeth's vision of beauty dies with her, since she cannot translate it into the social world around her; that social world cannot accommodate her sense of things. The continuation of *The Barracks'* narrative beyond the end of Elizabeth's life indicates that death has not released the narrative tensions but merely exposed them. Unlike Beckett's dismantling of narrative to reveal its drives and structures, McGahern relies on the structures and foundations of narrative to offer a social critique. He uses the account of Elizabeth's illness to express hidden truths and unspoken emotions. The third-person omniscient-narrative perspective McGahern employs allows him to depict not only the inner workings of Elizabeth's consciousness but also the perspective of the other characters who live in the barracks, including her husband, Reegan, whose own worries and concerns provide a wider view of life in rural Ireland. This technique emphasizes the limits of narrative and the unknowable nature of death that is concealed by the chores of everyday life. The threat of death challenges the boundaries of Elizabeth's world. She can no longer exist wrapped up in the needs of others, unconscious of herself and "whatever beauty had been left her," as she is at the beginning of the novel.³ The pain and physical suffering she must endure separate her from all that, forcing her to define her identity and beliefs.

At the center of *The Barracks* is Elizabeth's conflict between her knowledge that death is the end, the ultimate definer of reality—a painful but necessary disjuncture in the cycle of life—and her desire to believe in a Christian heaven that she initially finds comforting, with its promise of continuance and continuity. This theme of continuity surfaces at the end of the novel with a description of the funeral and burial rituals that follow Elizabeth's death as well as an account of the lives of Reegan and the children after her burial. Death functions as a trauma or point of rupture in the novel's plot, but the narrative continues despite the loss of Elizabeth's central voice.⁴ However, as the traumatic element of the novel, namely, Elizabeth's death, does not occur until the end of the book, the focus of this chapter is primarily on how the prospect of death shapes the novel's structure and the way that bodily pain is represented. This focus allows for an understanding of the way that death becomes traumatic rather than exploring its traumatic effects. The bodily pain associated with dying is even more pronounced in McGahern's novel than in *The Ante-Room* or *Malone Dies* in the sense that Elizabeth cannot express herself or her pain in writing as Malone can, nor is the pain described at a distance as it is in O'Brien's novel, where Agnes observes her mother's physical suffering but experiences it only secondhand. McGahern's narrative becomes a way for Elizabeth's life to gain expression, thus providing readers with a deeper understanding of how pain often deprives its victims of language, robbing them of their powers of expression. Elaine Scarry suggests that the problem of representing pain, both physical and mental, stems from its very inexpressibility, causing pain to become a tool of both creation and destruction. Scarry further suggests that the human power to create is the result of the intentional relationship between pain and imagination; it is a person's ability to imagine pain that makes it an active force in self-creation.⁵ In *The Barracks* Elizabeth is continually denied expression of her emotions and must instead find an outlet for self-expression through prayer and ritual. She occupies a liminal space between the desire to express her own feelings and society's denial of these feelings. Her physical pain shatters Elizabeth's connection with her social world, forcing her to assess her life and to construct a sense of self. The emotional pain of death is the ultimate reality that, because denied and diverted into ritual, continues to haunt the society that refuses its expression. Rather than simply rejecting ritual and its ability to give structure and meaning to life, McGahern instead stresses that the reality of death must be confronted and that doing so enhances our capacity to live well.

The theme of death, particularly the trope of the dying or dead mother, is one that McGahern returns to again and again. McGahern's first two novels, *The Barracks* and *The Dark*, deal with representations of the towering figures who shaped his early life experiences: his mother and father.[6] There are intriguing similarities between McGahern's fictional depictions of mothers and fathers and his own life. This connection between McGahern's life and his fiction was further strengthened by the publication of his autobiography, *All Will Be Well*, in 2005, which describes his troubled relationship with his father and close connection with his mother. After his mother's death from cancer when McGahern was nine, he was sent to live with his father in the police barracks. McGahern was forced to leave the home he shared with his mother several days before her death, and he was not allowed to attend her funeral. In the memoir McGahern poignantly describes how on the day of his mother's funeral he watched the clock and imagined the rituals of the funeral, going so far as to envision the four candles being lit around her coffin and the Latin incantations that accompanied the ceremony. He writes that he "followed the Mass from movement to movement, holding the clock in my hands, weeping."[7] This event obviously had a traumatic impact on McGahern's life, and it is particularly significant that he reenacts the funeral ceremony by imagining its rituals, as he will later re-create similar scenes in his fiction.

The painful impact of a mother's death features not only in *The Barracks* and in *The Dark*, where young Mahoney's mother has also died from cancer, but also in *Amongst Women*, where Moran's first wife is dead; in *The Leavetaking*, in which the protagonist's mother dies in a scene very similar to the one described in *All Will Be Well*; and in *The Pornographer*, where the protagonist visits his dying aunt in the hospital. McGahern's early loss of his mother has a particularly devastating impact on him because it was an "invisible death," one that was kept from him and his brothers and sisters and relegated to the private rooms of their old home, illustrating what Philippe Ariès would call part of modern society's "denial of death."[8] Dermot McCarthy cites the event of his mother's death and the guilt he felt at not fulfilling his promise of becoming a priest, as well as his incomplete farewell to her, as the forces driving McGahern's need to create narrative fiction.[9] The suggestion that this need to narrate arises from an early trauma helps to explain how death functions as a force driving plot and narrative. However, it is problematic to attempt, as McCarthy does, to project McGahern's creative impetus as a writer on to his fictional characters as if their desires and his were one and the same. Nevertheless, McGahern's traumatic experience with death furthers our understanding of the structure and narrative perspective of *The Barracks*. McGahern's choice of an omniscient narrator highlights the problems involved in narrating death and representing physical pain. While death compels narrative, it also defies representation. The physical pain involved in dying as well as the restrictions placed on her by society, which require her to assume the role of housekeeper and caretaker to her husband and children and to blindly accept Catholicism, limit Elizabeth's power of expression. The story cannot be told solely from her point of view because she does not have the means to narrate it fully.

The Barracks is unique in McGahern's oeuvre, as it does not simply depict the aftereffects of the loss of the mother; rather, it offers the story from her perspective. As such, the novel offers a glimpse into McGahern's creative imagination as well as insights into the way that death functioned in Irish society at the time. As Joe Cleary rightly argues, *The Barracks* reveals the "fundamental structure of feeling" that "shapes McGahern's imaginative world; a traumatized sense that death is always the ultimate and most visceral reality, and that an emotionally assimilated acceptance of one's own transience, and that of others, will afford the only decent response to this condition."[10] McGahern's depiction of a dying woman in rural Ireland reveals something fundamental about Irish cultural attitudes toward death, suggesting that death as a final end must be both acknowledged and accepted. Elizabeth is surrounded by people who do not want to face death and choose to ignore the fact that she is dying until it is too late. They then immerse themselves in ritual in order to escape death's harsh reality, promoting a false sense of continuity between life and death. McGahern's portrayal of Elizabeth's final illness has a dramatic impact on the reader, ending with a sense that death is not only the most ultimate reality but that the concealed nature of this reality results in a trauma—a break in time's continuity—that is bound to be repeated. Rather than focusing on McGahern's own processing of trauma or his creative imagination, this chapter focuses on the way that Elizabeth's dying is portrayed—how death compels her narrative and how bodily pain shapes its expression.

Situating *The Barracks* within a larger context of Irish novelistic depictions of death reveals how McGahern challenges modern attitudes toward dying and approaches to the end of life. McGahern uses the rupture that death creates to challenge assumptions about the nature of life. As David Malcolm notes, much of the critical analysis of McGahern's work has tended to focus on the relationship of the individual to the greater Irish community or on debates as to whether his view is ultimately pessimistic or optimistic or whether his work can be seen as experimental or traditionally realist.[11] Expanding such criticism, this chapter discusses the relationship between death and narrative in *The Barracks*, arguing that narrative telling becomes a way of revealing the tensions and traumas that pervade Irish society more broadly. For McGahern, the denial of death and the tendency to bury the pain of loss in ritual further serve to perpetuate suffering by promoting an illusion of continuity. Narrative offers a way of expressing suffering, even if it does not always alter reality.

When *The Barracks* was published in 1963, it was generally well received and marked McGahern's arrival on the Irish literary scene, winning him a McCauley fellowship. In her review of the novel in the *University Review* in 1964, Kate O'Brien comments on the simplicity of the story's outline and on McGahern's concern with the unities of place, time, and theme. She identifies the place as a Garda barracks in County Roscommon, the time as a single year around 1950, and the theme as family life and love in relation to death.[12] These "simple" outlining features of McGahern's novel remind the reader of the specific social context in which this story is set and how these factors all contribute to Elizabeth's attitude toward death. O'Brien's one criticism is that Elizabeth's philosophical reflections do not seem within the reach of her "simple form of consciousness."[13] O'Brien's suggestion that Elizabeth is incapable of such sophisticated thought highlights the contrast McGahern establishes between Elizabeth's inner consciousness and her social reality. Elizabeth's backward-looking narrative remembers her early years as a nurse in London—a period for her philosophical questioning and self-exploration.

O'Brien's comment about Elizabeth's limited intellectual capacity is particularly relevant when considering McGahern's work in relation to her own novel *The Ante-Room*. In addition to their similarly retrospective settings, both novels feature female protagonists who are heavily influenced by Catholic teachings and whose everyday lives are shaped by Catholic rituals and regulations. Most important, both women experience a crisis of faith in the face of death. Despite these similarities, O'Brien's Agnes is markedly different from McGahern's Elizabeth: Agnes remains bound to Catholic teachings, whereas Elizabeth's exposure to cosmopolitan life and modern ideas of selfhood have created within her a need to realize her desires. McGahern's depiction of Elizabeth's inner thoughts shows the influence not only of Catholicism but also of international philosophic thought shaped by two world wars on a woman living in rural Ireland. O'Brien views the existence of such a woman as an impossibility, but McGahern's depiction cannot simply be dismissed as unrealistic; his portrayal of Elizabeth may indicate a cultural shift away from the conception of the rural housewife as blindly faithful to Catholicism.[14] In fact, it is the contrast between Elizabeth's philosophical questioning and the naturalistic description of her surroundings that makes *The Barracks* such an important novel in its depiction of death and dying.

Critical work on *The Barracks* has tended to focus on the religious aspects of the novel and on McGahern's depiction of rural Irish life, viewing him as a chronicler of an Ireland that is slowly being lost.[15] Critics such as Eamon Maher and James Whyte stress the significance of the novel's depiction of a rural Ireland trapped between unattainable ideas and an inadequate reality.[16] McGahern's naturalist account of Elizabeth's illness in *The Barracks* is contrasted with his depiction of her decidedly existentialist concerns with self and subjectivity, freedom and authenticity, emphasizing the power of reality to deny individual expression.

Denis Sampson argues that McGahern's metaphysical concerns and use of symbolism and rhythm to represent the unconscious display a distinctly modernist style or aesthetic.[17] Despite the modernist traces inherent in McGahern's portrayal of time and his concern with consciousness and individuality, it is clear from the linear structure of his narrative that follows Elizabeth from the diagnosis of her illness until her death, and from his realistic depictions of life in the barracks, that the novel can ultimately be classified as naturalist, a style that ties it to the social reality of postindependence Ireland.[18] McGahern's depiction of Elizabeth's struggle with breast cancer further reflects his desire to engage with social issues. Brian Liddy calls McGahern's decision to give Elizabeth breast cancer an "active choice," noting the invasive nature of the illness as it attacks her individuality and sexuality.[19] Elizabeth's illness affects not only the way that she perceives the world around her but also the way that she is perceived, stressing the separation between the individual and society. Liddy notes that the religious rituals in the novel do not spring from Elizabeth's own moral leanings but are perpetuated by the community in which church teachings have been so deeply ingrained that most people cannot see beyond them. This insight is particularly relevant to Elizabeth's struggle to reconcile her own doubts, fears, and philosophical questioning with the Catholic society that surrounds her.

This chapter argues that McGahern's depictions of death and of bodily suffering in *The Barracks* do not merely reflect the social values of Ireland during this time, but also reveal how death becomes traumatic as a result of its being denied and repressed. For Elizabeth, death is the ultimate end. The narrative, however, continues beyond her life and thus suggests a historical time sequence that exists outside her life sequence, indicative of the natural life cycle that continues on in spite of death.[20] The opposition between Elizabeth's agonized, existentialist consciousness and her personal, social, and familial commitments underlines the competing values at work on the modern individual struggling to make sense of life and death in a rapidly changing world.

Employing a naturalist style to depict the harsh social conditions and religious restrictions that constrain Elizabeth and prevent her from attaining the authentic existence valued by existentialists, McGahern offers a critique of Irish Catholic society. However, he softens and avoids the absolute darkness, pessimism, and misery associated with naturalism through his close third-person narrative that focuses mainly on Elizabeth's point of view. Her perspective provides readers access to the joy and the natural beauty of everyday life, increasing the sense of tragedy when this vision dies along with Elizabeth at the end of the novel. Elizabeth's final acceptance of death is an expression of her own free will, which grants her freedom and peace. The great tragedy of the novel is that her subjective vision is ultimately consumed by the reality of her social conditions. Through the contrast between naturalism and subjectivism, McGahern suggests that death need not function as trauma but that an awareness and acceptance of life's brevity can enhance human existence.

McGahern's narrative structure and style are key to understanding the ways that he uses death to reveal the tensions that underlie Irish society. *The Barracks* follows Elizabeth from just before her diagnosis with breast cancer through the progression of her illness and finally to her death, ending with the effects of the loss on her family and community. The opening pages of the novel establish Elizabeth's connection to her social reality through her role as stepmother to Reegan's children and highlight her lack of a sense of self. The novel opens: "Mrs. Reegan darned an old woollen sock as the February night came on, her head bent, catching the threads on the needle by the light of the fire, the daylight gone without her noticing." This description is decidedly naturalist in its dark setting and grim but realistic focus on a woman's social surroundings. Elizabeth's first name is withheld here; instead, the narrator uses her married surname, indicating that her social identity takes precedence over her individual selfhood. She is so focused on her chores that she fails to notice the fading daylight. A page later, one of the children addresses her as Elizabeth, and she thinks how "her Christian name—Elizabeth—struck at her out of the child's appeal. She was nothing to these children." Here Elizabeth's name is a kind of insult that seems to strike at her as it reminds her that she is separate from the family and that she will never be a mother to these children. Her sense of her own uselessness is further enhanced by the fact that Elizabeth's attempts to conceive her own children had "come to nothing."[21] From the outset of the novel, Elizabeth views herself as a failure because all her attempts at creation have been fruitless.

The third-person omniscient-narrative perspective provides the reader with access to Elizabeth's thoughts and therefore offers an understanding of her physical pain, as well as exposing her own anxieties about her life. The portrait of Elizabeth created by McGahern highlights her personal failings but also, more important, underscores the negative influence of her social reality that denies her expression of her emotions. This denial is most apparent in Elizabeth's interactions with her husband, Sergeant Reegan. Reegan is not abusive, but he is self-centered and ignores her emotional needs. When thinking about Reegan, Elizabeth notes, "He'd have none of the big questions: What do you think of life or the relationships between people or any of the other things that have no real answers? He trusted all that to the priests as he trusted a sick body to the doctor and kept whatever observances were laid down as long as they didn't clash with his own passions."[22] Elizabeth's observation that Reegan refuses to deal with the "big questions" suggests that she does not blindly accept the world as he does. The reader is given access to Elizabeth's thoughts and doubts about her faith in God, but these ideas are never given voice through dialogue or written down by Elizabeth. The only way that Elizabeth's worldview achieves expression is through McGahern's representation of her interior private life.

Critics such as Maher, Sampson, and Whyte tend to view Elizabeth as an artist in her worldview, using McGahern's description of her as a "way of seeing" to buttress their arguments.[23] It is indeed significant that McGahern describes Elizabeth in such a way, as it indicates that, despite the close third-person omniscient-narrative perspective, she is the novel's primary lens through which the social world is perceived. However, despite the fact that Elizabeth does, at points, resemble an artist in her vision of everyday life, her artistic role is never fully realized; she cannot share her vision of beauty with anyone else. The removed third-person narrative is necessary, as Elizabeth is too embedded in the social reality of her life to adequately express her doubts and fears. This narrative aspect of McGahern's novel illustrates both the inexpressible nature of suffering and of death while also highlighting the restrictive aspects of Elizabeth's position.

The link between Elizabeth's vision and McGahern's artistic aesthetic is strengthened by the third-person narrative mode, a connection made much of by McCarthy, who sees McGahern's artistic vision as interchangeable with Elizabeth's. It is perhaps more constructive to interpret the omniscient narrator as a mediator between art and artist; that omniscient narrator supplies a voice that speaks for Elizabeth, who, deprived of language because of her physical pain, cannot speak for herself. As Scarry explains, "Because the person in pain is so bereft of the resources of speech, it is not surprising that the language for pain should sometimes be brought into being by those who are not themselves in pain but who speak *on behalf* of those who are."[24] The idea that physical pain deprives the sufferer of the power of expression helps to explain McGahern's choice of narrative mode. The omniscient narrator must speak on behalf of Elizabeth but also has the power to express the thoughts of Reegan and the other characters in the novel. This narrative perspective becomes increasingly important as the characters fail to express their feelings to each other through dialogue. Therefore, the only way to know how Reegan feels about Elizabeth's illness or to view Elizabeth from outside her own mind is through the omniscient-narrative voice, which affords a window into the communal consciousness that would otherwise be impossible. However, it is Elizabeth's experiences and thoughts that dominate the novel.

Elizabeth's imminent death drives the plot of the novel forward, with each of the novel's events focusing on her physical pain, her operation, and her final confinement to bed. Yet even as the plot progresses toward her death, Elizabeth's mind and conception of her self are ever changing and developing. As Elizabeth's life moves toward death, her memories disrupt the linearity of the plot. Her memory can, as Liddy notes, "transcend time; it moves in and out of time remembering an array of divided years in one present moment." However transcendent Elizabeth's memory might be, it is her knowledge of the severity of her illness that causes her to think back to her time as a nurse during the Second World War, a time when her love affair with Halliday exposed her to existential ideas that there is no God or afterlife and that a person's life has meaning only for that individual. McGahern's focus on individual existence and the way that death reveals the absurdity of life is characteristic of existentialist philosophy as elaborated by Jean-Paul Sartre. Yet McGahern does not fully endorse this view, either; Elizabeth does not completely accept that her life is meaningless and finds beauty in Catholic rituals. From the beginning of the novel, Elizabeth is aware of her inability to make sense of her own life: "She couldn't ever hope to gain an ordered vision of her life. Things were changing, going out of her control, grinding remorselessly forward with every passing moment."[25] Elizabeth is aware that the changes going on around her are drawing her only closer to death and will provide her with no true sense of her own life or what it means. As she gradually accepts the fact that she will die, her experience of the world around her takes on a deeper meaning. Though this acceptance of death while also living well converges with Sartre's philosophy, Elizabeth is not fully atheist, either. Religion forges a bond between her and reality; without it she has nothing by which to define herself.

Elizabeth's past work as a nurse means that she has cared for the dying and witnessed a great many deaths. When she first visits the local doctor after noticing the lump in her breast, the doctor treats her differently from other patients because she used to be a nurse, commenting that the knowledge granted by the profession allows doctors and nurses to "face up to the situation." Elizabeth is appalled by what she perceives as his snobbery and thinks about how no one dies better than anyone else. She reasons:

> She had seen doctors and nurses ill and getting well again and dying as she had seen people from every other way of making a living getting well and dying too; and it made small difference. No one was very privileged in that position. Money and a blind faith in God were the most use but there came a point when pain obliterated the comfort of private rooms and special care as it did faith and hope. The young and old, the ugly and the beautiful, the failure and the successes took on such a resemblance to each other in physical suffering that it seemed to light a kind of truth.[26]

Although Elizabeth has experience with the dying, she considers herself no more prepared for death than anyone else. Truth, unity, and connection to others are found not through pain and suffering. Elizabeth lists money and blind faith in God as useful tools for fighting off death, but notes that pain has the power to corrode both these things. Also evident here is the idea that all life is diminished in the end, as a person's failures or successes make no difference when facing physical pain. For Elizabeth, death does not bestow meaning on an individual life but serves to bind together people who, as a result of their suffering, have lost both their material comforts and their faith. Yet throughout the novel Elizabeth struggles with her loss of faith and her fears about death alone, finding no one to share in or understand her suffering.

The fact that Elizabeth remains relatively isolated from her community and that she faces the pain of dying alone is particularly poignant as it contrasts with her vision of death as an experience that everyone shares. The idea of pain as a unifying force has a wider application to Irish culture in general, or at least to the wider social problems as McGahern sees them. Scarry's analysis of the metaphors used to represent pain in Western culture is useful here: "It will gradually become apparent that at particular moments when there is within a society a crisis of belief—that is, when some central idea or ideology or cultural construct has ceased to elicit a population's belief either because it is manifestly fictitious or because it has for some reason been divested of ordinary forms of substantiation—the sheer material factualness of the human body will be borrowed to lend that cultural construct the aura of 'realness' and 'certainty.'"[27] According to Scarry, when ideologies begin to break down or fail to appear vibrant, real, or certain, the physical attributes of the human body will become appropriated away from that body and will become attributes of a cultural construct, lending it realness. Instead of a person experiencing the suffering caused by an ideological crisis or crisis of belief in their own body, they experience it through the pain of another. Christ on the cross is one such example of a symbol of physical suffering, which people identify with in moments of crisis and lends their own suffering certainty.

The Barracks depicts a world in which the Catholic Church still dominates social and religious life, but secular existentialist ideas are gaining a stronghold. This society deprives Elizabeth expression of both her physical and her emotional suffering. As a result of this denial of expression, she identifies with images of bodily pain such as Christ on the cross, which accords with Scarry's further assertion that the failure to express pain will result in its "appropriation and conflation with debased forms of power," whereas the successful expression of pain will work to "expose and make impossible that appropriation and conflation."[28] Elizabeth cannot express her pain herself, but McGahern's omniscient narrative allows the reader access to her thoughts, which serves as a way of articulating her suffering. In his portrait of a dying woman whose society refuses to acknowledge her suffering, McGahern exposes the way that Catholic images of bodily suffering gain power as belief wanes. McGahern makes it impossible for the reader to view Elizabeth's death as a necessary sacrifice for the greater good and refuses to in any way ameliorate the pain it causes.

McGahern does not suggest that Elizabeth's existential crisis is indicative of the inner consciousness of the average housewife in rural Ireland. Rather, he deliberately juxtaposes Elizabeth's inner questioning and past experiences with her present reality in order to locate the source of a larger crisis in Irish culture that he is looking toward. Her physical pain deprives her of any ordinary forms of comfort; instead, her shared conception of bodily suffering lends authenticity to her experience. Elizabeth struggles to reconcile her memories of her past and, with them, existentialist notions of death as meaningless, with her present Catholic-dominated reality that promotes a false sense of continuity and denies her expression of her pain. Rather than wholly accepting either view, Elizabeth attempts to find her own meaning in Catholic rituals, discovering in Christ's suffering a metaphor for her own pain. Through his depiction of Elizabeth's fatal illness, McGahern challenges Irish cultural attitudes toward death and dying that promote an unquestioning belief in the afterlife and insist on life's continuity. Instead, McGahern suggests that the individual life must be allowed expression and that it is only through a shared understanding of pain and suffering that the trauma of the past can be overcome.

From the moment Elizabeth first suspects that she has cancer, she has little doubt that she will die. The hospital visits and procedures only confirm what she already knows. Yet she has difficulty accepting the certainty of her own death, and when Catholicism fails her, she turns to the existentialist thoughts introduced to her by Halliday. Though she can now understand these philosophies better, she still finds them unpalatable. Remembering her affair with Halliday, Elizabeth thinks, "Everything was stripped down to the bone now and there was the pure nothingness he'd spoken about. Nothing could ever stay alive, nothing could go on living."[29] Elizabeth does not really believe in an afterlife and knows that death will not confer retrospective meaning on her life. She accepts that she must forge an authentic selfhood, since it will not be given to her by any other means. But even while she takes this existentialist atheism for granted, she never entirely renounces Catholicism. She may not wholly believe in Catholic dogma, nor does Catholicism provide her the comforts of common belief. But it gives her something that she seems to value, even though it is not always clear what exactly that something is.

In order to relieve her suffering, Elizabeth focuses on the natural world—the changing of the seasons and her observations of nature's pattern of death and rebirth—which help her to accept death. Part of this acceptance comes from the knowledge that she cannot control her own fate; there is no way of stopping the progression of time. In a departure from Christian traditions, such as the *ars moriendi* that instructed the dying person on how to prepare for death by ordering his or her life, Elizabeth makes little attempt to order her affairs or review her sins. She works as a housewife to Reegan and the children until she is too sick to continue. Elizabeth considers her own mortality and prepares with dread for an initial visit to the doctor: "She couldn't bear to think about it, she'd have to show her own ageing flesh to the doctor, and it was no use trying to think anything, it was too painful, it all got on the same claustrophobic road back to yourself, it was the trick always played you in the end."[30] Although Elizabeth recognizes the unrelenting progression of time toward death, as is evident in her description of her own aging flesh, she cannot bear to consider her mortality because she fears that it will lead deeper into herself and away from the community. She finds it necessary to ignore the severity of her illness in order to go on with life. While Elizabeth may be able to inwardly admit knowledge of her imminent death, she must outwardly continue as if she did not have this knowledge. Instead of an image of death as a release from the body, Elizabeth describes the process of dying as claustrophobic, a sinking away into oneself instead of expanding out into the greater world. The loss of the individual as the self becomes more tied to a declining body indicates the impossibility of projecting interior beauty onto reality.

McGahern's depiction of Elizabeth's moods, alternating between hope and despair, acceptance and denial, realistically portrays someone facing a grave illness. Her perpetual fluctuation between beliefs resembles Beckett's Malone as he struggles to establish his own identity so that he may die properly. A comparison with Beckett reveals the differing ways that death functions as a narrative limit. On the one hand, Beckett uses death to reveal and destroy the structures and bounds of narrative; on the other, McGahern's portrayal of death points out the societal constrictions that inhibit narration. Beckett, in his attempt to end his character's narrative by dismantling the structures that make sense of life and death, ends up revealing the drives and desires that impel narrative. McGahern similarly reveals the nothingness at the heart of human existence, but for him death both provokes narrative as well as restricts it. While the rituals and structures that give order to human existence appear empty in McGahern's novel, they retain the possibility of meaning, and McGahern attempts to restore their value. McGahern is, then, picking up where Beckett left off, revealing the possibilities of death as both a creative and a destructive force—one that compels narrative but also ends it.

A particularly poignant instance from *The Barracks* that bears the mark of Beckett's influence occurs just before Elizabeth undergoes her first operation to remove the cancer. She thinks of how the anesthetist will come and put her into a sleep from which she may not wake. She laments, "Oh, if she could clutch and suck every physical thing around her into her being, so that they'd never be parted; she couldn't let go of these things, it was inconceivable that she could die!" This notion of drawing physical objects to oneself is reminiscent of Malone's inventory in *Malone Dies*: "Perhaps I should call in all my possessions such as they are and take them into bed with me. Would that be of any use? I suppose not. But I may. . . . Then I shall have them all round me, on top of me, under me, in the corner, there will be nothing left, all will be in the bed, with me."[31] Both Elizabeth and Malone seek to draw the physical world into themselves. Unlike Elizabeth's desire to clutch and suck every physical thing in an effort to prolong and extend life, Malone's collection of objects is an effort to end the world outside of himself. The differences in these two characters illustrate the inherent differences between McGahern's and Beckett's fiction. Beckett expresses a loss of faith in the world and in narrative's ability to accurately describe that world, while McGahern finds narrative embedded in nature, contained and sometimes concealed by the rituals of everyday life. For McGahern, death does not just compel narrative; it remains a mystery that endows life with meaning.

The influence of Beckett's fiction on McGahern's novel is undeniable, especially in the existential concerns that both exhibit. Sampson correctly points out that the main difference between the two authors is that McGahern's fiction is more engaged with the material, social world and Beckett's with abstract landscapes. Yet Sampson's assertion that suffering for both serves as a way of opening a window into artistic experience is somewhat more questionable. In Sampson's view, Elizabeth and Malone are alike because of their efforts to understand suffering and death. However, Beckett's Malone is an artist not just in his efforts to understand these matters, but also in his attempts to express them in words, to write them down, whereas Elizabeth fails to project her artistic vision onto reality. Agreeing with Sampson's view of Elizabeth as an artist, Maher argues, "[Elizabeth] plays the role of the writer here, in a sense. She is wording the world, naming things, places and people."[32] The problem with this conception of Elizabeth as a writer is that she never finds expression through the medium of written words, and her pain remains accessible only through the third-person omniscient narrator. If anything, Elizabeth's constant revising of her own beliefs can be said to resemble an author's creative process, but she never fully realizes this role.

The most apparent instance of Elizabeth's failure to convey her emotions in written words occurs when she sits down to write a letter to an old friend from the London hospital. As she contemplates what to include, she realizes that she will be forced to describe her life with Reegan as well as her diagnosis of cancer and her growing indifference to life. Soon after she sets pen to paper, she finds herself crossing out her own words, unable to accurately convey her meaning. She finally decides that the whole exercise is useless: "She'd leave it so, it was a ridiculous thing to want to write in the first place, how could she have ever imagined she'd carry it through. She rose from the table and dropped the sheet of notebook paper into the fire, watched the flames crumple it like a hand closing a fist would, and the charred fragments float in the smoke."[33] Elizabeth's inability to represent her emotions in language is "ridiculous," suggesting that it is outside the limits of rational possibility. Importantly, the notebook page crumples into the image of a fist, a symbol of violence. The image of the flames closing around the paper symbolically represents the cancer that is closing in around Elizabeth's life, but also signifies the closed nature of the society in which she lives and the conventions that prevent her from expressing herself to others. Instead of envisioning the immortality her life will take on through communal remembrance of her accomplishments, Elizabeth sees her life reduced to charred fragments of ash.

The fist of flame closing in around Elizabeth's letter is indicative of her emotional and physical pain. The fact that her suffering finds expression through an image rather than through words suggests the extent to which Elizabeth has been denied powers of expression as pain begins to define her reality. Thinking of how her life can be measured or judged, Elizabeth reasons, "Her life was either under the unimaginable God or the equally unimaginable nothing: but in reality it was no lesser thing; and the reality continued, careless of whether the human accident was a child waking up in terror or two people bored together."[34] In his depiction of Elizabeth's spiritual crisis, McGahern searches for a way of reconciling the beauty and comfort of Catholic rituals with the existentialist knowledge that nothing exists beyond life. While these two views are not easily reconciled, Elizabeth's acceptance of death and of the absurdity of human existence allows her to find beauty in the idea of Christ's suffering for man. Pain binds Elizabeth to reality, a world colored and made real by death.

Scarry shares this concern with pain and suffering as absolute definers of reality, arguing that the world can be "made" through pain in that it assures one of earthly reality and is used to mediate power. However, the world can also be "unmade" by pain as it is used by torturers to reduce victims' lives to a state where they are unable to speak or imagine a reality outside of pain.[35] Both the processes of "making" and "unmaking" that are products of bodily pain are evident in

Elizabeth's "unmaking" (her struggle to express her emotion or imagine a reality beyond this worldly one) and her "making" (the new way of seeing brought on by her illness). In his portrayal of Elizabeth's physical suffering, McGahern highlights death's transformative power to destroy life, but also to endow it with meaning. For McGahern, death is a painful reality, but it has also the ability to provoke narrative creation, which offers the possibility of redemption from suffering through its expression of an individual vision.

McGahern's depiction of dying in *The Barracks* is focused on Elizabeth's attempt to reconcile Catholicism with existentialist philosophy, but, intriguingly, it does not endorse either view. The novel begins with Elizabeth's rejection of Catholicism, finding it meaningless and the thought of heaven of little use in easing her anxieties about death. By the end of the novel, Elizabeth has found few answers to the big questions of life and death, but she does find her own meaning in religious rituals and their power to ease emotional suffering. For Elizabeth, death is a philosophical question; more important, it is a social and religious concern. Catholicism is important to the novel because it shapes Elizabeth's social reality, a world to which she stands at some remove. Her illness and imminent death further separate her from this reality. As the novel progresses, Elizabeth finds that rituals such as the rosary allow her to connect to her social world, thus endowing these rituals with a personal significance.

Elizabeth's connection with the rosary raises the question of whether she is a religious character. Maher calls her the most religious of McGahern's characters in her attachment to rituals and ceremony and in her knowledge that there are deep mysteries of life that are not to be understood. Elizabeth's attachment to ritual is, however, best understood as her way of relating to the people around her. The meanings she derives from these rituals are not necessarily related to their customary religious function. At the beginning of the novel the nightly recitation of the rosary is a chore for her. As her illness progresses, the rosary takes on a deeper meaning. She does not pray the rosary for forgiveness or to atone for her sins but, rather, as an expression of her own inner joy: "The rosary had grown into her life: she'd come to love its words, its rhythm, its repetitions, its confident chanting, its eternal mysteries; what it meant didn't matter, whether it meant anything at all or not it gave her heart release, the need to praise and celebrate, in which everything rejoiced." Deprived of expression of her pain or, indeed, of her joy, Elizabeth finds release through ritual and prayer. Frederick Hoffman's distinction between the modern imagination and the religious one is useful for understanding Elizabeth as a character who still inhabits a religious world but possesses a modern consciousness. Hoffman makes the distinction between the religious imagination, which seeks to transcend time and to "will the existence of eternity," and the acceptance of death as a natural end to human time prevalent in modern literature, which sees time as an irreversible progression toward death, an attempt to "explore the quality of experience within time."[36] Bearing in mind Hoffman's description, Elizabeth's focus on her daily experience and her acceptance of death are more in line with the modern imagination than the religious. While she finds beauty in the idea of Christ's sacrificial suffering, Elizabeth ultimately fails to believe that his sacrifice grants eternal life. Although she does not believe in life after death and is therefore not a religious character in the truest sense of the word, Elizabeth does cling to aspects of Catholicism to make life bearable. Her reliance on ritual and prayer is most apparent at times of physical suffering or mental anguish in the form of loneliness. In these instances she prays in an attempt to alleviate pain and recites the rosary with her family to gain a sense of social belonging.

Elizabeth finds a particular connection to the way of Calvary, discovering a link between Christ's life and her own. The similarity between Christ's suffering and Elizabeth's bodily pain makes the latter endurable in her mind and elevates the pettiness of her own life to a higher level of meaning. Elizabeth considers this connection: "And if the Resurrection and still more the Ascension seemed shadowy and unreal compared to Calvary, it might be because she could not know them with her own life, on the cross of her life she had to achieve her goal, and what came after was shut away from her eyes." Elizabeth's description focuses attention on the human body by making a connection between bodily suffering and divinity and of the wounding of the body as a way of confirming God's divinity. The cross becomes a particularly important object here, especially given Scarry's argument that it serves as a way of mediating God's contact with humanity. Christ's suffering on the cross, unlike the wounds inflicted by weapons, inflicts pain over a long period of time rather than immediately, thereby depriving the executioner of power, destroying the relationship between power and pain, and allowing them to exist side by side.[37] This suffering over a long period is similar to Elizabeth's slow death from cancer that, while robbing her of expression, endows her with the power of seeing. Suffering, then, occurs within the context of creating while also functioning as a way of rendering powerless.

Elizabeth's inability to imagine a future life beyond suffering indicates her lack of belief, which, according to Scarry's definition, involves crediting an object with more power than oneself. Despite her identification with Jesus on the cross, Elizabeth does not believe in God's power the way she believes in her own experience. By prioritizing her own experience over her faith, she suggests that she is more of an existentialist than a religious Catholic. Yet Elizabeth does not seem to fully grasp the existentialist contention that the individual must find his or her own meaning from life and not from other religious or secular sources. According to existentialism, it is the individual's quest for and ability to find meaning that matters the most. In Elizabeth's view, the individual quest is neither possible nor imaginable, a failure that causes her to create a false opposition between existentialist belief in meaninglessness and a Catholic confidence in meaning. McGahern creates this false opposition in order to highlight one of the problems with existentialist thought as he sees it. He thinks that the existentialist focus on the individual quest for meaning must not forget that life is lived socially. Thus, he keeps at bay the existentialist reliance on the isolated individual and seeks some form of communal connection. In *The Barracks*, at least, this connection is maintained through Catholicism, which also stresses the communal.

Late in the novel, Elizabeth questions whether she would have been better off had she not met Halliday and been exposed to his existentialist thinking. She then thinks that she might have met someone else who would have had a similar influence and notes that her vision had never been the same as his and that "what he had woken in her grew so different that it could barely be recognized as the same thing." Elizabeth's exposure to existentialist thought has caused her to question her Catholic faith and has taught her to rely on her own experiences to make sense of the world. This sense of things has, partly as a result of her Catholic upbringing, turned into something different in her mind, resulting in the development of Elizabeth's own vision. As she lies in her sickbed, Elizabeth thinks, "All real seeing grew into smiling and if it moved to speech it must be praise, all else was death, a refusal, a turning back; refusal to admit she knew nothing and was nothing in herself, a creature of swift passage, moving into whatever reality she had, the reality she knew nothing about."[38] The emphasis Elizabeth places on "real seeing" suggests that she has achieved an authentic sense of self and no longer sees the world through someone else's vision. The only way to express this vision is through smiling and praise, optimistic gestures that are puzzling in the face of physical suffering and death. In her rejection of the idea that she is "nothing in herself," Elizabeth is rejecting existentialism, refusing to simply accept herself as "a creature of swift passage," and instead praising the world, affirming life and its mysteries. At the same time, she is not wholly religious, as she does not fully believe in God and in the afterlife.

As *The Barracks* progresses, Elizabeth's physical world diminishes from the whole of the barracks to a single bedroom. The reduction of Elizabeth's life to a smaller and smaller sphere of experience until the limits of her reality extend no further than the sides of her sickbed corresponds to Scarry's assertion that "to have a body, a body made emphatic by being continually altered through various forms of creation, instruction (e.g. bodily cleansing), and wounding, is to have one's sphere of extension contracted down to the small circle of one's physical presence."[39] While Scarry's account of pain focuses on prisoners of war, her analysis of the way that pain is expressed and the way that it is used to control power has a useful application in McGahern's novel. As Elizabeth's physical world constricts, her mind grows ever more expansive as she remembers her childhood home and the familiar streets of London. Her illness awakens a heightened awareness of all that she is losing.

In the last weeks of her sickness when she finally takes to bed, it seems to her that "the whole vital world was in herself, contracting or going outwards to embrace according to the strength and direction of her desire, but it had nothing to do with what someone else thought or felt."[40] The physical situation that Scarry describes of a world reduced by pain, defined by the immediate surroundings, describes Elizabeth's situation both physically and mentally. The sicker she becomes, the more confident Elizabeth becomes in her own vision. But as her condition deteriorates, she also loses all power of extension out into the world. Her physical pain isolates her from her family and social surroundings because it prevents her from performing household duties and deprives her of language with which to express her feelings.

Despite her lack of faith, Elizabeth does find expression through ritual. Though she finds Reegan's devotion to the rosary tiresome, it does allow Elizabeth a release from the burden of her own worries. The extent to which the rosary allows for an expression of her suffering is evident at the beginning of the novel when no one notices that she says twelve Hail Marys in a row because she feels sick; at another point she is touched by Reegan's offering the rosary for an unnamed "special intention" the night before she gets the test results from her doctor. The rosary beads were given to Elizabeth by a priest she nursed in London and were brought from Spain and are more than a hundred years old. They hold a special significance for Elizabeth: "She felt the warm wood of the beads in her fingers. They were old and rather rare, she knew, and there was a relic of St. Teresa of Ávila enclosed in the carved crucifix." There is a significant parallel to be drawn between Saint Teresa's life and Elizabeth's, as Teresa also questioned her faith, suffered from illness, and stopped praying. Elizabeth, too, is unable to pray when she suffers terribly after the initial operation to remove the cancer: "She couldn't pray. *I believe, O God. Help my unbelief,* rose to her lips and sounded as dishonest as something intended to be overheard, she'd never made it part of her life, it was not in her own voice she spoke."[41] Elizabeth desires a way to express her own authentic voice and beliefs. It is not simply that she does not believe in God, but that she needs to experience things in order to believe in them.

This perspective is similar to Saint Teresa's, whose conversion was inspired by her religious experiences and visions. Teresa developed a form of mental prayer focused on the individual's relationship with God, and her writing is unique among mystical theologians because she relies so heavily on the personal experiences that she describes in her autobiography, *The Life of Saint Teresa of Ávila*.[42] The link between Teresa's life and Elizabeth's is strengthened by this reliance on personal experience and on finding an individual way of praying. Elizabeth is caught between being fully atheist or entirely religious. She finds that rituals, even when emptied of religious meaning, can take on a personal significance. In one sense Elizabeth lives very much within the religious structures of rural Irish society, but its promise of heaven provides no comfort for her.

As she nears death, the rules of society and religion come to hold even less meaning for her, especially in the face of physical pain. What distinguishes Elizabeth is her desire to believe, even though she knows that there is nothing worth believing in. The unsharable nature of her pain, and also her philosophical questioning, isolates her and deprives her of any sense of catharsis. She tries to tell Reegan that she is unlikely to recover from her illness, but he refuses to accept it. Elizabeth thinks that it was "as if he was afraid that if he shared with her the knowledge of her approaching death he'd be forced in some way to share her dying too. No one at all would help her." What would really help Elizabeth it seems is for others to just acknowledge that she is dying. Their denial is intended to comfort her, but it really only comforts others.[43]

Catholicism and secular humanism alike fear death too much to acknowledge it. McGahern's novel suggests that this failure to acknowledge death ultimately diminishes everyone. Elizabeth considers how "she'd have to go on as she had lived, alone. She'd have to pretend to believe she was going to get well, whether she did or didn't, and the worst was thinking it happened to be the one thing in the world she wanted to believe."[44] Elizabeth pretends to believe in order to maintain a bond to the community she lives in, regardless of what she believes. Yet this feigning of belief is not entirely false, as Elizabeth wants desperately to believe that she will live. However, she finds that she cannot escape death. Unable to convince herself that she is going to get well, she must pretend, offering an appearance of hope while her inner despair remains unacknowledged.

Elizabeth's outer conformity and inner resistance to Catholicism become even more apparent in her dying moments, when the deathbed confessional is reduced to a formula. McGahern does not attempt to dismantle the idea of the deathbed confessional itself—the ritual remains intact—but it is in a hollowed-out form. By separating Elizabeth's thoughts from the words she speaks to the priest, McGahern emphasizes the rupture between thought and action and renders the significance of the confessional void by denying its power to grant absolution. As the priest administers the sacrament to Elizabeth's sickbed, she thinks of all the patients she has prepared for the same rite and how this ritual they have been brought up to believe in is ultimately meaningless. She considers how she never let this priest close to her and notes that "in the confessional she put everything into formula. She didn't let him know any of her thoughts. . . . Her thoughts had been with her too long, they had changed themselves too often for her to want to change them now because of another's interpretation of a law big enough to include every positive position of honesty; and if her own truth wasn't within herself she didn't see how it could possibly concern her anyhow."[45] This notion of truth being within herself is key to how religion functions in Elizabeth's life. While she "puts everything into formula," conforming outwardly to the rules of Catholicism to give her life shape and structure, she retains a private world within herself.

As Elizabeth dies, she is drawn further into herself, destabilizing the physical world dominated by the rules of Catholicism. Her inward journeying awakens a desire to establish her own beliefs and allows her to see the unbounded natural beauty of the world. She cannot envision a world beyond death and therefore has no illusions about a heaven that awaits her. Instead, Elizabeth struggles to establish a sense of self before she dies. She realizes that by accepting death, her own perception of the world has been enhanced. However, she never fully realizes this vision or expresses it. She dies with "her fingers groping the sheets, the perishing senses trying to find root in something physical."[46] Without a way of sharing her beliefs with others or to impact her social reality, Elizabeth's life is rendered meaningless in the end, her final attempt at permanence reduced to a groping for something physical to cling to.

The great tragedy of *The Barracks*, and the cause of the greatest trauma for the reader, is that Elizabeth dies before fully realizing her identity and before she has found a means to express her unique vision of reality, the terrible beauty born of her physical pain. There is no catharsis after Elizabeth's death—the novel's supposed climax—as the event of her passing away is reduced to a generic ritual that shows little of her spirit or individuality. Death, the event that should function as the plot's ultimate realization, a moment of clarity and summing up, is reduced to a ritual that functions as a regressive turning back, as Elizabeth herself predicted in her statement that speech must be praise, "all else was death, a refusal, a turning back."[47] The last scene repeats the novel's opening with Reegan's son, Willie, asking his father, instead of Elizabeth, if he can light the lamps. McGahern ends with this repetition in order to emphasize how little impact Elizabeth's questioning has actually had on reality and suggesting that death's traumatic impact, when denied expression, ends up being repeated.

The ending of the novel functions as a trauma not only for the readers but also for the novel's fictional society. Highlighting the traumatic effects on the community, Elizabeth's death is described as a "shock"; this description is surprising, considering that the novel was building toward this end all along: "After the first shock, the incredulity of the death, the women, as at a wedding, took over: the priest and the doctor were sent for, the news broken to Reegan on the bog, the room tidied of its sick litter, a brown habit and whiskey and stout and tobacco and foodstuffs got from the shops at the chapel, the body washed and laid out—the eyes closed with pennies and her brown beads twined through the fingers that were joined on the breast in prayer."[48] The parallel drawn between a happy event like a wedding and a sorrowful one like a funeral returns to Joyce's merging of deathbed with the marriage bed and focus on the woman's body as a site of both birth and death, as well as indicating a reduction of life to ritual, regardless of the emotions involved. The depiction of Elizabeth's body is particularly poignant, as it seems not even to belong to her anymore and certainly gives no indication of individual identity. Her hands and eyes are described not as hers but are identified by the impersonal article "the." The only thing that belongs to "her" is the rosary beads, further strengthening the connection between her life and Saint Teresa's.

The novel does not end with Elizabeth's death—the climax toward which it has been building—but continues on for several pages, describing Reegan's long-awaited resignation from the police force, prompted by Elizabeth's death and the reckless notion that he has nothing left to lose. In this sense, Elizabeth's death can be said to have some impact on the living and is therefore given some significance. However, any hope that Elizabeth's life might have positively impacted her family and community is destroyed by the novel's closing scene. This scene, referred to above, which repeats the opening of the novel only this time without Elizabeth, most poignantly indicates the traumatic effect her death has had on her family and community. In both scenes the scarlets and golds of the religious pictures have faded owing to the darkening night, and the Sacred Heart lamp on the mantelpiece turns "reddish." In the final scene, there "seems a red scattering of dust from the Sacred Heart lamp," whereas in the earlier scene there is no mention of the dust, but the wind and rain at the windowsills are part of a "spell of silence." The scene can be read symbolically, with the fading religious images suggesting a decline of faith and the eagerness to illuminate the encroaching darkness as indicative of an unwillingness to explore life's darker mysteries. Most important, however, is the spell of silence and "their fear of the coming night" that Willie breaks with "visible strain" to ask if he can light the lamp.[49] Willie's fear of darkness is greater than his fear of asking about the lamp, but his anxiety about the question is indicative of the way that fears are often denied expression. Elizabeth's death is the realization of the novel's linear plot, but the temporality of the children's lives and of Reegan's is not broken by this death but continues on, suggesting that the significance of Elizabeth's death has been repressed. This repetition is also indicative of the nature of trauma that inflicts a hurt so profound and unutterable that it must be repeated to be understood.

McGahern's novel, then, although closer to O'Brien's in style and subject matter, shows hints of Beckett's existentialism and echoes Joyce's interest in the woman's body as a site of making and unmaking. *The Barracks* contributes to our understanding of death and dying in the modern Irish novel not only in that it offers a distinctly Irish view of death in its depiction of suffering and of a purgatorial sense of being caught between Christian notions of an afterlife and secular existentialism, but also because of its emphasis on the power of narrative to preserve cultural norms as well as to challenge them. Elizabeth, the mother figure, is the central narrative point of view, but she is denied expression of her suffering, finding emotional release in rituals that take on a personal meaning for her while also connecting her with the larger community. The threat of death provokes Elizabeth to question the purpose of human existence. The introduction of death as trauma at the end of *The Barracks* demonstrates how death regulates narrative and, more important, how it reveals the repressed narratives that, when expressed in novel form, have the power to both capture and challenge society's values.

This notion of narrative as a way of expressing the physical and emotional pain of death and loss that inflicts a traumatic wound in Irish society finds further articulation in Anne Enright's *The Gathering*, whose traumatized narrator, Veronica, must write out her past in order to understand it. However, McGahern is much more forgiving than Enright in his attitudes toward Catholicism and the importance of ritual in coping with grief. While Enright suggests that an airing of past grievances will provide a way of moving forward, McGahern is much more aware of the failure of narrative to provoke social change and acknowledges the human need for ritual to relieve suffering.

McGahern's final novel, *That They May Face the Rising Sun* (2002), exhibits a much less critical attitude toward Irish Catholic society and the rituals that attend the dead than his first novel, *The Barracks*. This last novel suggests that McGahern found a way of reconciling the individual and society, of both lamenting the loss of a way of life that is passing while also offering consolation for that loss. For the novel's main character, Ruttledge, the process of laying out the body of his friend Johnny "made death and the fear of death more natural, more ordinary." Ruttledge later remembers how Patrick Ryan ordered Johnny to be buried with his head lying to the west so that "when he rose with all the faithful he would face the rising sun," in accordance with Catholic belief in the resurrection of the dead.[50] Unlike the generic rituals that take over after Elizabeth's death in *The Barracks*, which obscure the importance of her life, the significance given to the processes of laying out and burying the dead in *That They May Face the Rising Sun* indicates the power of ritual to naturalize death without denying its reality. In his depictions of death and dying, McGahern attempts to reconcile the reality of human experience with its perceived meaning and significance. For McGahern, there are no easy answers to the questions these issues raise, but an acknowledgment of these mysteries can enhance the quality of an individual life. Narrative cannot solve the problem of death, but, like ritual, it can assuage grief and suffering.

5

Death without Resurrection and the Modern Wake

Anne Enright's *The Gathering*

Set in Ireland during the economic boom period of the "Celtic Tiger," *The Gathering* (2007) tells the story of Veronica Hegarty as she mourns the suicide of her favorite brother, Liam. Narrated by Veronica as she journeys to England to retrieve Liam's body and attempts to assemble the disparate members of the Hegarty clan—who are spread between Ireland, England, and South America—for his wake, the novel's plot is structured around the communal act of grieving. However, Veronica feels separated from her family by her grief, her mind perpetually moving backward, remembering a time before Liam's death. *The Gathering* is a novel concerned with death as a break in continuity, forcing a backward look on the part of the bereaved even as life continues to move forward. It is this gap between the past and the present that most interests Enright, as it mirrors the holes in memory created by traumatic experience that must be repeated in order to be overcome.[1] As well as relying on collective funerary rituals to bestow meaning on life, Veronica finds that written narrative can endow personal, subjective experience with a communal value. In Enright's novel the act of writing functions as a way not merely of accessing traumatic memories but also of working through grief in an attempt to understand life through death.[2]

In *The Gathering* death provides an impetus for Veronica's narrative and provokes her to interrogate the past in the hope of arriving at the truth. The dead haunt Veronica's memories, and she feels morally obligated to write their stories down so that they will not be lost. This relationship between death and the act of creating a written narrative calls to mind Peter Brooks's suggestion that novelistic narrative is a way of making sense of death. The reading of novels is then motivated by the desire to understand life through fictional death.[3] Enright's novel works through many of these same ideas about writing as a way of easing human anxieties concerning mortality, but it focuses attention on the traumatic wound that results from repressed histories. Utilizing the popular trope of the Irish wake, *The Gathering* interrogates Ireland's relationship to death by comparing it with British funeral practices. Rather than defusing the cultural tensions between religious and secular approaches to death, *The Gathering* opens up the wounds of the past and suggests that the act of narrative can provide a way of healing these wounds, even if it does not compensate for past losses.

Structured around the act of gathering, both Veronica's family members and her memories, the plot oscillates between Veronica's account of her current life, descriptions of events in the recent past, memories of her childhood, and an imagined account of her grandmother Ada's life from 1925 onward. Many critics would classify *The Gathering*'s style as postmodernist owing to the novel's fragmented structure that deliberately resists assimilation into linear narrative, along with the self-conscious mode of narration, dark humor, and suspicion of the authority of grand narratives. Yet the novel's concern with individual consciousness and attempts to reconcile the individual's subjective experience with a larger cultural history prevent Enright's novel from being easily classified as realist, modernist, or even postmodernist. *The Gathering* breaks with what Gerardine Meaney calls the "residual modernism" that remains "integral to much Irish writing and Irish writers' self presentation." Meaney goes on to argue that *The Gathering* challenges the distinction between postmodernism and realism, as "the narrative's realism resides in its self-reflexive uncertainty."[4] Indeed, it is Veronica's doubts about the truth of her claims that establish a world outside of her own consciousness. Veronica's distrust of reality is in part owing to Liam's suicide that works to unravel the separations between the real and the not real.⁵ Death does not serve as the ultimate definer of reality, as it does in McGahern's fictions; rather, it brings the past into the present. Veronica's description of her life since Liam died can best be classified as surreal in the sense that while strange, nothing that happens in the novel defies the rules of reality: even the corpse that Veronica envisions occupying her car turns out to be a headrest. Death destabilizes narrative authority and calls into question the nature of memory, of historical narrative and the power of words to accurately convey any kind of truth of the past. Sharing a modernist concern with the complex workings of the individual psyche, Enright's novel exhibits a more immediate interest in how these individual memories fit into a larger familial and ultimately cultural history. This chapter employs narrative theory to argue that Enright uses postmodern techniques such as the self-conscious and unreliable narrator to call into question the nature of memory (particularly of the dead), finding in the act of written narrative a way of opening the future by accessing its unlived potential.⁶

The Gathering marks a return to the themes of death, suicide, and memory evidenced in Enright's first novel, *The Wig My Father Wore* (1995), which details the interactions between Grace, a young Dubliner, and an angel named Stephen, who committed suicide and has been sent back to earth to guide lost souls. The novel also, as Hedi Hansson notes, "lacks a linear plot" and instead "traces a kind of reverse development where Grace [the protagonist] regresses from cynical experience to hopeful innocence and a promise of a new beginning at the end."⁷ *The Gathering*, while sharing many of these concerns, manages to connect the surreal elements of death with the reality of Irish life in a way that the earlier novel does not.

Winning the 2007 Man Booker Prize for *The Gathering* served as a turning point in Anne Enright's career and awakened an international interest in the novel.⁸ *The Gathering* depicts an Ireland at odds with itself—at once enjoying the fruits of economic prosperity while also lamenting the inability of this material wealth to heal old wounds. Enright's attempts to understand Irish culture are striking in that they are made in relation to death: the contrast between British and Irish funeral practices, Veronica's various departures and returns to Ireland, the depiction of Liam's wake itself—an event that carries with it cultural stereotypes such as drunkenness and wild celebration, while also serving as an important cultural ritual, particularly in its affirmation of life over death.[9] The plot of *The Gathering* is dictated by Veronica's task of collecting her brother's body from England. This process not only provides Enright's novel with a structure and form, but also proves therapeutic for Veronica, as it forces her to come to terms with her troubled past.

As she sets about the task of making the arrangements for Liam's funeral, Veronica is confronted with old family secrets. Determined to separate fact from fiction, Veronica uses the act of writing to access memories of her childhood as well as the imagined life of her grandmother Ada. The narrative is written in a style that, as Margaret Mills Harper notes, resembles psychotherapy, as it is made up of a series of short chapters that are episodic and not clearly progressive, but ultimately liberating.[10] The narrative oscillation and temporal ruptures of the novel, along with the use of the present tense, often make it difficult for the reader to fix a definite chronological sequence to the narrative. However, Veronica's narration of her grandmother's past remains distinct, as these sections are written in a close third-person narrative mode, which separates narrator and character by using the pronoun "she" instead of "I," while also communicating the thoughts of the character to the reader. Framed by Veronica's current state—disconnected from her life by her desire to write her family history—the novel is endowed with a metafictional quality, as Veronica repeatedly questions the reliability of memory.

In the first few pages, Veronica makes it clear that her act of writing is an attempt to console the dead for the past. The possibility of consolation is found in the process of remembering, with Veronica replaying Liam's life (as well as her own) over and over again in a kind of Freudian repetition compulsion. For Freud, the repetition compulsion reveals that human destiny is controlled not only by the life instinct (*Eros*) but also, more important, by the death instinct (*Thanatos*), an "ego instinct" that manifests in the compulsion to repeat. Brooks applies Freud's theory to novelistic narrative: "Repetition, remembering, reenactment are the ways in which we replay time so that it may not be lost."[11] Liam's death disturbs Veronica's life, and the return of repressed memories provokes within her a need for repetition. Writing, then, serves as a way of reclaiming the past by repeating it, ensuring its survival. However, Veronica's project does not merely involve remembering but also includes uncovering hidden traumas. Imagination, often linked to the future, is opposed to memory, which is linked to the past, and both are used in *The Gathering* to access Veronica's grandmother's history, tying the future to the past. As a boundary of all that can be known, death endows life with meaning through retrospection. Enright's novel is suspicious of the closure provided by death and seeks to interrogate the boundaries that fix meaning and separate present from past.

Beginning with a scene of Veronica and her daughters on the beach where she expresses her desire to write, the narrative moves back to the recent past, where she must tell her mother that Liam has died, and from there to a further imagined past: to the moment when Ada first met Lamb Nugent and her future husband, Charlie Spillane, and then back to memories of her childhood with Liam. The plot is split between her physical movement to England to retrieve Liam's body and return it to Ireland and her psychic journey into the past. The realization of the novel's plot comes at Liam's wake when the past is made real and becomes personal, allowing her to access the further repressed memory of her own possible sexual abuse.

Death in *The Gathering* also prompts a backward look, a narrative retrospection inherent in literary depictions of death. This sense of backwardness is largely manifest in the novel in the form of ghosts (those of Liam, Uncle Brendan, Ada, and Nugent) who contrast with the modern architecture of Veronica's house and with the technologies (a car, a train, an airplane, and a moving walkway) that allow her to move more quickly through time. The uncanny appearance of the past in the present is suggestive of the rupture between the two. Death—toward which life is being propelled and also the cause of retrospection—brings these two temporalities together. In the absence of collective social rituals that bestow meaning upon the dead, the act of writing functions as a subjective way of realizing the deaths of the marginalized as well as allowing Veronica to figuratively die in order to live.

Proclaiming her desire to write down what happened in her grandmother Ada's house when she was eight, Veronica expresses a need to bear witness to an "uncertain event" that she feels "roaring inside her."[12] The need to know this uncertain event echoes the ideas underlying much trauma theory and literature, fitting Enright's novel in a wider British and North American trend of present-tense narration (and trauma narratives). As with many postmodern novels, trauma fiction is distrustful of totalizing narratives that ignore marginalized histories and that are told from the perspective of the culturally or economically dominant. Like other early-twenty-first-century Irish novels such as Sebastian Barry's *The Secret Scripture*, and Patrick McCabe's *Winterwood*, *The Gathering* is concerned with the way that history is represented and understood. But while the metafictionality of Enright's novel fits into wider trends in contemporary literature, the novel is most interested in the specific way that Ireland conceives of itself through narrative.[13]

While Veronica's status as a traumatized narrator makes her unreliable, the metafictional quality of *The Gathering* endows the text with a realistic quality as she depicts her life as it is. From the start of the novel, the reader is aware of the impossibility of Veronica's ever determining an objective truth. She tells herself, "I do not know the truth, or I do not know how to tell the truth. All I have are stories, night thoughts, the sudden conviction that uncertainty spawns."[14] For Veronica, the truth is contained not in objective reality but rather in "night thoughts," implying a distrust of the visible world and an interest in the inner working of the mind. Her statement that these thoughts are formed from the "sudden conviction that uncertainty spawns" is inherently contradictory, since uncertainty is incapable of spawning conviction. Veronica remains aware of the insubstantial nature of memories and turns to writing as a way of making sense of them.

The temporal structure of Enright's novel allows remembered past, imagined past, recent past, and present to be spliced together in the hopes of arriving at truth. As Veronica notes early in her narrative, everything stops for death, and it is this point of suspension that she remains confined to for the duration of the novel.[15] The plot, then, mirrors this liminal position from which the story is told. The deviations from this main plot form the crux of Enright's novel, as Veronica's mind drifts back to memories of her childhood and adolescence with Liam and then forward to more recent memories of him and to her own life. According to Brooks, the plot of a novel is made up of deviance and error in accordance with Freud's "Beyond the Pleasure Principle," which maintains that the narratable part of an organism's existence is sustained by the "dynamic interactions of Eros and the death instinct." In a similar pattern of deviance and error, Veronica's memories divert the plot from its progress toward Liam's body, delaying the revelation of his (and possibly Veronica's) sexual abuse and postponing her reengagement with her own life. The return of Liam's body to Ireland, one possible ending of the novel, reveals that the novel's plot is centrally about Veronica's awakening to life rather than simply an account of Liam's death. In this way, as Brooks's theory suggests, the repetition of the past in Enright's novel suspends the temporal processes and creates an alternating shuffle between past and present in an effort to bring all these different moments together.[16]

Veronica's writing also bridges the gap between her thoughts and her actions, fictionally containing her life and making the workings of her mind visible to herself. Her interest in the past is psychoarchaeological in the sense that she seeks to reconstruct it not through artifacts and objects but through memory and imagination. Veronica notes the absurdity of her existence since Liam died: "I stay downstairs while the family breathes above me and I write it down, I lay them out in nice sentences, all my clean, white bones."[17] The act of writing separates Veronica from her family and forces her into a nocturnal existence. For Veronica, the process of writing is like that of laying out bones, both suggestive of the laying out of the corpse in Irish funerary practice and vividly evoking the practice of disinterment when the bones of the dead are dug up after the flesh has fallen away, often signifying the end of the period of mourning.[18] The disinterment of bones is also connected to the archaeological project of recovering truths about the past. From the Middle Ages on, in Britain and elsewhere, bones were regularly disinterred to answer specific questions about death or as objects of study for medical purposes.[19] In the Irish context, the disinterment of corpses is often motivated by religion or politics.[20] Veronica's reference to her writing as bones suggests that she wants to dredge up a buried past that is not only personal but also connected to cultural memory. The fact that the bones are "clean" and "white" signals the way that Liam's death functions in the text as a truth-revealing device.[21] Yet Veronica is skeptical of linear histories and of a past that leaves no room for the complicated aspects of life. Veronica's reference to bones brings to mind ancient folk beliefs that the indestructible part of a human or animal—its soul—is found in or connected to its bones.[22] The comparison of writing to laying out bones indicates her desire to reassemble the past in a more truthful light than memory can provide. However, the notion of truth is constantly called into question by Veronica's inability to separate her memories from her imagination. She makes no assertions of narrative authority. Rather, the act of narrative interrogates the past and reveals its gaps.

The laying out of Veronica's "bones" recalls the laying out of a corpse, suggesting that there is something unresolved left to mourn. According to Claire Connolly, Irish death rituals are intimately connected to the Irish novelistic tradition. Connolly refers to John Banim's early-nineteenth-century novel *The Nowlans*, noting, "Laid-out bodies of this kind carry the burden of the representation of the past within Irish romanticism."[23] Veronica's reference to laying out her bones, with its connotations of folkloric beliefs concerning bones and laid-out corpses, connects Veronica's narrative to the end of life rather than to its beginning. The bones serve to frame the structure of Veronica's narrative, a structure that she is perpetually rearranging. The purity Veronica associates with death is evident in several Irish literary texts. From the consolation provided to Michael's family by his "clean burial" at sea in J. M. Synge's *Riders to the Sea* to the bar of soap Leopold Bloom carries in his pocket to Dignam's funeral in *Ulysses*, death rites in the Irish tradition involve purification and anointment by water. As the body decays, the bones are the only reminder of any lingering wounds. However, these wounds are often invisible on the bones themselves and can be known only through narrative reconstruction. Veronica's reference to bones also carries connotations with one of W. B. Yeats's *Noh* plays, *The Dreaming of the Bones*, which features a fugitive from the 1916 Easter Rising who encounters the ghosts of Dermot and Dervorgilla on a Connaught hill. Yeats's blurring of a historical moment (the Easter Rising) with legendary figures from Irish history (the chieftain Diarmuid, whose theft of his wife, Dervorgilla, from another prince resulted in a war involving the Normans and ultimately contributed to Britain's deployment of colonizing forces in Ireland) is similar to Enright's distorted temporalities.[24] Both Yeats's play and Enright's novel exhibit a concerted interest in understanding the present through the past.[25] In both, bones reanimate the past, disturbing ghosts that seek release from suffering. The dead who are deprived of ritual remain trapped in sin. Yeats's play, going against traditional *Noh* structure, ends with a refusal of forgiveness and a sense that the past will be repeated. In Enright's novel, death rituals fail to provide the necessary relief from suffering, but the act of narrative assuages pain.

Speculating about Lamb Nugent and his involvement with Liam, Veronica notes, "I think you might call it a crime of the flesh, but the flesh is long fallen away and I am not sure what hurt may linger in the bones."[26] She distinguishes between human "flesh," which is perishable, and "bones," which contain some of the "hurt." Veronica's words indicate a need to dig up the remaining artifacts in order to recover something that has been lost. However, Veronica's laying out of the bones is not in fact an archaeological project, nor is she laying out her brother's actual bones. Her project is, rather, a literary one, and the bones she refers to are figurative, making up the structural formation of the narrative itself. In order to fully understand how death operates as a way of revealing truth in this narrative, it is necessary to understand its mode of telling.

※

A distinctive feature of *The Gathering* is the testimonial mode in which the story is told. Veronica's narrative style can be situated more widely in the contemporary culture of confession described by Brooks that is deeply influenced by the model of the Roman Catholic confessional.[27] The confessional aspect of narrative itself is directly related to early novelistic relationships with death in the form of the deathbed confessional, a feature of many Victorian novels.[28] In the early days of the Catholic Church, the confession of sins was a public act of penance and, as such, was humiliating and therefore done only once in a person's lifetime. As the confession was privatized and restrictions on its practices were relaxed, it became a verbal and private exchange between the individual confessor and priest. This exchange cannot exist without a sense of selfhood, individuality, and self-narrative. Therefore, confession becomes a way of achieving deeper self-knowledge. Brooks further argues, "The confessional model is so powerful in Western culture, I believe, that even those whose religion or non-religion has no place for the Roman Catholic practice of confession are nonetheless deeply influenced by the model."[29] Similarly, the novel form, while a product of secularization, is still influenced by aspects of religion such as the confessional but is also instrumental in shifting the power of the confession away from the church and into secular hands in the form of written narrative.

The development of the novel form is strongly tied to the Protestant Reformation and its altered practice of confession, which was understood to be a private practice of self-scrutiny and was primarily written rather than shared orally.[30] Ian Watt argues that this Protestant tradition of introspection and private scrutiny occurs even or especially when "religious conviction has weakened."[31] Since Ireland's eighteenth- and nineteenth-century novelistic output is not nearly so accomplished as the British and French traditions, one can expect a different development in the Irish novel, particularly in relation to secularization. In the semisecular culture of Enright's novel, Veronica's confession is not made to a priest or even to a therapist, but instead takes the form of written narrative. In this sense, Enright's confessional mode of narrative calls to mind the Protestant origins of the novel form, situating *The Gathering* in a novelistic tradition of confessional narrative. However, Veronica's confessional mode of writing does not have a religious function, nor is it strictly private. Veronica is confessing not only her own sins but the sins of the community that have gone unspoken for years. Through her written narrative, Veronica hopes finally to grant peace to the souls of her dead relatives (including Liam) and also to achieve a deeper understanding of her place in contemporary culture. Rather than featuring a deathbed scene where a dying character confesses his or her sins, the narrative of *The Gathering* itself takes on this function of purging and absolution, with Veronica's narrative expunging the sins of her whole family.

The culture of confession described in *The Gathering* is centered on the media and radio programs that feature personal accounts of individual trauma and were instrumental in revealing the child sexual-abuse scandals involving the Catholic Church during the 1990s. Indeed, the resurgence in the cultural popularity of the confessional mode not only provides Veronica with a way of accessing her memories (as well as a voice in which to narrate them), but also changes the way she views the past. Thinking about Nugent's sexual abuse of Liam, Veronica notes the changes in Ireland that have allowed her access to these memories. She reflects on how "over the next twenty years, the world around us changed and I remembered Mr. Nugent. But I never would have made that shift on my own—if I hadn't been listening to the radio, and reading the paper, and hearing about what went on in schools and churches and in people's homes. It went on slap-bang in front of me and still I did not realize it."[32] The contemporary culture of confession that Brooks refers to has cleared the way for Veronica to express her own traumatic memories. It also situates Enright's novel in a larger Western culture of confession. While it does not alleviate her guilt, Veronica's confession opens the wounds of the past as well as the possibility of the future.

The contemporary phenomenon of the culture of confession described above is prevalent not only in Ireland but in England and North America as well. This relationship between death and confession becomes particularly complicated in the Irish novel, as, unlike the British or American novel, deathbed confessionals were not a prominent feature of the nineteenth-century Irish novel. Instead, as Derek Hand argues, individual wakes and funerals in the nineteenth-century novel became "a symbol for the death of traditional Irish culture that could be played out again and again."[33] As elaborated in chapter 1, representations of death in James Joyce's *Ulysses* mark a transition from anthropological depictions focused on collective death customs to a twentieth-century novel focused on the meaning of individual death. In Enright we see the influence of contemporary Western cultures of confession that assert the authority of individual experience above all else. Yet Enright is wary of this model as a way of making sense of the world because of its unreliability. Instead, Veronica's written confessional and her imagining of her grandmother's past extend the realm of experience beyond herself to other members of her family and to a past she can never know. In her depiction of Veronica's efforts to write an account of her grandmother's history, Enright highlights how fictional narrative can shape cultural attitudes toward the past through a purging of traumatic experiences and an interrogation of cultural memory.

The Gathering is a novel crucially concerned with the troubled relationship between the present and the past, which is poignantly dramatized in Enright's portrayal of Veronica's family.[34] Although Enright provides a list of the Hegarty family's attributes, these characters remain more caricatures of people than fully developed characters. Enright deliberately describes them in this nonspecific way in order to merge the individual with the communal and to show the effects of trauma on an entire generation rather than on specific individuals. Enright's novel also explores trauma's metaphoric possibility as a tool for destabilizing narrative authority. Veronica's personal experience of loss is linked to wider Irish cultural changes. However, Liam's wake does not function on a symbolic level for the death of Irish culture; rather, it serves as a moment when the past is brought into the present. Trauma as a disruption of narrative authority also destabilizes the notion of death as a point of closure, bestowing meaning upon life.

The Gathering portrays death as that which forces a reconsideration of the past. The fact that Ada, Liam, and Mr. Nugent are all deceased adds to Veronica's sense that her memories of the past are somehow fictional or invented.[35] The knowledge that her perceptions of the past can no longer be confirmed or denied also has benefits, as it allows her to access any hidden truths that the past may contain. After journeying from Ireland to England to retrieve Liam's body, Veronica must return to Ireland without her brother's remains, owing to British restrictions preventing the corpse's release. On the plane Veronica sees Liam's ghost a few rows away from her. As she feels Liam's gaze on her, she recognizes how "uncanny and dead" he looks, commenting that the dead want only the truth; "it is the only thing they require."[36] Interesting here is the use of the word "uncanny," a term that Freud popularized and discussed with relation to death, dead bodies, revenants, spirits, and ghosts.

According to Freud, the uncanny "often arises when the boundary between fantasy and reality is blurred, when we are faced with the reality of something that we have until now considered imaginary, when a symbol takes on the full function and significance of what is symbolizes, and so forth."[37] For Freud, then, the uncanny is something familiar that reappears after being repressed, but it also marks the actualization of something imaginary that has now been given material form. Certainly, this definition fits Enright's novel exceptionally well, as the appearance of ghosts (Liam's and others) indicates the emergence of hidden family secrets and repressed memories that haunt Veronica's consciousness. Freud's further suggestion that the uncanny arises either "when repressed childhood complexes are revived by some impression, or when primitive beliefs that have been *surmounted* appear once again confirmed" can be productively applied to Enright's novel in which primitive beliefs surrounding death take on an added significance.[38]

In her earlier novels such as *The Wig My Father Wore* and *What Are You Like?* (2000), Enright used uncanny doubles in the form of angels and twins to investigate what Jeanett Shumaker identifies as the "conflict between religious ideals and the technophiliac materialism of contemporary Ireland" as well as the relationship between "identity and the universal fear of death." In *The Gathering* Enright elaborates these themes and uses the experience of the uncanny to reveal Veronica's repressed memories and to confirm the continued relevance of premodern rituals and superstitions. Building on Freud's definition, Nicholas Royle's association of the uncanny with "a strangeness of framing and borders, an experience of liminality," accurately describes Veronica's life since Liam died. The unnatural aura of unrest evoked by Veronica's lines, "This is how I live my life since Liam died. I stay up all night. I write, or I don't write. Nothing settles here. Not even the dust," are suggestive both of her liminal position and of the strangeness of borders. Unconventionally framed, *The Gathering* challenges the borders dividing fact from fiction and living from dead. The narrative moves between present and past, infusing the experience of reading with a sense of the uncanny. While Freud only briefly mentions that neurotic men can find women's genitals uncanny, as they are representative of his mother's womb or the "entrance to man's 'old home,' the place where everyone once lived," implying a connection with the death drive, Royle elaborates this idea. For Royle, the feeling of the uncanny is also bound up with the notion of home and "extreme nostalgia or 'homesickness'; in other words a compulsion to return to an inorganic state, a desire (perhaps unconscious) to die, a death drive."[39] This association of the uncanny and the death drive is particularly relevant to a discussion of the forces driving novelistic plot. The appearance of the uncanny awakens in Veronica an unconscious desire to die or to know death vicariously through Liam. The narrative's completion is driven by Veronica's desire to reengage with her own life.

When Veronica collects Liam's body, she must deal with the grim details of his suicide. She confesses, "There were facts about the way that Liam died, that I wish I did not know. All the things that I have forgotten in my life, and I cannot forget these small details." Significantly, Veronica uses the past tense here, in a novel that mostly uses the present. "There were facts" is in the past, while "I wish I did not know" is in the present, suggesting that Liam's death marks a break in temporality. Veronica's tense shift can be best understood through Cathy Caruth's description of the link between the psychological experience of trauma and the body. Caruth usefully describes how unlike the body, the mind's barrier of consciousness protects the organism by placing events in an ordered experience of time: "What causes trauma, then, is a shock that appears to work very much like a bodily threat but is in fact a break in the mind's experience of time." Veronica's confused temporalities can therefore be read as indicative of the traumatic impact of Liam's death. The facts that Veronica does not want to know—Liam was wearing a fluorescent yellow jacket when he died; he had stones in his pockets; he wore no underpants— tell her about her brother's mind-set at his time of death. Liam wore the jacket so that his body would be found easily; the stones were to weigh him down. What Veronica finds most unsettling is Liam's lack of socks and underwear, items he removed because they were unclean. She notes that Liam "probably thought, as the cold water flooded his shoes, cleansing thoughts." Here again death, and especially death by sea, is cleansing and purifying. The nominative implies that, for Liam, suicide is the only way of redeeming the sins of the past. However, Liam's suicide, which provides relief from only his own suffering, further buries the truth of the past. Veronica's narrative is an alternative to this kind of an end—it is a way of clearing her own consciousness that allows her to reengage with life. Veronica explicitly attempts to expunge the sins of the past when she resolves that "it is time to put an end to the shifting stories and waking dreams. It is time to call an end to romance and just say what happened in Ada's house, the year that I was eight and Liam was barely nine."⁴⁰ Despite this resolution, Veronica's only access to the past is through imagination. Shifting notions of truth and the unreliability of memory are problems that prevent Veronica from achieving definite answers. The dead are reminders of the past, keepers of facts, and their appearances serve as an impetus to reassess.

The reality of the past lies with the dead, and Veronica must fight her imaginative urge to romanticize it. Yet it becomes impossible for her to give an account of her family history that is not influenced by emotion. Though she cannot articulate the reasons, Veronica has a sense that the cause of Liam's suicide might be related to the time they spent in their grandmother's house and, in particular, to their interactions with Lamb Nugent, their grandmother's landlord: "The seeds of my brother's death were sown many years ago. The person who planted them is long dead—at least that's what I think. So if I want to tell Liam's story, then I have to start a long time before he was born. And, in fact, this is the tale I would love to write: history is such a romantic place, with its jarveys and urchins and side-buttoned boots. If it would just stay still, I think, and settle down."⁴¹ Despite her desire to escape into a romantic vision of history, Veronica knows that it is not a fiction she is writing and that, unlike other idealized views, her family history will not "settle down" into a linear narrative. Veronica must imagine a time before Liam was born, and before her own birth, in order to know the end of Liam's life.

This sense of the plot moving backward to a time before the narrative or even before the birth of the narrator recalls Freud's theory of the death drive as a desire to achieve a prebirth state of quiescence. The function of the death drive in narrative can be best understood through Brooks's assertion that the death drive is behind any aspects of repetition in a text. While the drive toward the end and the repetition it entails move the plot forward, it also retards the text's forward movement. Examples of this recur throughout *The Gathering* in Veronica's constant narrative shifts between her present and past. The repetition of her family's history as well as her own enables Veronica's narrative to move both backward and forward because, as Brooks argues, the terms have "become reversible: the end is a time before the beginning."[42] In order to know the end of Liam's life, the reader must understand what came before his death, before Veronica's birth, and before the beginning of the novel. Liam's death is the end, but it is also the beginning point of telling. However, throughout the novel Liam remains an elusive figure, known only vaguely through Veronica's memories. His impermanence, his nebulous presence, in many ways mirrors death itself, which, despite all attempts to know it, remains unknowable.

Despite its interest in the indecipherable aspects of the past, *The Gathering* is actually a novel about the present. Robert Garratt distinguishes "Irish trauma novels" as those books characterized by a concern with an individual's struggle to discover a catastrophic past and to depict the process by which a character comes to know the traumatic moment. Enright's novel, though in many ways similar to the other novels that Garratt terms trauma novels, such as John McGahern's *Amongst Women* and Sebastian Barry's *The Secret Scripture*, is distinguished by its self-awareness of itself as a trauma novel. Garratt cites Barry's *The Secret Scripture* as "standing as a model for all the trauma novels under discussion" in the way that it "suggests that a narrative of past events can become truly a part of memory, things remembered as over with and finished, breaking the cycle of traumatic repetition."[43] The sense of closure Garratt describes here, with the past relegated to memory, is something that Enright's novel is deeply suspicious of. For Enright, narrative does not serve to overcome the past but puts it into dialogue with the present.

By narrating in the present, Veronica creates a sense of immediacy in the reader—the past is happening again now—while also emphasizing that the past is being told from the perspective of the present. The importance of this last point is that the social concerns of the present influence the way the past is being told. The sense of narrative as being dictated by the concerns of the present is strong in Enright's novel, as it consciously engages with prominent themes in contemporary Irish culture, including suicide and child sexual abuse. As Harper rightly notes, "[*The Gathering*] evokes social contexts in contemporary Ireland (and elsewhere), including the scandals of clerical abuse that rocked Ireland in the 1990s, set forth in chilling public documents like the Ferns Report (2005) and the Ryan Report (2009)."[44] These issues arise out of Veronica's grief and the task of making funeral arrangements, gathering family members, and burying the dead. Veronica's narrative uses the retrospective insight endowed by death to make sense of the present.

Throughout *The Gathering* Veronica is torn between the technologically sophisticated present that propels her rapidly into the future and her memories as her mind runs backward to the past. These split temporalities are made particularly apparent in Veronica's experience with modern travel. As she sits on the train to Brighton during her voyage to collect Liam's body, Veronica notes that the landscape shifts speeds as it moves past her. She tries "to find the line along which the landscape holds still and changes its mind, thinking that travel is a contrary kind of thing, because moving towards a dead man is not moving at all."[45] Travel provides a person with a sense of movement and therefore of progress. However, moving toward a dead man is not actually making progress, as there is nothing to be gained at the end—the deceased has no future left to fulfill. Veronica's sense of her own movement hints at Freud's theory of the death drive as an inevitable, biological urge toward death, but also suggests a critique of the rate at which modern society moves. Trains do not usually move backward, and Veronica, a passenger on a train, is moving forward whether she changes her mind or not. The reader's experience of the novel is broken by these jumps in time that threaten to disrupt the narrative stability. Yet the persistence of present-tense narration creates an illusion of continuity, fostering a sense that the remembered past, imagined past, and future are all contained in the present moment.

As the dead return to haunt Veronica, she finds that her life cannot move forward without first moving backward. This sense of life and death coming together is apparent in the preparations for Liam's wake. During her train journey to Brighton, Veronica's sister Bea calls to inform her that their mother would like to have Liam waked at home. Veronica is reluctant to fulfill her mother's wishes, as she associates this kind of wake with antiquated notions that do not match the contemporary moment. However, Bea insists that it is what their dead father would have wanted: "Meanwhile, the train chunters through England, clicketty-clack, and Bea talks on, sitting on my dead father's knee with a ribbon in her hair, like the good little girl that she has always been, and I look at the hills, trying to grow up, trying to let my father die, trying to let my sister enter her adolescence (never mind menopause). And none of these things is possible. None of them. There is a line on the landscape that refuses to move, it slides backwards instead, and that is where I fix my eye."[46] Veronica's uncanny experience of the train voyage in which her grown sister and dead father appear to her in one temporally confused image accurately describes her narrative as well as her current state. As she moves forward through space and time, her mind moves backward, making her present composed of memory, imagination, and reality. In Veronica's mind Bea is a still a child, and this image of Bea in the past is brought together with a current image of their father who remains dead, even in Veronica's memory. The sense here, as throughout the novel, is that the dead cannot truly die and that the lives of the living cannot progress owing to some unspoken aspect of the past. At the same time, Veronica's impulse to look back is pulling her into the future.

Veronica's inability to fully engage with her life can be attributed to her fear of death. According to Brooks, the fear of death, of ending improperly, is in tension with the desire for life, the need to divert the plot in an effort to prolong it. In *The Gathering*, the (dual) function of death as that which is associated with backwardness is contrasted with its ability to impel forward movement. Veronica first manifests her fear of ending improperly when she is assigned the task of choosing a casket for Liam. Although she has already chosen a limed oak casket, Veronica feels compelled to explore other options when she arrives at the funeral parlor. While she does not remember the mortuary or leaving it, she comments, "But I know I will remember this, the hinterland of the funeral parlor, suburban and pastel: a desk with a chair on either side and, up on a swivel stand, a laminated catalogue of coffins, all kinds and varieties of them, except, when I enquire for the sake of distraction, the eco-warrior's coffin."[47] Veronica's inquiry about the "eco-warrior's" coffin "for the sake of distraction" is a deviation from the plot, which indicates her desire to prolong the process of arranging the funeral in order to forestall the final end when Liam is put into the earth. When Veronica asks the funeral director about this coffin, he inquires if Liam was concerned with protecting the environment. Veronica answers that he was not. This instance is indicative of modern changes to death and burial practices in Ireland and elsewhere, which have expanded the amount of choices available for caskets, services, and burials and reflect an attempt to match a person's death to his or her life. In other words, death practices have become personalized, focused on the individual's life and commodified in ways that distract from the reality of death as a final departure from the world.[48]

These highly individualized modern funeral practices that are offered to Veronica in England contrast with the way that Liam is waked and buried in Ireland. Veronica's descriptions of this event emphasize that it is "ancient" and out-of-date.[49] Liam himself is described as an anachronism: "My emigrant brother makes an old-fashioned ghost, and when he died, I dressed him in worn-out Wellington boots, as the Irish seventies dipped back into the fifties in my mind." Although Liam emigrated, separating himself from his country and associating himself with the cosmopolitan, to Veronica he remains associated with an Ireland of another era. Again, Liam's death is in the past tense and marks a divide between Veronica's mind and her actions. The sense of confused temporalities finds further elaboration in the figure of Veronica's mother, who mistakes Liam's wake for her dead husband's. When she tells her children that "he" would be proud of them, Veronica explains, "We know she means, not Liam, but our father. She has got her funerals mixed up. Either that or all funerals are the same funeral now."[50] The sense of all funerals becoming the same funeral now depersonalizes Liam's funeral a step further, making it universal. While the wake rituals seem old and strange to

Veronica, they bring back the past in a tangible way that allows her access to personal truths.

The contradictory fear of death and desire for life become particularly apparent at Liam's wake when Veronica's husband, Tom, remembers how Veronica wouldn't go near a graveyard when she was pregnant with their first child. Veronica remembers that this superstition is called "*Cam reilige* which is Irish for *the twist of the grave*," and walks away from Tom feeling "the shadow of a child in me, the swoop of the future in my belly, black and open."[51] While these references to Irish phrases and traditional practices suggest Veronica's adherence to superstitious beliefs that the dead can contaminate the future, this moment marks the first time in the novel that Veronica feels the future inside of her. Building on this notion of *Cam reilige*, Liam Harte makes a link between traumatic stasis and another Irish phrase, "*marbhfháisc*, which translates as 'death band' and refers to the strip of cloth placed around the face of a corpse to keep the mouth closed in Irish funerary tradition."[52] This ritual, like many others in the Irish tradition, is meant to ensure peace to the dead and to prevent them from returning to haunt the living. In Irish folk tradition, after a person has died the curtains are drawn, the mirror and all glass surfaces are covered, and the clock is stopped. Though the exact motivations behind each of these customs are uncertain, these practices may stem from a belief that the soul of the dead might be incorporated into something else as it leaves the body.[53] The suggestion here is that the dead can possess even inanimate objects like mirrors, which must be covered over to prevent them from inhabiting them. Clocks are stopped to indicate a corresponding pause in time. These practices are meant to ensure the silence of the dead and to banish the past from the world of the living. Significantly, the dead populate Veronica's world in the form of inanimate objects; car headrests double as corpses, and ghosts appear on airplanes and moving walkways.[54] In the absence of rituals to close the gaps in memory, to bind the mouths of the dead and unify reality in one linear narrative, the line separating real from imagined is dissolved, and the dead come to mingle with the living. The dead's uncanny presence in the text do not simply represent the return of repressed childhood complexes but also, more important, confirm primitive beliefs, such as Irish wake rituals, which gain a new potential through their redeployment.[55]

What is particularly striking about Veronica's perceptions of Liam's wake is that she views the scene in an abstract way. As she stares at the coffin, Veronica considers how she cannot see Liam's face properly from where she sits: "The wood of the coffin angles down, slicing across the bulge of his cheek. I can see a dip in the bone where his eyes must go, but I do not get up to see if this dip is correctly filled, or if the lids are closed. This lift and fall of bone is all I want to see of him for the moment, thank you very much."[56] Veronica does not care about Liam's corpse itself and whether his body has been prepared properly; her real interest is in the outline of his face and in his bones, which she believes hold the truth of the past. The image of Liam's body as a disjointed series of angles, slopes, and inclines highlights Veronica's tendency to abstract reality in order to understand it objectively. Liam's wake forces her to deal with the emotions aroused by death, bringing her own buried truths to light.

Veronica is initially resistant to traditional wake rituals, seeing them as remnants of the past. But her grudging adherence to these rituals ultimately proves cathartic, bringing new and old together in surprising ways. Enright's description of Liam's wake highlights the distinctive features of the Irish wake, which is made up of a compilation of pagan rituals and Catholic traditions and, as such, represents a place where conflicting and often contradictory beliefs coexist. In the eighteenth and nineteenth centuries, the Irish wake, or so-called merry wake, traditionally included games, keening, and merrymaking that served as an alternative to orthodox Christian values. The "merry wake" became, as Gearóid Ó Crualaoich argues, "a central social mechanism for the articulation of resistance—or at least reaction—on the part of the Irish peasantry to new forms of civil and clerical control in Irish society in early modern and modern times."[57] This notion of the Irish wake as a site of resistance to Catholicism begins to disappear in the twentieth century, as the elements of paganism and the clerical satire of mock marriage ceremonies began to fade.[58] Enright's depiction of Liam's wake, where the dead come to life, returns to the earlier associations of the wake as a kind of "liminal interface of life and death in the community" and serves to restore the social order that death has disrupted.[59] The difference on this occasion is that only Veronica sees the ghosts of Liam, Ada, Nugent, and Uncle Brendan, and the narrative remains focused on her personal experience of grief. It is not the wake itself that restores the social order that has been disrupted by death; it is, rather, Veronica's act of narrative that connects her personal experiences to a larger cultural history.

The partially secular culture of Enright's novel contains remnants not only of pagan superstitions but also of Catholic imagery apparent in Veronica's comparison between her grandfather Charlie's corpse and Liam's. While Charlie looked like himself, even in death, Liam is transformed. Religious imagery seeps into Veronica's secular consciousness as she explains: "If you ask me what my brother looked like after he was dead, I can tell you he looked like Mantegna's fore-shortened Christ in paisley pajamas. And this may be a general truth about the dead, or it may just be what happens when someone is lying on a high mortuary table, with their feet towards the door."[60] More interesting than the comparison of Liam and Christ is the reference to the work of Italian Renaissance artist Andrea Mantegna. *The Lamentation over the Dead Christ* (ca. 1480), painted by Mantegna for his personal devotional use (he wanted the painting hung in his burial chamber), depicts a grief-stricken Mary and Saint John lamenting over Christ's corpse. Praised for its technique, the painting uses foreshortening to make Christ's body appear realistic and to emphasize his wounds and suffering.[61] Veronica's vision of Liam's body as Mantegna's foreshortened Christ wearing paisley pajamas creates a sense of playfulness and lightens the somber mood of both the painting and the novel. Veronica's association of Liam and Mantegna's Christ at once elevates Liam's corpse to an impossible level by equating it with Christ's, while lowering the seriousness of this association by dressing him in paisley pajamas. The novel is infused with such bloody and martyr-like imagery: Veronica's memory of how she used to cut herself in college, the descriptions of her stylish but sterile modern home, and bodies full of holes (her mother's, Liam's), all of which lead back to the Catholic figure of the crucified Christ. Enright's novel does not simply condemn the Catholic Church for the problems of the past; it acknowledges the role of human weaknesses in perpetuating abuse. The bloody religious images that appear throughout the novel indicate the extent to which the past has damaged the present, but they also serve as reminders of suffering that must be endured in order to live. Enright's characters appear to be almost completely secular, yet they retain a need to believe in something.[62]

The traditional Irish "merry wake" involved a centering of "the life of the community into a traditional assembly with both sacred and social significance." However, in *The Gathering*, the ritual of the wake seems foreign to Veronica, out of touch with modern life and also lacking in the sacred significance it once had. When she arrives at her childhood home for Liam's wake, Veronica is told that not many mourners have arrived yet. Veronica thinks, "'What do you expect?' I want to say. 'Who's going to come and look at a dead body in your living room, when there isn't even a decent glass of wine in the house?' But I do not say this." The Irish wake portrayed in popular culture is a riotous affair dominated by whiskey consumption, fighting, poetic laments, and music. Enright plays with this stereotype, setting it against the reality of modern Ireland, where heavy drinking at wakes has been curtailed by strict drunk-driving laws and busy work schedules prevent people from leaving work for two or three days to attend a wake. Veronica's desire for a "decent glass of wine" is indicative of a need to fulfill old customs while at once updating that need: it is wine she wants, not whiskey or stout. After most of the guests have departed and Veronica is alone with her siblings, they do find a bottle of "decorative-looking" whiskey and decide to drink it: "This ritual is strange for us because, although the Hegartys all drink, we never drink together." This notion of the ritual as strange is furthered when, having decided that the whiskey tastes awful, Veronica's brother goes to a liquor store to get wine: "One by one we finish and sit, ready to uncork the wine when it arrives. And when it does arrive, we do not toast the dead but merely drink and chat, as ordinary people might do."[63] Drinking the wine is normalizing, separating the siblings from the facts of death and preventing them from having to deal with the past in the manner that toasting the dead may have occasioned. Yet despite all these alterations to wake rites, Veronica and her siblings still adhere to the tradition of sitting up all night with the corpse to prevent spirits from entering it.[64] It is this ritual that has the most significance for Veronica, as she must now deal with the ghosts of the past as they appear to her.

Going upstairs to check on her mother, Veronica attempts to draw from her truths about her grandmother and Lamb Nugent. Despite her efforts, she fails to communicate with her mother, never voicing her suspicions about Nugent's molestation of Liam. Veronica then finds a box containing all of her mother's old records, including letters between Ada and Nugent and payment registers. Only after she opens the box does Veronica realize the repercussions of what she has done: "But I have disturbed the ghosts. They are outside the door of the room, now, as the ghosts of my childhood once were; they are behind the same door. Their story is there, out on the landing of Griffith Way, waiting for me one more time."[65] At this moment the full consequences of Veronica's narrative undertaking become apparent—her story is not simply a narrative about Liam and the reasons for his suicide but extends across generations to all those whose stories lie buried beneath the surface. The function of Veronica's narrative is here revealed to be twofold: on one level, she is responsible for exposing the truth of the past in order to assure the dead peace; on the other, the act of narrative is a way of accessing her own consciousness, enabling her to get on with her life. The fact that this is a story about Veronica is significant because her act of narrative becomes a way not merely of making peace with the past but of bringing it into the present.

The appearance of the dead on the night of Liam's wake brings the past undeniably into the present, allowing Veronica access to further repressed memories of her own possible sexual abuse. She comments that the revelation of her own abuse "comes from a place in my head where words and actions are mangled. It comes from the very beginning of things and I cannot tell if it is true."⁶⁶ Veronica's sense of having found the "beginning of things" is reminiscent of the death drive, indicating the narrative's function as a journey through death, ending at the beginning.⁶⁷ Beginning her novel with death and ending with Veronica's reengagement with life, Enright disrupts the boundaries that hold narrative in place and destabilizes narrative authority. *The Gathering* provides no easy answers, but it does attempt to address the problems of contemporary Ireland, suggesting that the traumas of the past must be dealt with before the future can be realized. Integral to this vision of the future is the inclusion of the voices of the dead, who rather than being exorcized must be given expression.

The Irish wake is portrayed in the novel as an outdated tradition but one that is, nonetheless, useful in exhuming the past and forcing the living to confront painful memories. This process is stalled by the fact that Liam died in England and his body must be brought back to Ireland. As she awaits the arrival of Liam's body, Veronica comments, "The British, I decide, only bury people when they are so dead, you need another word for it. The British wait so long for a funeral that people gather not so much to mourn, as to complain that the corpse is still hanging around." The fact that the whole Hegarty family has to wait for Liam's body disrupts the traditional Irish practice of waking the dead in the home shortly after death. A different word for death is needed for how the British handle it, implying that the British and Irish do not share the same vocabulary in regard to death and that, by implication, the Irish have a unique way of handling death. As she welcomes Liam's ex-girlfriend to his funeral, Veronica thinks, "And I suddenly feel very Irish as I reach out to take her hand in both my hands, to thank her for making the journey, to welcome her in and allow her to grieve." What makes Veronica feel "Irish" is not any particular ritual pertaining to the burial of the dead but rather the simple act of allowing another to grieve. The denial of death seems then to be a symptom of British society. Despite her ability to allow others to grieve, Veronica is incapable of properly mourning the loss of her favorite brother. Describing her own behavior, Veronica observes, "My face sets into the mask of a woman weeping, one half pulled into a wail that the other half will not allow. There are no tears." The church funeral does not allow for the release of emotion that Veronica hoped for, and instead of actually expressing her grief, she dons a mask that makes her look as if she were crying. Her grief does arrive later, at the funeral dinner at a hotel when her sister Kitty sings Liam's favorite song and Liam's three-year-old son tells everyone to shut up. At this moment Veronica thinks, "I have never been to a happier funeral."[68] This last sentiment captures the very essence and paradox of the Irish wake that laments death while also celebrating life. At this point Liam's corpse disappears from the narrative, and readers are left with the image of his young son, symbolizing the promise of the future.

Beginning the narrative with Veronica laying out the bones of the past, *The Gathering* works in reverse order as a process of coming to life rather than of dying. From bones, the ghosts of the past are brought back and at Liam's funeral figuratively become flesh and blood again through Veronica and her family. In the absence of religious faith through which to express her grief or relieve her suffering, Veronica turns to narrative to make sense of Liam's death. The act of confessional narration purges Veronica's consciousness, allowing her to separate her thoughts from her actions in order to observe her own life. In this sense the act of narrative allows Veronica a kind of fictional death from which she can emerge at the end ready to begin again. Enright's interest in narrative then does not simply lie in understanding the past or unearthing some ultimate truth but rather lies in understanding Ireland's position in a global world by exposing its dialectical relationship between tradition and modernity, the religious and the secular. What is striking about *The Gathering*'s fictional depiction of the Irish wake is that the old rituals are abstracted and unfamiliar. Despite Veronica's resistance to the traditional rituals attending the dead, her adherence to these rituals reaffirms the wake's folkloric connotations of rebirth and affirmation of life. In *The Gathering* death is positioned at the beginning so that the backward look it instigates becomes associated with the process of moving forward, with memory and imagination functioning as implements that propel Ireland into the future rather than dragging it back to the past.

***

The Gathering depicts an Ireland that is at odds with itself, a country that seeks to move rapidly into the future without confronting its past. Death and grief have no place in this modern life with its sleek surfaces, advanced technologies, and virtual communities. Liam's death exposes the unreal nature of the novel's world, revealing the gap between the individual and the communal. For Veronica, Liam's death functions as a point of rupture, pausing her life and plunging her into a liminal state where she must interrogate her family history in order to reengage with life. The novel contrasts Irish funeral practices with British rites, emphasizing the Irish wake as a place where these conflicts between traditional and modern are acted out. While Veronica sees the rituals of the wake as impulses that are out-of-date, the very act of dealing with the body of the dead ultimately proves cathartic, aiding her in working through her memories and overcoming her traumatic past.

In Enright's view, what distinguishes Irish death practices from British ones are their demand for the body of the dead to be present at the funeral, their preference that the wake occur as close as possible to the time of death, and their insistence that traditional rituals attend the corpse's disposal. The process of retrieving Liam's corpse serves as a way of reviving the past, bringing the dead and the living together. The written narrative that accompanies this process reads like a psychiatric session, a working through of Freud's death drive, which functions as a kind of "talking cure" by which trauma is overcome by repetition and telling.[69] Veronica's past memories and her narrative of the present are joined by the bodies of the dead and the truth that lingers in their bones.

Poised on the edge of an unknown future, Enright's novel ends in a similar way to other novels in this study, leaving its readers with little closure or consolation. Now that the bones of the past have been excavated, Enright indicates, the characters can begin to live their lives authentically. Enright's depiction of death does not serve to expose a gap between Catholic conceptions of the afterlife and existentialist ideas of nothingness or the incompatibility of these notions, as in O'Brien or McGahern, but rather serves to excavate the past. In many ways, Enright's depictions of death are like Joyce's in that both seek to insert death into life, blurring temporalities and creating a narrative that feeds off the past. However, Enright's novel ultimately returns the dead to their graves, indicating a separation between past and present that needs to be acknowledged in order to open the possibilities of the future. Veronica's role as narrator allows her a retrospective view of her family history. In her liminal state Veronica can order and make sense of her life and Liam's. In this way, her memories take on a fictional quality through their narrative reordering that resembles the process of novelistic composition. The suggestion at the end of the novel is that Veronica's act of narrative has allowed her to imaginatively work through death, allowing her to return to life.

What is ultimately unclear from the ending of Enright's novel is how this excavation of the past can serve to reconcile the individual with the community or to address the larger questions concerning death and dying. Enright's novelistic depiction of the Irish wake may serve to remind readers of the importance of ritual in dealing with death, but it does not fully resolve the question of how religious narratives fit together with the liberal-humanist focus on life and the fulfillment of human desires. The ambiguity of *The Gathering*'s ending indicates a wider impasse in contemporary Irish society as it struggles to reconcile the religious and the secular. Veronica's abstraction of death, and her offering of consolation to the dead rather than the living, suggests that the religious and the secular cannot come together in any productive way until amends have been made for past injustices.[70]

Enright's novel highlights the necessity of rituals to cope with grief, and Catholic imagery features in the novel as a reminder of mortal suffering and redemption. While the religious is allowed to coexist with the secular, there is little sense that they are working together to provide consolation for death or to make sense of the world. In the end, Enright's novel demonstrates that the ways that the Catholic focus on bodily suffering and privileging of the afterlife over earthly existence overlap with the liberal-humanist focus on self-fulfillment and the realization of human desires within mortal time have yet to be resolved. Novelistic narrative holds the possibility not only of working through the past and exposing its lost histories, but also of bringing together living and dead, providing a way of interrogating death's function in society and forcing the individual to confront his or her mortality.

The Gathering explores the state of contemporary Ireland in new and complex ways, depicting Irish society as neither entirely secular nor entirely religious. Enright's experimental style and structure express the ruptures in memory created by trauma and produce an intriguing break with the realist or naturalist style in which many other Irish novels are written. Yet Enright's use of the confessional form, her portrayal of Veronica's liminal state, her use of death as an impetus for narrative, and, particularly, her depictions of the rituals attending the wake all situate *The Gathering* in a distinctly Irish novelistic trajectory of writing about death and dying. Death in novelistic narrative serves to reveal the novel's underlying tensions and provides a way of working through human anxieties concerning mortality. While the novel form cannot offer any concrete answers for the modern individual struggling to make sense of death and the afterlife, it can integrate his or her concerns into a larger communal narrative where conflicting worldviews can coexist. Enright's novel reaches a kind of balance between Catholic and liberal-humanist conceptions of death, and, though it does not offer much insight into how these worldviews might work together to make sense of death or offer consolation for its losses, the possibility of reconciliation offers hope for the future.

CONCLUSION

"As You Were before You Rested"

Death and the Afterlife of the Irish Wake

During the time period that the novels in this study were published (1922–2007), Ireland underwent profound economic and sociological changes that had deep impacts on Irish culture: from poverty and emigration in the early twentieth century to the economic success of the "Celtic Tiger" in the late 1990s and the return to financial crisis in 2008, from an almost wholly Catholic country to a largely secularized one, and from a rural to a more urban and globalized society. These changes undoubtedly altered the way that Ireland was perceived internationally, resulting in the commodification of Irish culture and impacting the way that Ireland conceived of itself. These dramatic swings from poverty to wealth and prosperity and back to economic crisis have not only impacted everyday Irish life but also had considerable effects on cultural attitudes toward death and how the end of life is perceived. As recent controversies over end-of-life care and questions raised about what constitutes human life can attest, death and dying remain vital issues in Irish culture and society. While novels cannot necessarily provide answers to these questions, they can reveal the conflicting worldviews, unconscious desires, and unfulfilled potentials that underlie human life and often come to a head at the point of death.

This book has traced Irish novelistic treatments of death and dying in order to understand and probe some of these questions in ways that are possible only through the imaginative powers of fiction. Medical technologies have now made it possible to extend life indefinitely, forcing into relief conflicts between the rationality of science and the more intangible dealings of religion and spirituality. Without the structure provided by religion or traditional ritual, modern society has lost its ability to deal with death and has turned instead to medicine and science to provide answers to life's big questions. As Irish physician Seamus O'Mahony observes, we have lost the common script for dying, and death is now banished from our thoughts: "In our atomized world, death is far more shocking for us because we cannot imagine anything beyond this self, this life."[1] As this study has confirmed, novels are necessary because they offer us something that medicine cannot supply and that other genres of life writing such as illness blogs or memoirs fail to provide: a way of coping with death by granting readers a chance to imaginatively place themselves into a life and a world beyond their own.

In the modern Irish novel, the prevalence of wakes, funerals, and rituals attending the dead is indicative of an abiding cultural interest in death. These fictional depictions of the end of life reveal the uneasy coexistence of religious and secular conceptions of human existence and the afterlife. Read together, these novels do not simply trace a shift from Catholic to secular conceptions of death but, rather, illustrate the ways in which ideas about death and dying are altered and shaped by the interactions between these two worldviews. Even as secular conceptions gain ground, these novels remain resistant to the idea of death as a final and absolute ending, suggesting a need for some sort of consolation in the face of death, whether religious or otherwise.

Death is undoubtedly a grim topic, but in the Irish context representations of the Irish wake and novelistic treatments of the dead often feature humorous elements as well. The anxious laughter provoked by Bloom's comic vision in *Ulysses* of Paddy Dignam's corpse falling from the funeral carriage to the road or by Malone's futile efforts to end his life by narrating his own death in *Malone Dies* serves to remind us that reading about death need not be an entirely depressing encounter. In the Irish novel, the nearness of death triggers images of beauty and macabre humor, suggesting that death is not simply a destructive force that ends life, but that it is also a creative force that generates new life and impels the formation of narrative.

This study ends with Anne Enright's *The Gathering*, in which the reader is presented with a version of a modern Irish wake that features many of the old customs and superstitions. The characters in *The Gathering* adhere to traditions such as waking the dead at home, staying up all night with the corpse, and drinking. However, in the urban secular context in which these characters live, many of these rituals have lost their meaning. Enright's novel leaves the reader with a sense that, while these rituals may seem out-of-date, they still hold some power to relieve the pain of grief in a secular world that offers few alternatives. While funeral rituals in Ireland now feature a blend of Catholic and secular elements, the struggle between these two worldviews and their conceptions of death has not been entirely resolved. As recent debates around assisted death and euthanasia suggest, the conflicts between religious and secular humanist worldviews continue to pose new moral conundrums in the twenty-first century.

The medical advancements and technologies that have made it possible to extend life and to grant even terminal patients a few extra days or even months of life have also resulted in a conception of death as failure. According to O'Mahony, "Death in modern hospitals still has the faint whiff of an industrial accident, a failure of medical intervention."[2] Questions continue to be raised about the cost of these advancements and the ethical issues surrounding the end of life. What constitutes a "good death" and how that kind of death is achieved continues to be a much-discussed topic. The notion of an ideal death has shifted from the religious *ars moriendi*, which instructed the dying on how to die a "good death" by atoning for their sins, mending personal relationships, and ordering worldly affairs, to a more secular ideal death, in which the dying person experiences little to no pain and dies comfortably, surrounded by friends and family. What is particularly interesting about this shift is that a "good death" in the secular sense described above is not seen as something that is difficult to achieve but is, rather, viewed as a basic human right. The fact that medical professionals now view death as a "failure" and people debate about the right to die seems to suggest that death is within the grasp of human control. Yet in spite of this illusion of control that modern medicine provides, death still happens at the most unexpected and inconvenient of times and without consideration of the wishes or rights of the people involved.

These technological advancements and conflicts surrounding death raise new moral concerns, bringing religious and secular worldviews into contact in fascinating ways. Recent memoirs and novels exploring these questions suggest that literary narrative continues to provide a form where these questions can be addressed and worked through. In her memoir, *An Act of Love: One Woman's Remarkable Life Story and Her Fight for the Right to Die with Dignity*, Marie Fleming details her battle with multiple sclerosis and the legal battles she undertook in order to fulfill her wish to die with dignity, at home with her family rather than in pain and suffering. Fleming lost the case in the Supreme Court of Ireland, where she argued that the ban on assisted suicide violated her constitutional rights. Her case did, however, succeed in bringing attention to end-of-life care and the rights of the dying and disabled. Her memoir was published after her death on December 20, 2013. Denied the right to take her own life, Fleming succumbed to her disease in the end, but nevertheless died peacefully in her home, surrounded by her partner and children. Fleming's landmark right-to-die case and the memoir that followed it opened a new public forum for the discussion of the moral issues surrounding death and dying and raised questions about what constitutes a "good death" and how this kind of death is to be achieved or even if it is always attainable.

In his recent novel *Every Single Minute*, Hugo Hamilton offers a fictionalized account of the time he spent with Nuala O'Faolain and a group of other writers in Berlin in the final weeks of O'Faolain's life. The trip to Berlin fulfilled O'Faolain's dying wish, and Hamilton describes how she seemed to revise the view she so poignantly described in her interview with Marian Finucane, that the world "went black" as soon as she found out she was dying. According to Hamilton, on the Berlin trip O'Faolain "wanted to see everything and she spoke with extraordinary optimism." Indeed, this portrait of the end of O'Faolain's life offers a much more hopeful view of things than her final interview with Finucane suggested. Hamilton further comments on O'Faolain's time in Berlin: "It was a strange contradiction, that the closeness to death gave great urgency to living."[3] It seems odd that Hamilton should describe this contradiction as "strange," because this is a fairly standard and almost banal view of the end of life. While O'Faolain's interview laid bare the anxieties and fears surrounding secular death and refused any kind of consolation to ease the pain of dying, Hamilton's novel offers a much more conventional and optimistic view of the end of life as sad but meaningful. Though these two portraits of O'Faolain might seem to contradict one another, causing one to wonder if Hamilton did not simply invent a fictional character loosely based on the writer in order to offer a more hopeful view of her death, it is entirely possible that these two accounts are both accurate and reveal the complicated and conflicting emotions that surround the end of life. Hamilton's novel, as a work of fiction, does not promise truth or accuracy but, rather, blurs the lines between fact and fiction, calling into question fixed notions of life and death. However, rather than using the form to his advantage in exploring some of the difficult questions raised by O'Faolain's interview, Hamilton seems here to be stressing the fictional quality of the novel and using it to defer these questions. Instead, the novel offers a beautiful memory of O'Faolain's last days and therefore provides a more comforting view of her death.

Despite human attempts to tame or control death, it remains something that can never be fully understood. The novel is the ideal form for interrogating death and the religious and moral questions it raises not only because of its dialogic nature but also because it deals with emotions and imagination rather than solid facts, allowing for a greater elasticity in thinking about these matters. While *Every Single Minute* seems in many ways to soften the bleak view of death that O'Faolain herself described, it does not dissolve or diminish that view. It is very possible that O'Faolain's last days not simply were characterized by unmitigated despair but also featured a series of contradictory feelings that vacillated between optimism and depression, between fear and tranquility. It is also conceivable that O'Faolain accepted death in the end and that this acceptance eased her anxieties and gave her a sense of hope. Novelistic portrayals of death and dying allow these conflicting and contradictory emotions to exist side by side, allowing for a realistic and multilayered view of the experience of dying.

While the novel provides no answers to the questions surrounding human existence and does not offer instructions on how to die properly, it can shape and interrogate the ways we conceive of death and the ways that we deal with the loss, suffering, and grief that accompany the process of dying. In a modern world dominated by medical and technological advancements that are focused on life and how to live longer, death is often denied. However, there is also an increasing tendency for those individuals who suffer extreme physical pain to view death as a desired end, one that promises relief from their anguish. This tension between the dread of death, its association with failure, and death as a final choice that one has a right to make will undoubtedly continue to provoke much debate and even to inspire many interesting new novels.

This study began with a desire to understand the ways that death and dying structure and shape the form of the Irish novel and what that awareness might reveal about larger conceptions of death and the afterlife, particularly in the context of Ireland's complex history of famine, war, colonial occupation, and nationalist martyrdom. The loss of life during the Great Famine and the inability of the survivors to care for and bury the dead left an indelible mark on the Irish literary imagination. Similarly, the cult of sacrifice and martyrdom that characterized the Irish War of Independence and subsequent Irish Civil War greatly impacted the ways that the Irish conceived of death, converting it from abject failure to final triumph. To complicate matters further, the lack of ritualized burial that characterized the loss of life during World War I and the horrors of the concentration camps during World War II resulted in a shift in the conception of death as a natural and acceptable end to human life to something that was appalling and absurd. While these historical circumstances are not explicitly referenced in, say, Beckett's *Malone Dies* or Anne

Enright's *The Gathering*, the ways that these events impacted cultural conceptions of death and dying undoubtedly influenced the ways that these novels conceive of their subject. However, what links these five novels together is not simply the context but also the way that they use death to interrogate the religious structures that fix meaning in place and divide the world of the living from that of the dead. Despite attempts by authors such as Joyce to break down these boundaries and defy death by creating a narrative with endless possibilities, in the end these novels cannot provide us with the answers to questions of death or the afterlife but force us to face that which we dread most. By requiring us to confront our own mortality, these novels work to make us less afraid of our final end and give these fears and anxieties a form and structure. In this way, the Irish novel continues to offer valuable material for future interrogations of death and dying.

The focus of this book was largely on religious and secular conceptions of death, but there remain many different ways of approaching the topic and much further research to be done. Recent initiatives such as the "Forum on End of Life in Ireland," established by the Irish Hospice Foundation, promote public debate on issues relating to death, dying, and bereavement.[4] Initiatives like this one suggest that there is a wider cultural interest in these issues, and they also indicate a shift in the way that death is discussed and dealt with. These debates on death and the ways that it is being discussed in terms of individual rights will undoubtedly shape the way that writers, artists, and filmmakers approach the topic. It is evident from Irish films, such as *Waking Ned Devine* (1998), *Kings* (2007), and, more recently, Bernadette Manton's short film *The Wake* (2014), that the topic of death, funerals, and the wake continues to be of great interest in Irish popular culture. Though the Irish wake remains a popular trope in Irish culture, it is perhaps of even greater interest to foreign audiences. The portrayal of the Irish American wake in novels like Alice McDermott's *At Weddings and Wakes* (1992) or in popular television shows like *The Wire* (2002) undoubtedly influences how Ireland is perceived abroad.

The interest in the Irish wake and the association of Irish culture with death and mourning have their roots in nineteenth-century travelogues such as those written by John Gamble and Thomas Crofton Croker, which recorded the games, stories, and rituals observed at wakes throughout the Irish countryside for the consumption of a largely British audience. Though many of these practices (particularly the games played at wakes) were altered or faded away over time, the perception of the Irish as people who know how to "do" death still persists. Despite the negative aspects of Catholic domination of Irish society, O'Mahony claims that the structures provided by its rituals are part of what make Irish death rituals so effective: "The Irish, for all our many failings, still—just—do mourning well. The old ritualistic Catholic sequence—first the rosary, then the removal, and finally the funeral mass and burial, still survives." Despite these successes, O'Mahony warns that these rituals are slowly dying, particularly in cities, along with the wake itself, which is now rare in Ireland and tame compared to the descriptions of them featured in Ó Súilleabháin's *Irish Wake Amusements*.[5] Interestingly, this yoking together of the Catholic structure and ritual sequence with the pagan and semisecularized wake that characterize Irish death practices in the late twentieth and early twenty-first centuries seems to be lacking in popular conceptions of the wake outside of Ireland. Indeed, even as the practice of the wake might be declining in Ireland, the Irish wake remains a popular trope elsewhere.

The popularity of the Irish wake is so pervasive, particularly in North American culture, that it has become almost synonymous with the concept of a "good funeral" put forth by Thomas Long and Thomas Lynch.[6] The most basic reason that the Irish wake has become interchangeable with the "good funeral" is that it offers a celebratory alternative to more somber rituals. Television shows such as *The Wire* depict the wake in an exaggerated way as a drunken, riotous affair. In one such scene, the corpse of a minor character is laid out on the pool table of the local pub, Kavanagh's, and friends and colleagues offer toasts in honor of the deceased, highlighting the humorous and merry aspects of death rather than the grim or morbid ones. Later in the series, one of the main characters, Jimmy McNulty, is given a similar send-off in a scene nearly identical to the earlier wake. The only difference here is that McNulty is not dead but is leaving the police force. This example of a "fake wake" indicates the social death McNulty endures as a result of his departure from his detective job. Despite the Irish American stereotypes that proliferate—exemplified by the Pogues' song "The Body of an American," which the characters sing along to—the wake scenes in *The Wire* are true to the traditional Irish wake in that they serve a similar function: both represent a moment where narrative tensions are released and social significance is bestowed on the life of the deceased or the seemingly deceased, as the case may be. However, the risk of such portrayals is that they solidify the notion of the Irish wake as a carnivalesque party rather than as part of a process of mourning that involves the acceptance of death. When taken out of context, this idea of the wake as a wild party can become reappropriated in such a way that it loses its normalizing function and becomes a way of further enhancing modern society's denial of death by obscuring its reality and glossing over the suffering that results from grief and loss.

Perhaps one of the most distinctive features of the Irish wake is the idea of the dead returning. Indeed, the name "wake" itself comes from the custom of the living staying awake all night to keep watch over the deceased, making sure he or she was truly dead. Part of the function of the Irish wake is not only to ensure that death has taken place but also to give narrative shape to the life of the deceased by eulogizing and telling stories. However, the idea of staying awake with the corpse also offers the mourner the hopeful possibility that their loved one is not dead at all but merely sleeping. Thus, the Irish wake is often associated with irrationality or magic, with the idea that the dead might suddenly come to life.

This notion of the Irish wake as magical or fantastical is a trope that Joan Didion uses in her memoir, *The Year of Magical Thinking*, which describes her grief following the sudden death of her husband. Didion details the medical facts of her husband's demise but realizes that these statistics will not help her to accept his death because her grief exceeds rational thinking: "Had I been operating from my rational mind I would not have been entertaining fantasies that would not have been out of place at an Irish wake."⁷ Here Didion contrasts the rational world of medicine with the irrationality of her own grief. She can find no relief from sorrow in the facts of her husband's death, but the idea of an Irish wake allows her to entertain fantasies of her husband's return and offers her the possibility of imagining him having dinner with chef Julia Child, who is also recently deceased and whom Didion's husband admired. Not only are this ability to imagine a life for the dead beyond this one alongside the belief that the dead still occupy space within human temporality things that Didion associates with an Irish wake, but they are also thoughts that allow her to get on with her life. Such examples suggest that even as modern medicine attempts to regulate and control death, it still occurs unexpectedly and without reason, leaving those individuals left behind with few ways of making sense of the loss. The Irish wake therefore offers the bereaved imaginative possibilities often denied by Western culture, creating a zone of contact in which living and dead, religious and secular, coexist.

While Didion's reference to an Irish wake is a positive one, acknowledging both the fantastical and the realistic elements of the wake, it is also indicative of the way that the wake is becoming commodified within American culture. Popular portrayals of the wake do not focus on its power to subvert dominant ideologies but, rather, view it as a material object: a drunken party at which the deceased is remembered and praised. For instance, the purpose of the inclusion of an "Irish Wake Tent" at Irish American festivals across North America may be to educate the public about Irish death rituals, but such events often have the unwanted effect of commercializing the wake rather than highlighting its communal importance. Recently, the Irish wake has been further commodified by reality television shows such as *The Bachelorette*, a dating show that featured one of its contestants being given a mock "Irish wake" and laid in a coffin with a flask of whiskey clutched between her hands, while her suitors gave eulogies praising her. The danger of such examples is that they make a mockery of death, highlighting its unreality rather than fostering an acceptance of the end of life. This disturbing example of a fake wake illustrates the ways that the event has been reappropriated and misunderstood.

As has become evident from the brief discussion here, the narrative possibilities offered by death in the Irish context extend far beyond the novel form. Future studies might usefully explore representations of the Irish wake in American popular culture and could reach as far back as the nineteenth-century notion of an "American wake," a party thrown for loved ones immigrating to America. The difficulties of accepting death and making sense of the end of life are problems that will become only more complicated as medical and technological advancements progress. Studies such as this one do not provide us with answers to many of these large questions, but they do offer us insight into the ways that we conceive of death, revealing the power of narrative to retrospectively give order and meaning to life and to open an imaginative space of contact between the living and the dead.

Notes

Bibliography

Index

Notes

Introduction

1. Nuala O'Faolain, "The Saturday Interviews."
2. For a classic account of the invisibility of death in modern society, see Philippe Ariès, *The Hour of Our Death*, 87–106. For a recent work on death in the modern Irish context, which also comments on O'Faolain's dying interview, see John Waters, *Beyond Consolation; or, How We Became Too Clever for God . . . and Our Own Good*, 1–47.
3. O'Faolain, "The Saturday Interviews."
4. Waters, *Beyond Consolation*, 1. Waters views this moment as a summing up of "the condition of human existence at a frozen moment in Irish life." The word "frozen" here implies stasis when in fact the interview reveals a moment of change that challenged public perceptions of dying and opened the discussions surrounding death.
5. Tom Inglis, *Moral Monopoly: The Catholic Church in Modern Irish Society*, 21; Gearóid Ó Crualaoich, "The 'Merry Wake,'" 173.
6. The wake as a drunken, riotous affair features in a great deal of Irish fiction and song. The Irish American folk song "Finnegans Wake" tells the tale of a fight that breaks out at a funeral, causing whiskey to be spilled on the corpse, who revives and joins the party. The Celtic punk band the Pogues pay tribute to the wake in their song "The Body of an American," and their rowdy concerts themselves have, particularly in recent years, been described as Irish wakes. Nineteenth-century Irish fiction such as Maria Edgeworth's *Castle Rackrent* (1800) features a fake wake. Synge's *In the Shadow of the Glen* (1903) also features a wake hoax, and his more famous play *The Playboy of the Western World* (1907) is bookended by offstage wakes.
7. Ó Crualaoich, "The 'Merry Wake,'" 199, 174, 199.
8. Patrick Corish, *The Irish Catholic Experience: A Historical Survey*, 212–13.
9. Edward Peters, ed., *The 1917 Pio-Benedictine Code of Canon Law in English Translation*, 412–29. Canon 1239 forbade the ecclesiastical burial of those individuals who died without baptism, with the exception of catechumens. Canon 1240 denied burial rites to those "who killed themselves by deliberate counsel" as well as those

"who order that their body be handed over for cremation and other public and manifest sinners."

10. Caroline Smyth, Malcolm MacLachlan, and Anthony Clare, eds., *Cultivating Suicide? Destruction of Self in a Changing Ireland*, 16–20.

11. See Ó Crualaoich, "The 'Merry Wake.'"

12. See Peters, *1917 Pio-Benedictine Code of Canon Law*, canons 1239, 1240, 1241; and Canon Law Society of America, *Code of Canon Law: Latin-English Edition*, canons 1176, 1183, 1184.

13. Ariès, *Hour of Our Death*, 571; Geoffrey Gorer, *Death, Grief and Mourning* (Garden City, NJ: Doubleday, 1965); Ariès, *Hour of Our Death*, 585–88.

14. Thomas G. Long and Thomas Lynch, *The Good Funeral: Death, Grief, and the Community of Care*, 59–60, 197, 189.

15. Ibid., 80, 212.

16. Raymond Williams, *Marxism and Literature*, 122, 123. Williams explains: "A residual cultural element is usually at some distance from the effective dominant culture, but some part of it, some version of it—especially if the residue is from some major area of the past—will in most cases have to be incorporated if the effective dominant culture is to make sense in these areas."

17. Garrett Stewart, *Death Sentences: Styles of Dying in British Fiction*; Elisabeth Bronfen, *Over Her Dead Body: Death, Femininity and the Aesthetic*; Frederick Hoffman, *The Mortal No: Death and the Modern Imagination*; Alan Warren Friedman, *Fictional Death and the Modernist Enterprise*; David Sherman, *In a Strange Room: Modernism's Corpses and Mortal Obligation*.

18. Lawrence Taylor, "*Bás InÉirinn*: Cultural Constructions of Death in Ireland," 183–84. Taylor discusses how, for the immigrant, burial in Ireland serves as a means of reincorporation into the culture after the separation "death" that occurred at departure.

19. Peter Brooks, *Reading for the Plot: Design and Intention in Narrative*, 6; Ian Watt, *The Rise of the Novel: Studies in Defoe, Richardson, and Fielding*, 84.

20. See Mikhail Bakhtin, *The Dialogic Imagination: Four Essays*, 276–77, 314.

21. See Theodore P. Fraser, *The Modern Catholic Novel in Europe*; Malcolm Scott, *The Struggle for the Soul of the French Novel: French Catholic and Realist Novels, 1850–1970*; and Thomas Woodman, *Faithful Fictions: The Catholic Novel in British Literature*. For more on the Irish Catholic novel, see Eamon Maher, *Crosscurrents and Confluences: Echoes of Religion in Twentieth-Century Fiction*; and Eamon Maher and Eugene O'Brien, eds., *Breaking the Mould: Literary Representations of Irish Catholicism*.

22. Brooks, *Reading for the Plot*, 22.

23. Ibid., 61.

1. Death and Narrative Regeneration

1. James Joyce, *Ulysses*, 732.

2. See Mary Lowe-Evans, *Catholic Nostalgia in Joyce and Company*, 12–13, 22. Lowe-Evans argues that Joyce's grief over his mother's death served as an impetus for the writing of *Ulysses*. She cites similarities between May Dedalus's deathbed scene and that of Joyce's mother, described in his letters, as evidence of Joyce's desire to control memory and overcome the finality of death.

3. See Derek Hand, *A History of the Irish Novel*, 140, 149. Hand contends that the Irish wake and funeral have always been of extreme interest to novelistic audiences, particularly those outside of Ireland. He further asserts that in the nineteenth-century novel, the wake and funeral scene were representative of the death of Irish culture and, rather than mourning an individual life, became expressions of cultural death.

4. For major critical works that argue that Joyce is anti-Catholic, see Roy Gottfried, *Joyce's Misbelief*; Frederick K. Lang, *"Ulysses" and the Irish God*; and Geert Lernout, *Help My Unbelief: James Joyce and Religion*. For major critical works that argue for a Catholic Joyce, see Robert Boyle, *James Joyce's Pauline Vision: A Catholic Exposition*; Lowe-Evans, *Catholic Nostalgia*; and J. Mitchell Morse, *The Sympathetic Alien: James Joyce and Catholicism*.

5. Pericles Lewis, *Religious Experience and the Modernist Novel*, 36.

6. See Frank Kermode, *The Sense of an Ending: Studies in the Theory of Fiction*, 8. Kermode contends that literature allows us to see or understand human existence by creating an imagined beginning and end. He notes, "We project ourselves—a small, humble elect, perhaps—past the End, so as to see the structure of the whole, a thing we cannot do from our spot in the middle."

7. Joyce refines this idea of narrative as a communal consciousness in *Finnegans Wake*. Seamus Deane argues that in *Wake*, Joyce depicts a communal unconscious because "at the conscious level so much has been repressed that amnesia is the abiding condition." See Deane, introduction to *Finnegans Wake*, by James Joyce, xi.

8. For Freud, melancholia isolates the individual and is directed against the ego. My understanding of melancholia's function here is similar to Dominick LaCapra's less strictly Freudian reading in that I view melancholia as a more active force that allows a traumatized subject to articulate memories from the past. See Sigmund Freud, "Mourning and Melancholia"; and Dominick LaCapra, *Writing History, Writing Trauma*, 65–66.

9. Brooks, *Reading for the Plot*, 140. Brooks argues that novelistic plot is driven by its desire for ending, but also, paradoxically, resists closure as it signifies the end of desire. The plot of the novel, then, functions as a working through of Freud's death instinct.

10. Karen Lawrence, *The Odyssey of Style in "Ulysses,"* 8.

11. Luke Gibbons, *Joyce's Ghosts: Ireland, Modernism and Memory*, xiv–xv.

12. Freud, "Mourning and Melancholia," 244–47; Sigmund Freud, "The Ego and the Id," 24.

13. For more on the shifting styles in Joyce's novel, see Lawrence, *Odyssey of Style*.

14. Brooks, *Reading for the Plot*, 268.

15. Seamus Deane, "Joyce and Nationalism," in *Celtic Revivals: Essays in Modern Irish Literature, 1880–1980*, 98. Deane argues that Joyce dismantles the relationship between author and reader and, instead, "insists on the dependence of the story and the very idea of fiction upon language. Given that, he can then make language constitutive of reality, not merely regulative of it."

16. See Benedict Anderson, *Imagined Communities: Reflections on the Origin and Spread of Nationalism*, 12. Anderson argues that as religious worldviews declined, so too did their ability to transform fatality into continuity. In secular society the idea of nation performed the same function that religion had previously served.

17. Lang, *"Ulysses" and the Irish God*, 16, 25. While Lang contends that Joyce's fiction reveals that he was "consistently anti-Catholic," he does note that Bloom's introduction of the word "Reincarnation" early in the novel indicates a "return to the human flesh as the proper object of worship." Contrary to Lang's assertion, it would seem that rather than positioning human flesh as an object of worship, Joyce is returning religion to the mortal, everyday world.

18. Sherman, *In a Strange Room*, 130.

19. Ariela Freedman, *Death, Men, and Modernism: Trauma and Narrative in British Fiction from Hardy to Woolf*, 3–5, 15–16. Freedman argues that in modernist novels, young dead men indicate a crisis in masculinity and a failure of modernity. Without the shared significance of religion, the individual becomes wholly responsible for making sense of death.

20. Richard Ellmann, *James Joyce: New and Revised Edition*, 244. Ellmann notes, "That the dead do not stay buried is, in fact, a theme of Joyce from the beginning to the end of his work; Finnegan is not the only corpse to be resurrected."

21. Lewis, *Religious Experience*, 171; Lawrence L. Langer, *The Age of Atrocity: Death in Modern Literature*, xii–xiii, 40.

22. Daniel Moshenberg, "What Shouts in the Street, 1904, 1922, 1990–93," 129.

23. Sherman, *In a Strange Room*, 25–31. Sherman's history of the corpse in the twentieth century is largely focused on England and America. For more background on Irish capital and culture during this period, see Joe Cleary, "Capital and Culture in Twentieth-Century Ireland," in *Outrageous Fortune: Capital and Culture in Modern Ireland*, 76–111.

24. Deane, *Celtic Revivals*, 102. He writes: "In breaking away from the restrictions of a local nationality and from the kinds of identity conferred upon him by tradition, Joyce achieved a language which, by the sheer number of its polyglot associations, appears to be all-inclusive and yet which, by the sheer complexity of its narrative orders, manages to be almost willfully exclusive."

25. Joyce, *Ulysses*, 97.

26. Ibid., 101.

27. Emer Nolan, *James Joyce and Nationalism*, 58–59. Nolan comments that although *Ulysses* is not a linear story and is instead composed of many different stories, these narratives function in a complementary manner and are tied together by the persistence of "underlying narrative paradigms."

28. Mark S. Cladis, introduction to *The Elementary Forms of Religious Life*, xxii.

29. For more on *Ulysses*'s connection to everyday life, see Declan Kiberd, *"Ulysses" and Us: The Art of Everyday Life in Joyce's Masterpiece*.

30. Joyce, *Ulysses*, 447, 539.

31. Ibid., 3.

32. Don Gifford with Robert G. Seidman, *"Ulysses" Annotated: Notes for James Joyce's "Ulysses*," 13.

33. Joyce, *Ulysses*, 10; *The Layman's Missal* (1962), cited in Gifford with Seidman, *"Ulysses" Annotated*, 19.

34. Joyce, *Ulysses*, 10.

35. Robert Garratt views Stephen as a "true trauma victim" who is "overwhelmed and stymied" by the traumatic experience of his mother's death. While Stephen is clearly haunted by his mother's death, the assertion that he is a trauma victim suggests that this is something that can be worked through, overcome, and then divided from the present. I argue that Joyce, rather than dividing present from past, seeks to further blur these boundaries. See Robert Garratt, "History and Trauma in *Ulysses*," 40.

36. Joyce, *Ulysses*, 10.

37. Ibid., 8; Nolan, *James Joyce and Nationalism*, 60.

38. See Jeremy Taylor, *The Rule and Exercises of Holy Dying*.

39. See Nancy Lee Beaty, *The Craft of Dying: A Study of the Literary Tradition of the "Ars Moriendi" in England*.

40. Joyce, *Ulysses*, 6.

41. Ellmann, *James Joyce*, 67; Gifford with Seidman, *"Ulysses" Annotated*, 10; Joyce, *Ulysses*, 9; Stanislaus Joyce, *My Brother's Keeper*, 134; Jean Kimball, "Love and Death in *Ulysses*: 'Word Known to All Men.'"

42. Joyce, *Ulysses*, 48, 540.

43. Richard Ellmann, *"Ulysses" on the Liffey*, 147, 174. Ellmann asserts that this word is "love." He supports this point in his review of Gabler's edition of *Ulysses* by citing a passage from "Scylla and Charybdis" recovered by Gabler. See Richard

Ellmann, "The Big Word in *Ulysses*: Review of *'Ulysses': A Critical and Synoptic Edition* by James Joyce, Prepared by Hans Walter Gabler, by Wolfhard Steppe, by Claus Melchoir." This goes against Hugh Kenner's contention that the word is "death." See Hugh Kenner, *Ulysses*, 129.

44. Kimball, "Love and Death in *Ulysses*," 156.

45. Joyce, *Ulysses*, 85.

46. See Julieann Ulin, "'Famished Ghosts': Famine Memory in James Joyce's *Ulysses*," 30. Ulin notes, "Although this custom returned in 1904, Simon's remark conceals the fact that the tradition is not without a very significant interruption. Famine burials in mass graves, the inability to obtain a coffin for remains, and corpses devoured by wild animals along the road represent an unspeakable history contained in Simon's statement."

47. Sherman, *In a Strange Room*, 130; Joyce, *Ulysses*, 94–95.

48. Friedman, *Fictional Death*, 23. Friedman suggests that modern society has made death unnatural: "Whether hiding or forestalling death in hospitals or enacting it massively in wars, modern technology removed death from the home and rendered it artificial, arranged, civilization's chief product; its dehumanized subjects were distanced from what had long been the 'natural' site and processes of living and dying."

49. Gibbons, *Joyce's Ghosts*, 224–25. He asserts that traumatic memory acts as "an ethical resource, providing glimpses of alternative futures" rather than shutting down the past. In a similar way, I argue that Joyce uses death to open possibilities rather than close them. However, unlike traumatic memory, which haunts the narrative telling, death impels the very act of narrative itself. Thus, in order to undo the function of endings, Joyce must break down the novel's form and structure even as he creates it.

50. Joyce, *Ulysses*, 84, 104, 110.

51. Kiberd, *"Ulysses" and Us*, 104–5.

52. Zvi Sobel and Benjamin Beit-Hallahmi, *Tradition, Innovation, Conflict: Jewishness and Judaism in Contemporary Israel*, 84.

53. Joyce, *Ulysses*, 92; Friedman, *Fictional Death*, 47.

54. For an excellent account of how monuments function in Joyce's work, see Ellen Carol Jones, "Ghosts through Absence."

55. Joyce, *Ulysses*, 92.

56. R. M. Adams, "Hades," 99–100. He notes, "It is probably natural that 'Hades' (an episode described as using the primary technique of 'incubism') should carry out, more than any other unit of *Ulysses*, the major theme of *Dubliners*, that Ireland is a land of walking ghosts and barely vitalized corpses."

57. In a similar reading, Ellen Carol Jones asserts that the absent spaces of the city and the "unsaid of the subaltern" in *Ulysses* "claim the possibility of a future

conditional, a future that is non-telic and unknowable but open to alternative imagining." See Jones, "Ghosts through Absence," 143.

58. Friedman, *Fictional Death*, 137. Friedman comments on Stephen's failure to pray for his dying mother and notes, "Joyce implies that the refusal of one ritual, bedside prayer for the dying, ruined another: the funeral and mourning for Stephen's mother that are also elided."

59. Ibid., 8. For Friedman, these "improper" deaths serve as devices that unbind the narrative rather than causing it to cohere. In this sense, the improper deaths in *Ulysses*, whether inappropriate in themselves or made so through the failure of ritual, serve as disruptive forces that blast apart the structures and conventions of the novel form.

60. Joyce, *Ulysses*, 92.

61. Gifford with Seidman, *"Ulysses" Annotated*, 111.

62. Joyce, *Ulysses*, 95.

63. Jessica Mitford, *The American Way of Death*, 91, 164. Mitford describes the process by which a corpse is embalmed and transformed into a beautiful memory picture for the living to remember the dead. Bloom's comments here indicate a similar desire to hide death's horror or ugliness.

64. Joyce, *Ulysses*, 5.

65. Sherman, *In a Strange Room*, 116.

66. Joyce, *Ulysses*, 100, 45–46, 49. In "Telemachus" Stephen associates the sea with his mother and, in particular, the china bowl that held her vomit on her sickbed. In "Proteus" Stephen describes his father as "a drowning man" and laments, "I could not save her. Waters: bitter death: lost."

67. Ibid., 104.

68. Gifford with Seidman, *"Ulysses" Annotated*, 105.

69. Joyce, *Ulysses*, 84; Adams, "Hades," 111; Joyce, *Ulysses*, 449; Adams, "Hades," 111; Gifford with Seidman, *"Ulysses" Annotated*, 105.

70. Freud, "Mourning and Melancholia," 246–52, 257. He later alters these views and redefines the self in a less rigid relation to the object. See Freud, "Ego and the Id," 24.

71. Joyce, *Ulysses*, 447, 62; Lawrence, *Odyssey of Style*, 153.

72. Joyce, *Ulysses*, 540, 542, 555.

73. As Karen Lawrence contends, "Circe" does not represent a "radical change in the characters" but allows the reader to "feel where the climax *would have been* in a more conventional novel." Lawrence, *Odyssey of Style*, 161.

74. For John Paul Riquelme, "'Circe' is a writerly text. It enables us to reconfigure its language in various ways that depend on our assumptions about narrative, literary style, and consciousness. And whatever our attitudes, it always defies them." Riquelme, *Teller and Tale in Joyce's Fiction: Oscillating Perspectives*, 140.

75. Joyce, *Ulysses*, 564.
76. Ibid., 565; Gifford with Seidman, *"Ulysses" Annotated*, 529.
77. Lawrence, *Odyssey of Style*, 160. She also contends that the fact that Rudy does not speak to Bloom indicates the incompleteness of the vision, a lack that is expressed in the fragmented dialogue.
78. Gifford with Seidman, *"Ulysses" Annotated*, 527.
79. See Seamus Deane, "*Ulysses*: The Exhaustion of Literature and the Literature of Exhaustion."
80. Joyce, *Ulysses*, 110.
81. Ibid., 691.
82. Ibid., 723.
83. Ibid., 724, 728.
84. Ibid., 732; Roland Barthes, *The Pleasure of the Text*, 40–41.
85. As Riquelme confirms, "Molly's 'yes' marks two boundaries as if they were one; the boundary between the unwritten and the written and between what can and cannot be written. Joyce shows us simultaneously where language stops and where it starts." Riquelme, *Teller and Tale*, 229.
86. Seán Ó Súilleabháin, *Irish Wake Amusements*, 159–60.
87. Ilana Harlow, "Creating Situations: Practical Jokes and the Revival of the Dead in Irish Tradition," 142.
88. Ibid., 153.
89. James Joyce, *Finnegans Wake*, 3, 628. This notion of a circular narrative is apparent in *Finnegans Wake* in which the novel's first sentence, "riverrun, past Eve and Adam's, from swerve of shore to bend of bay, brings us by a commodious vicus of recirculation back to Howth Castle and Environs," is a fragment that ends the last sentence of the novel: "A way a lone a last a loved a long the."

2. The Eve of All Souls and the Death of Desire

1. See Declan Kiberd, *Inventing Ireland: The Literature of the Modern Nation*, 395–410.
2. Eibhear Walshe, *Kate O'Brien: A Writing Life*, 118. Walshe notes, "Like Joyce, Kate appropriated much of her aesthetic of the novel to her Irish Catholic education."
3. Ibid., 2.
4. Declan Kiberd, *Irish Classics*, 559. Kiberd notes, "[O'Brien] is unusual in her alertness to the spiritual dilemmas posed for conscientious young intellectuals by [Catholicism's] exacting claims."
5. Eamon Maher, "Tracing the Imprint: Catholicism in Some Twentieth Century Irish Fiction," 491. Maher identifies *The Ante-Room* as "the closest an Irish writer

has come to being a truly 'Catholic' novel, not in the sense of indulging in apologetics or promulgating dogma but of being a narrative that could only be understood by readers with a certain knowledge of Catholicism and the obligations it imposes."

6. Kiberd, *Irish Classics*, 560.

7. The nineteenth-century deathbed narrative was modeled on documents such as Jeremy Taylor's *The Rule and Exercises of Holy Dying*. Taylor's book is an extension of the medieval manual on the art of dying well, known as the *ars moriendi*. Like the *ars moriendi*, Taylor argues for a tranquil death, achievable by following certain steps that require the dying person to set his or her house in order, heal family relationships, and encourage religion in others. For more on the *ars moriendi*, see also Beaty, *Craft of Dying*; and Sister Mary Catherine O'Connor, *The Art of Dying Well: The Development of the "Ars Moriendi."*

8. Sigmund Freud, "Civilization and Its Discontents," 756–60, 122.

9. Ibid., 764.

10. See Anne Fogarty, "'The Business of Attachment': Romance and Desire in the Novels of Kate O'Brien," in *Ordinary People Dancing: Essays on Kate O'Brien*, edited by Eibhear Walshe, 111.

11. Kate O'Brien, *The Ante-Room*, 221; Kiberd, *Irish Classics*, 571.

12. For more on novelistic death scenes, see Stewart, *Death Sentences*, 5–7, 11.

13. Walshe, *Kate O'Brien*, 58–59. For more on O'Brien's view of *The Ante-Room* as the greatest of her novels, see also Kiberd, *Irish Classics*, 557; John Jordan, "Kate O'Brien: A Note on Her Themes," 55–59; and Vivian Mercier, "Kate O'Brien."

14. Walshe, *Kate O'Brien*, 58.

15. For a contemporary review of *The Ante-Room*, see M. L., "Review of Kate O'Brien's *The Ante-Room*," 121. The reviewer notes, "A macabre setting for an illicit love, and perhaps most readers will feel that in real life death is too absorbing an affair to leave room for the terrors and ecstasies of such passion."

16. Lorna Reynolds, *Kate O'Brien: A Literary Portrait*, 56; Adele Dalsimer, *Kate O'Brien*, 32.

17. See Emer Nolan, *Catholic Emancipations: Irish Fiction from Thomas Moore to James Joyce*, 47. Nolan describes the rise of the Catholic middle class in Ireland during the late nineteenth century, arguing that their claim to political power was based on distinguishing themselves from the masses while asserting their ability to control those same masses: "Hence the enormous stress on self-repression in Catholic propaganda—and not only on the repression of sinful desires (especially the thirst for alcohol) but also of violent language and spontaneous protest."

18. E. Estyn Evans, *Irish Folk Ways*, 73, 277.

19. Heather Ingman, *Twentieth-Century Fiction by Irish Women: Nation and Gender*, 122.

20. O'Brien, *The Ante-Room*, 7.

21. Ibid.
22. Ibid., 13–14.
23. Hoffman, *Mortal No*, 3–4.
24. O'Brien, *The Ante-Room*, 15.
25. Ibid., 27.
26. See Gibbons, *Joyce's Ghosts*, xiv.
27. O'Brien, *The Ante-Room*, 28.
28. Ibid.
29. Ibid., 29.
30. Ibid., 65.
31. Ibid., 69.
32. Ibid., 63.
33. For a Kristevian reading of *The Ante-Room*, see Heather Ingman, "The Feminine and the Sacred," in *Twentieth-Century Fiction*, 115–41.
34. O'Brien, *The Ante-Room*, 65.
35. Ibid., 66.
36. Ibid., 91, 32.
37. See Sigmund Freud, "Beyond the Pleasure Principle," 42.
38. O'Brien, *The Ante-Room*, 53.
39. See Edward Muir, *Ritual in Early Modern Europe*, 78–79.
40. O'Brien, *The Ante-Room*, 128, 130.
41. Ibid., 132–33.
42. Ibid., 141–42.
43. Ibid., 147.
44. Kiberd, *Inventing Ireland*, 396.
45. O'Brien, *The Ante-Room*, 166.
46. Ibid., 173.
47. Ibid., 172–73.
48. Brooks, *Reading for the Plot*, 95.
49. O'Brien, *The Ante-Room*, 173.
50. Ibid., 177.
51. Ibid., 178.
52. Ibid., 203.
53. Ibid., 207, 217.
54. Ibid., 218.
55. Ibid., 220.
56. See Freud, "Civilization and Its Discontents," 754. Freud summarizes his own argument in "Beyond the Pleasure Principle": "Starting from speculations on the beginning of life and from biological parallels, I drew the conclusion that, besides the instinct to preserve living substance and to join it to even larger units,

there must exist another, contrary instinct seeking to dissolve those units and bring them back to their primaeval state. That is to say, as well as Eros there as an instinct of death."

57. Kiberd, *Irish Classics*, 572.

3. Deathbed Confessions and Unraveling Narration

1. David Weisberg, *Chronicles of Disorder: Samuel Beckett and the Cultural Politics of the Modern Novel*, 1.

2. Anthony Cronin, *Samuel Beckett: The Last Modernist*, 390.

3. *Godot* was not performed or published until 1953.

4. James Knowlson, *Damned to Fame: The Life of Samuel Beckett*, 323–24.

5. Seamus Deane, *A Short History of Irish Literature*; David Lloyd, *Anomalous States: Irish Writing and the Post-colonial Moment*, 42–155; Kiberd, *Inventing Ireland*, 530–50; Seán Kennedy, ed., *Beckett and Ireland*; Emilie Morin, *Samuel Beckett and the Problem of Irishness*; Patrick Bixby, *Samuel Beckett and the Postcolonial Novel*.

6. Deane, *Short History of Irish Literature*, 188; Morin, *Beckett and the Problem of Irishness*, 162; Kiberd, *Inventing Ireland*, 535, 537.

7. Vivian Mercier, *The Irish Comic Tradition*, 46, 76; Christopher Ricks, *Beckett's Dying Words: The Clarendon Lectures, 1990*, 43.

8. Critics such as Richard Begam have argued that Lemuel represents Samuel Beckett himself, the name Lemuel acting as an analogue to Samuel. Begam, *Samuel Beckett and the End of Modernity*, 146.

9. Declan Kiberd, *Irish Classics*, 574–684. Kiberd argues that the treatment of dying in *Malone Dies* bears a resemblance to the Irish-language modernist novel *Cré na Cille* (Graveyard Clay) by Máirtín Ó Cadhain published in 1949. Both explore the liminal zones between life and death and are interested in language as a way of delineating between these two states.

10. Rónán McDonald, "The Ghost at the Feast: Beckett and Irish Studies," 24–25. McDonald further asserts that "looking at Beckett from the point of view of his Protestant background has the virtue of breaking the implied monolith of Irishness into constituent micro-narratives."

11. Kiberd, *Irish Classics*, 454. Kiberd suggests that the influence of Protestantism is apparent in Beckett's confrontation with the themes of the "puritan conscience: work, effort, reward, anxious self-scrutiny, the need for self-responsibility, and the distrust of artifice and even of art. His work seems like an answer to Shaw's prayer for a writer who would redefine Protestantism."

12. Steven Barfield, Matthew Feldman, and Philip Tew, eds., *Beckett and Death*, 2.

13. Mark Nixon, "'Writing Myself into the Ground': Textual Existence and Death in Beckett," 25. Nixon argues that in *Malone Dies*, the process of writing is

equated with living and that Malone as author remains torn between leaving the last things unsaid and giving voice to the end.

14. Thomas J. Cousineau, *After the Final No: Samuel Beckett's Trilogy*.

15. Michel Foucault, "What Is an Author?," 124–27, 116. It is interesting to note that Foucault's famous antihumanist text argues that Beckett's *Texts for Nothing* raises one of the "fundamental ethical principles of contemporary writing" by asking what matter is it who is speaking.

16. Brooks, *Reading for the Plot*, 58.

17. Ibid., 323.

18. See Weisberg, *Chronicles of Disorder*, 137–49. Weisberg argues that while Beckett's fiction expresses a loss of faith in the ability of literature to generate new forms of fiction, he nevertheless succeeds in representing this meaninglessness.

19. For an interesting account of how the trilogy serves as a kind of autobiography for Beckett, see H. Porter Abbott, *Beckett Writing Beckett: The Author in the Autograph*.

20. Freud, "Civilization and Its Discontents," 754.

21. For more on Beckett and Sterne, see Patrick Murray, "The Shandean Mode: Beckett and Sterne Compared."

22. Kiberd, *Irish Classics*, 43.

23. See Beaty, *Craft of Dying*.

24. Drew Gilpin Faust, *This Republic of Suffering: Death and the American Civil War*, 6.

25. Knowlson, *Damned to Fame*, 168, 251.

26. Erik Tonning, "Beckett's Unholy Dying: From *Malone Dies* to *The Unnamable*," 109.

27. Ibid., 109, 112.

28. Samuel Beckett, *The Trilogy: "Molloy," "Malone Dies," "The Unnamable"*, 179.

29. Tonning, "Beckett's Unholy Dying," 117; Beckett, *Trilogy*, 288.

30. This inventory of possessions is foreshadowed early in *Molloy*: "Doubtless I shall speak of [my hat and greatcoat] later, when the time comes to draw up an inventory of my possessions." This serves to strengthen the idea that Malone is simply an older Molloy under a different name. Beckett, *Trilogy*, 14.

31. Ibid., 181, 250.

32. Ibid., 207; Friedman, *Fictional Death*, 23.

33. John L. Murphy, "Beckett's Purgatories," 111. "Purgatory remains the most Beckettian position of the three realms assumed in Catholic afterlife. His heaven and hell lie static; purgatory suggests energy and vitality."

34. Jacques Le Goff, *The Birth of Purgatory*, 199.

35. Pascale Casanova, *Samuel Beckett: Anatomy of a Literary Revolution*, 49–50.

36. Peggy O'Brien, *Writing Lough Derg: From William Carleton to Seamus Heaney*, xxii.

37. Beckett, *Trilogy*, 180; J. Taylor, *Rule and Exercises*.

38. Tonning, "Beckett's Unholy Dying," 114.

39. Beckett, *Trilogy*, 279.

40. Stewart, *Death Sentences*, 321.

41. Abbott, *Beckett Writing Beckett*, 11; Beckett, *Trilogy*, 23.

42. See Beckett, *Trilogy*, 7.

43. Brooks, *Reading for the Plot*, 104.

44. Freud, "Beyond the Pleasure Principle," 53–54; Freud, "Civilization and Its Discontents," 764.

45. Beckett, *Trilogy*, 226.

46. Ibid., 209, 210.

47. Stewart, *Death Sentences*, 327; Beckett, *Trilogy*, 180.

48. Murray, "Shandean Mode," 64.

49. Beckett, *The Trilogy*, 182, 181.

50. Eric P. Levy, *Beckett and the Voice of Species: A Study of the Prose Fiction*, 84; Brooks, *Reading for the Plot*, 104.

51. Beckett, *Trilogy*, 184.

52. Stewart, *Death Sentences*, 325; Beckett, *Trilogy*, 184.

53. Beckett, *Trilogy*, 208.

54. Ibid., 225.

55. Julieann Ulin, "'Buried! Who Would Have Buried Her?': Famine 'Ghost Graves' in Samuel Beckett's *Endgame*," 202; Mercier, *The Irish Comic Tradition*, 49.

56. Eric P. Levy, *Trapped in Thought: A Study of the Beckettian Mentality*, 224, 93, 99.

57. Elizabeth Barry, "Beckett, Augustine, and the Rhetoric of Dying," 76; Beckett, *Trilogy*, 290.

58. Beckett, *Trilogy*, 32.

59. In this sense *Molloy*, in which the title character tries and fails to give an account of his birth and development, can be read as the opposite of *Malone*, which charts the same character's decline and death.

60. Elaine Scarry, *Resisting Representation*, 92.

4. Ritual and Denial in a World Stripped of Illusion

1. John McGahern, *All Will Be Well: A Memoir*, 125. This quotation was cited in McGahern's obituary in 2006 in the *Guardian*. The book was published in Ireland and the United Kingdom simply under the title *Memoir*.

2. See Charles Townshend, *Ireland: The 20th Century*, 168–77; J. J. Lee, *Ireland, 1912–1985*; and Terence Brown, *Ireland: A Social and Cultural History, 1922 to the Present*.

3. John McGahern, *The Barracks*, 32.

4. Dermot McCarthy, *John McGahern and the Art of Memory*, 77. McCarthy argues that the novel's final scene functions not so much to "close the narrative circle" as to "draw attention to the emptiness now at its centre: the echo of the beginning accentuates the hollowness of the family without the mother-figure present." I suggest that this closing scene not only draws attention to Elizabeth's absence but is also indicative of a wider social problem stemming from a modern desire to move on from the past without working through its traumas.

5. Elaine Scarry, *The Body in Pain: The Making and Unmaking of the World*.

6. McCarthy, *McGahern and the Art of Memory*, 23. McCarthy argues that the death of McGahern's mother is the defining moment not only in his early life but in his entire fictional oeuvre.

7. McGahern, *All Will Be Well*, 141.

8. Ariès, *Hour of Our Death*, 595. Ariès is deeply critical of what he views as modern society's denial of death in which the dying and dead are removed from daily life, offering little opportunity to grieve or mourn. Important here is the idea that modern death gave birth to two beliefs: that nature seemed to eliminate death—in the natural world everything that is lost is then renewed or restored in the earth's process of decay and regeneration—and that technology would replace nature and eliminate death more surely.

9. McCarthy, *McGahern and the Art of Memory*, 10.

10. Cleary, *Outrageous Fortune*, 159.

11. David Malcolm, *Understanding John McGahern*, 5.

12. Kate O'Brien, untitled review, 59–60. See also Eamon Maher, "Circles and Circularity in the Writings of John McGahern." Maher has noted that O'Brien ranks among the Irish writers McGahern admired and draws similarities between O'Brien's and McGahern's novels. He argues that O'Brien's novels mark an end of the world of genteel Catholicism and that McGahern's depiction of rural Ireland in the twentieth century functions in a similar way.

13. O'Brien, untitled review, 59.

14. See Clair Wills, *The Best Are Leaving: Emigration and Post-war Irish Culture*, 41–42. Wills describes how the expansion of the labor market in postwar Ireland "contributed to the redefinition of marriage as an economic unit," resulting in women who sought "emotional fulfillment as well as financial security within marriage, as romance, sexual intimacy, and compatibility became increasingly accepted as rightfully part of the marriage contract."

15. For recent publications that attempt to situate McGahern's work in a wider European context, see Richard Robinson, *John McGahern and Modernism*; Frank

Shovlin, *Touchstones: John McGahern's Classical Style*; and Stanley van der Ziel, *John McGahern and the Imagination of Tradition*.

16. See Eamon Maher, *John McGahern: From the Local to the Universal*; and James Whyte, *History, Myth and Ritual in the Fictions of John McGahern: Strategies of Transcendence*.

17. Denis Sampson, *Outstaring Nature's Eye: The Fiction of John McGahern*, 21.

18. See R. Robinson, *John McGahern and Modernism*, for more on the modernist elements in McGahern's fiction.

19. Brian Liddy, "State and Church: Darkness in the Fiction of John McGahern," 112.

20. For more on time sequences and the historical novel, see Bakhtin, *Dialogic Imagination*, 216–17. Bakhtin argues that the motif of death undergoes a transformation with the emergence of the temporal sequence of an individual life that runs parallel to that of the historical time sequence. The challenge to the author of the modern historical novel is to unite these two sequences, finding historical aspects to private life. When this unity of time disappears, nature becomes a mere backdrop for action.

21. McGahern, *The Barracks*, 7, 8.
22. Ibid., 57.
23. Whyte, *History, Myth and Ritual*, 42.
24. Scarry, *Body in Pain*, 6.
25. Liddy, "State and Church," 110; Jean-Paul Sartre, *Being and Nothingness: An Essay on Phenomenological Ontology*; McGahern, *The Barracks*, 50.
26. McGahern, *The Barracks*, 84.
27. Scarry, *Body in Pain*, 14.
28. Ibid.
29. McGahern, *The Barracks*, 90.
30. Ibid., 55–56.
31. Ibid., 119; Beckett, *Trilogy*, 252.
32. Sampson, *Outstaring Nature's Eye*, 19; Maher, *John McGahern*, 16.
33. McGahern, *The Barracks*, 187.
34. Ibid., 59.
35. Scarry, *Body in Pain*, 20–22.
36. Maher, *John McGahern*, 18, 20; McGahern, *The Barracks*, 220; Hoffman, *Mortal No*, 349–50.
37. McGahern, *The Barracks*, 195; Scarry, *Body in Pain*, 213–14.
38. McGahern, *The Barracks*, 211.
39. Scarry, *Body in Pain*, 207.
40. McGahern, *The Barracks*, 218.
41. Ibid., 73, 123.

42. Teresa of Ávila, *The Life of Saint Teresa of Ávila by Herself.*
43. McGahern, *The Barracks*, 199. This kind of denial is in line with the cultural shift in modern attitudes toward death that Philippe Ariès observed in French culture in *The Hour of Our Death* and that Seamus O'Mahony has more recently discerned in Irish culture in *The Way We Die Now.*
44. McGahern, *The Barracks*, 199.
45. Ibid., 217.
46. Ibid., 221.
47. Ibid., 211.
48. Ibid., 222.
49. Ibid., 7, 222, 7.
50. John McGahern, *That They May Face the Rising Sun*, 294, 314.

5. Death without Resurrection and the Modern Wake

1. For more on trauma theory, see Cathy Caruth, ed., *Trauma: Explorations in Memory*; LaCapra, *Writing History, Writing Trauma*; and Laurie Vickroy, *Trauma and Survival in Contemporary Fiction.*
2. See LaCapra, *Writing History, Writing Trauma*, 183. This view of literature as a way of accessing trauma is in line with Caruth's theories. However, LaCapra criticizes Caruth's analysis of trauma because of its implication that "literature in its very excess can somehow get at trauma in a manner unavailable to theory." LaCapra questions how literature does this and seeks a distinction between structural and historical trauma.
3. Brooks, *Reading for the Plot*, xi–xxv.
4. Gerardine Meaney, "Waking the Dead: Antigone, Ismene and Anne Enright's Narrators in Mourning," 151, 146. Meaney argues that Enright's fiction inhabits the "aesthetic territory on the borderlines of what Julia Kristeva describes as the 'true-real'; where the outside of language manifests itself in language, a territory which Jean-François Lyotard made paradigmatically postmodern, where that which cannot be represented is present in representation." She suggests that Enright's fiction exceeds this paradigm by reconfiguring these forces in order to be able to live.
5. Freedman, *Death, Men, and Modernism*, 8. Freedman argues that death in modernist literature serves as a process of unbinding.
6. Robert F. Garratt's *Trauma and History in the Irish Novel: The Return of the Dead* argues that recent Irish fiction (between 1970 and 2000) differs from other historical novels because of their "retrospective narrative that focuses on memories of events of a previous generation" and in their emphasis on "traumatic experience rather than historical events" (4). He further asserts that symptoms of trauma can be relieved through acknowledgment and eventual narration.

7. Hedi Hansson, "Beyond the Local in *The Wig My Father Wore*," 51.

8. Hansson speculates that *The Gathering* garnered such prestigious recognition because it was organized around "the well-known Irish literary theme of the wake and dealing with the familiar topic of the dysfunctional Irish family." Ibid., 53.

9. For more on the Irish wake, see Evans, *Irish Folk Ways*; John Gamble, "An Irish Wake"; Ó Crualaoich, "The 'Merry Wake'"; and Ó Súilleabháin, *Irish Wake Amusements*, 282–95.

10. Margaret Mills Harper, "Flesh and Bones: Anne Enright's *The Gathering*," 79.

11. Sigmund Freud, *The Standard Edition of the Complete Psychological Works of Sigmund Freud*, vol. 92, "Beyond the Pleasure Principle," "Group Psychology," and Other Works, 44–63; Brooks, *Reading for the Plot*, 299.

12. Anne Enright, *The Gathering*, 1.

13. Garratt, *Trauma and History*, 16, 17. Garratt argues that Irish trauma novels are both "about and of history" and therefore "situate themselves within the current discussion of Irish historiographical practice." According to Garratt, this rediscovery of the past is necessary to open the future. However, as this study has shown, death in the modern Irish novel serves as a point of retrospection as well as prompting a consideration of the future.

14. Enright, *The Gathering*, 2.

15. Ibid., 27. On her way to the airport to fly to England to retrieve her brother's body, Veronica thinks of all the responsibilities she is leaving behind. Enright writes, "There is something wonderful about a death, how everything shuts down, and all the ways you thought were vital are not even vaguely important."

16. Brooks, *Reading for the Plot*, 139, 100.

17. Enright, *The Gathering*, 2.

18. For an excellent account of disinterment in the modern period, see Diane O'Rourke, "Mourning Becomes Eclectic: Death of Communal Practice in a Greek Cemetery." O'Rourke focuses on disinterment in rural Greece, but the changes in modern mourning practices are indicative of larger shifts in Europe.

19. Sarah Tarlow and Liv Nilsson Stutz, eds., *The Oxford Handbook of the Archaeology of Death and Burial*, 17.

20. L. Taylor, "*Bás InÉirinn*," 175. Taylor notes that despite the fact that there is no "cult of death" in Irish Catholicism, "attention to the fact and possibility of death is maintained in both religious and ordinary language." The "cult of death" emerges in the political realm. For more on disinterment in sixteenth- and seventeenth-century Ireland as it pertained to power struggles between Catholics and Protestants, see Clodagh Tait, *Death, Burial and Commemoration in Ireland, 1550–1650*.

21. Enright, *The Gathering*, 125. According to Veronica, "That was Liam's great talent—exposing a lie." Liam's ghost demands that Veronica expose the truth in a way that he could not.

22. See Daniel G. Brinton, "Folk-Lore of the Bones," 18. Brinton explains how the word "bonfire" is derived from the word "bone-fire," or in Irish *cnaimh theinne*. This ancient practice of sacrifice involved the burning of man or animal in order to reveal the soul.

23. Claire Connolly, *A Cultural History of the Irish Novel, 1790–1829*, 164–99 (quote on 193).

24. W. B. Yeats, *The Dreaming of the Bones*, in *Four Plays for Dancers*.

25. See Yeats, "Note on *The Dreaming of the Bones*," ibid. Yeats writes, "The conception of the play is derived from the world-wide belief that the dead dream back, for a certain time, through the more personal thoughts and deeds of life."

26. Enright, *The Gathering*, 1.

27. Peter Brooks, *Troubling Confessions: Speaking Guilt in Law and Literature*, 2.

28. For more on Victorian deathbed scenes and their relationship with modern fiction, see Stewart, *Death Sentences*, 8, 50, 101–2, 142, 321.

29. Brooks, *Troubling Confessions*, 91–92, 97, 2 (quote).

30. Jo Gill, introduction to *Modern Confessional Writing: New Critical Essays*, 1–11, 5.

31. Watt, *Rise of the Novel*, 74, 75.

32. Enright, *The Gathering*, 172–73.

33. Hand, *History of the Irish Novel*, 149.

34. Recent articles by Carol Dell'Amico, Margaret Mills Harper, and Liam Harte rightly point out the double function of Veronica's narrative as an attempt to gain personal understanding as well as evoking a wider social consciousness. See Dell'Amico, "Anne Enright's *The Gathering*: Trauma, Testimony, Memory; Harte, "Mourning Remains Unresolved: Trauma and Survival in Anne Enright's *The Gathering*"; and Harper, "Flesh and Bones."

35. Claire Bracken and Susan Cahill, "An Interview with Anne Enright," in *Anne Enright*, edited by Bracken and Cahill, 30–31. Enright comments on the role of memory in *The Gathering*: "I mean, *The Gathering* is interested in the edges between, certainly fantasy or imagination and memory, between memory and history and where we let go of memory, where it ossifies and turns into history, where it becomes static, when people die."

36. Enright, *The Gathering*, 156.

37. Sigmund Freud, *The Uncanny*, 150–51. For an excellent elaboration of Freud's concept, see also Nicholas Royle, *"The Uncanny": An Introduction*.

38. Freud, *The Uncanny*, 155.

39. Jeanett Shumaker, "Uncanny Doubles: The Fiction of Anne Enright," 107; Royle, *"The Uncanny": An Introduction*, 2; Enright, *The Gathering*, 36; Freud, *The Uncanny*, 151; Royle, *"The Uncanny": An Introduction*, 2.

40. Enright, *The Gathering*, 141; Cathy Caruth, *Unclaimed Experience: Trauma, Narrative, and History*, 61; Enright, *The Gathering*, 142.

41. Enright, *The Gathering*, 13.

42. Brooks, *Reading for the Plot*, 102, 103.

43. Garratt, *Trauma and History*, 4–7, 146 (quote).

44. Harper, "Flesh and Bones," 84.

45. Enright, *The Gathering*, 41.

46. Ibid., 43–44.

47. Ibid., 74.

48. For an account of how American funerals have become commodified, see Thomas Lynch, "Our Own Worst Enemies," in *Good Funeral*, edited by Long and Lynch, 141–46.

49. Enright, *The Gathering*, 42. Veronica describes, "Some ancient impulse of my mother's means that she wants the coffin brought back to the house before the removal, so Liam can lie in state in our ghastly front room. Though come to think of it I can't think of a better carpet for a corpse, as I say to Bea; all those oblongs of orange and brown." Here the unattractive interior of the Hegarty family home is the perfect place for a corpse. The fact that the interior is "ghastly" implies a terrifying or frightening aspect to the room that matches the shock and horror of the corpse.

50. Ibid., 191, 206.

51. Ibid., 205.

52. Harte, "Mourning Remains Unresolved," 201.

53. For more on Irish beliefs surrounding wake rites, see Dáithí Ó hÓgáin, *The Sacred Isle: Belief and Religion in Pre-Christian Ireland*. For an account of these beliefs in a wider European and North American context, see Lewis R. Aiken, *Dying, Death and Bereavement*, 137–38.

54. Enright, *The Gathering*, 132, 155, 158.

55. See Freud, *The Uncanny*, 155.

56. Enright, *The Gathering*, 193.

57. Ó Crualaoich, "The 'Merry Wake,'" 173.

58. Corish, *Irish Catholic Experience*, 213.

59. Ó Crualaoich, "The 'Merry Wake,'" 191.

60. Enright, *The Gathering*, 64.

61. Ronald Lightbown, *Mantegna*, 136–38.

62. Enright, *The Gathering*, 228. Veronica comments, "Belief needs something terrible to work, I find—blood, nails, a bit of anguish." While far from advocating Catholic belief, Enright presents a nuanced view of contemporary Ireland that is largely secular but in which religious images possess a persistent power.

63. Ó Crualaoich, "The 'Merry Wake,'" 191; Enright, *The Gathering*, 192, 208, 209.

64. Ó Súilleabháin, *Irish Wake Amusements*, 15, 166–67. Ó Súilleabháin describes how the corpse must not be left unattended for the duration of the wake, a ritual designed to protect the dead from evil spirits.

65. Enright, *The Gathering*, 215.

66. Ibid., 221–22.

67. Enright seems to be taking a distinctly Lacanian view of the death drive not as a biological drive to a prebirth but as a prelinguistic and therefore presymbolic state experienced in infancy. See Jacques Lacan, *Écrits: A Selection*, 102.

68. Enright, *The Gathering*, 182, 241, 243, 248.

69. Harper, "Flesh and Bones," 79. Discussing the process of reading *The Gathering*, she notes: "The reader of the novel is placed in the position of the analyst in a psychoanalytic setting, the book itself to be read as the couch, the scene of a 'talking cure.'"

70. Enright, *The Gathering*, 2, 156. At the beginning of the novel, Veronica muses, "You cannot libel the dead, I think, you can only console them." Later in the novel, she reasserts a similar sentiment: "The truth. The dead want nothing else. It is the only thing they require." Indeed, Veronica's point in writing a narrative of her grandmother's life is to undercover the truth that will bring peace to the dead.

Conclusion

1. O'Mahony, *Way We Die Now*, 60.

2. Ibid., 9.

3. John Spain, review of *Every Single Minute*, by Hamilton.

4. For more information on the "Forum on End of Life in Ireland," see http://hospicefoundation.ie/what-we-do/forum-on-end-of-life/forum-on-end-of-life/.

5. John Gamble, *Sketches of History, Politics and Manners in Dublin and the North of Ireland in 1810*; Thomas Crofton Croker, *Researches in the South of Ireland: Illustrative of the Scenery, Architectural Remains and the Manners and Superstitions of the Peasantry with an Appendix Containing a Private Narrative of Rebellion of 1798*; O'Mahony, *Way We Die Now*, 56–57. See also Seán Súilleabháin, *Irish Wake Amusements*.

6. See Long and Lynch, *Good Funeral*.

7. Joan Didion, *The Year of Magical Thinking*, 205.

Bibliography

Abbott, H. Porter. *Beckett Writing Beckett: The Author in the Autograph*. Ithaca, NY: Cornell Univ. Press, 1996.

———. "The Harpooned Notebook: *Malone Dies* and the Conventions of Intercalated Narrative." In *Samuel Beckett: Humanistic Perspectives*, edited by Morris Beja, S. E. Gontarski, and Pierre Astier, 71–79. Columbus: Ohio State Univ. Press, 1983.

Adams, R. M. "Hades." In *James Joyce's "Ulysses": Critical Essays*, edited by Clive Hart and David Hayman, 91–115. Berkeley: Univ. of California Press, 1974.

Aiken, Lewis R. *Dying, Death and Bereavement*. 4th ed. London: Psychology Press, 2001.

Alvarez, Al. *The Savage God: A Study of Suicide*. London: Bloomsbury, 2002.

Anderson, Benedict. *Imagined Communities: Reflections on the Origin and Spread of Nationalism*. London: Verso, 1983.

Ariès, Philippe. *The Hour of Our Death*. Translated by Helen Weaver. Oxford: Oxford Univ. Press, 1981.

Arnold, Matthew. *The Study of Celtic Literature*. London: Kennikat Press, 1905.

Bakhtin, Mikhail Mikhailovich. *The Dialogic Imagination: Four Essays*. Edited by Michael Holquist. Translated by Caryl Emerson and Michael Holquist. Austin: Univ. of Texas Press, 1981.

Barfield, Steven, Matthew Feldman, and Philip Tew, eds. *Beckett and Death*. London: Continuum, 2009.

Barry, Elizabeth. "Beckett, Augustine, and the Rhetoric of Dying." In *Beckett and Death*, edited by Steven Barfield, Matthew Feldman, and Phillip Tew, 72–88. London: Continuum, 2009.

Barthes, Roland. *The Pleasure of the Text*. Translated by Richard Miller. New York: Farrar, Straus, and Giroux, 1975. Originally published as *Le plaisir du texte*. Paris: Éditions du Seuil, 1973.

Beaty, Nancy Lee. *The Craft of Dying: A Study in the Literary Tradition of the "Ars Moriendi" in England*. New Haven, CT: Yale Univ. Press, 1970.

Beckett, Samuel. *Endgame*. 1957. Reprint, London: Faber and Faber, 2012.

———. *The Trilogy: "Molloy," "Malone Dies," "The Unnamable."* London: Calder, 1959.

Begam, Richard. *Samuel Beckett and the End of Modernity*. Stanford, CA: Stanford Univ. Press, 1996.

Bell, Robert H. "'Preparatory to Anything Else': Introduction to Joyce's 'Hades.'" *Journal of Modern Literature* 24, no. 3 (2001): 363–499. http://www.jstor.org/stable/3831763.

Benjamin, Walter. "The Storyteller." In *Illuminations: Essays and Reflections*, translated by Harry Zohn. New York: Schocken Books, 1968.

Benstock, Bernard. *Narrative Con/Texts in "Ulysses."* Urbana: Univ. of Illinois Press, 1991.

Bixby, Patrick. *Samuel Beckett and the Postcolonial Novel*. Cambridge: Cambridge Univ. Press, 2009.

Boulter, Jonathan. *Interpreting Narrative in the Novels of Samuel Beckett*. Gainesville: Univ. Press of Florida, 2001.

Boyle, Robert. *James Joyce's Pauline Vision: A Catholic Exposition*. Carbondale: Southern Illinois Univ. Press, 1981.

Bracken, Claire, and Susan Cahill, eds. *Anne Enright*. Dublin: Irish Academic Press, 2011.

Brinton, Daniel G. "Folk-Lore of the Bones." *Journal of American Folk-Lore* 3 (1890): 17–22.

Bronfen, Elisabeth. *Over Her Dead Body: Death, Femininity and the Aesthetic*. New York: Routledge, 1992.

Bronfen, Elisabeth, and Sarah Webster Goodwin, eds. *Death and Representation*. Baltimore: Johns Hopkins Univ. Press, 1993.

Brooks, Peter. *Reading for the Plot: Design and Intention in Narrative*. Oxford: Clarendon Press, 1984.

———. *Troubling Confessions: Speaking Guilt in Law and Literature*. Chicago: Univ. of Chicago Press, 2000.

Brown, Norman O. *Life against Death: The Psychoanalytical Meaning of History*. Middletown, CT: Wesleyan Univ. Press, 1985.

Brown, Terence. *Ireland: A Social and Cultural History, 1922 to the Present*. Ithaca, NY: Cornell Univ. Press, 1985.

Bryant, Clifton, and Dennis Peck, eds. *The Encyclopedia of Death and Human Experience*. Thousand Oaks, CA: Sage, 2009.

———, eds. *The Handbook of Death and Dying*. Vol. 1, *The Presence of Death*. London: Thousand Acre, 2003.

Cahalan, James. *The Irish Novel: A Critical History*. Boston: Twayne, 1988.

Canon Law Society of America. *Code of Canon Law: Latin-English Edition*. Vatican City: Canon Law Society of America, 1983.

Caruth, Cathy, ed. *Trauma: Explorations in Memory*. Baltimore: Johns Hopkins Univ. Press, 1995.

———. *Unclaimed Experience: Trauma, Narrative, and History*. Baltimore: Johns Hopkins Univ. Press, 1996.

Casanova, Pascale. *Samuel Beckett: Anatomy of a Literary Revolution*. Translated by Gregory Elliot. London: Verso, 2006.

Catanzaro, Mary. "Whose Story Is It? Samuel Beckett's *Malone Dies* and the Voice of Self-Invention." In *Literature and the Writer*, edited by Michael J. Meyer, 119–35. Amsterdam: Rodopi, 2004.

Cleary, Joe. *Outrageous Fortune: Capital and Culture in Modern Ireland*. Dublin: Field Day, 2006.

Commission to Inquire into Child Abuse. *Commission Report* [Ryan Report]. Dublin: Government Publications, 2009. http://www.childabusecommission.ie.

Connolly, Claire. *A Cultural History of the Irish Novel, 1790–1829*. Cambridge: Cambridge Univ. Press, 2011.

Corish, Patrick J. *The Irish Catholic Experience: A Historical Survey*. Dublin: Gill and Macmillan, 1985.

Cousineau, Thomas. *After the Final No: Samuel Beckett's Trilogy*. London: Associated Univ. Press, 1999.

Crofton Croker, Thomas. *Researches in the South of Ireland: Illustrative of the Scenery, Architectural Remains and the Manners and Superstitions of the Peasantry with an Appendix Containing a Private Narrative of Rebellion of 1798*. 1824. Reprint, Shannon: Irish Univ. Press, 1968.

Cronin, Anthony. *Samuel Beckett: The Last Modernist*. London: HarperCollins, 1996.

Cronin, John. *The Anglo-Irish Novel, 1900–1940*. Belfast: Appletree, 1990.

Cusack, George, and Sarah Goss, eds. *Hungry Words: Images of the Famine in the Irish Canon*. Dublin: Irish Academic Press, 1006.

Dalsimer, Adele. *Kate O'Brien*. Boston: Twayne, 1990.
Davies, Douglas. *Death, Ritual and Belief*. London: Continuum, 2002.
Deane, Seamus. *Celtic Revivals: Essays in Modern Irish Literature, 1880–1980*. London: Faber and Faber, 1985.
———. Introduction to *Finnegans Wake*, by James Joyce. London: Penguin, 1992.
———. *A Short History of Irish Literature*. South Bend, IN: Univ. of Notre Dame Press, 1994.
———. "*Ulysses*: The Exhaustion of Literature and the Literature of Exhaustion." In *Ulysses: Cinquante ans après*, edited by Louis Bonnerot, 263–74. Paris: Didier, 1974.
Dell'Amico, Carol. "Anne Enright's *The Gathering*: Trauma, Testimony, Memory." *New Hibernia Review* 14, no. 3. (2010): 59–74. doi:10.1353/nhr.2010.0014.
Didion, Joan. *The Year of Magical Thinking*. New York: Alfred A. Knopf, 2005.
Dollimore, Jonathan. *Death, Desire and Loss in Western Culture*. London: Penguin, 1998.
Donnelly, James S., and Kerby A. Miller, eds. *Irish Popular Culture, 1650–1850*. Dublin: Irish Academic Press, 1998.
Durkheim, Émile. *The Elementary Forms of Religious Life*. Translated by Carol Cosman. Oxford: Oxford Univ. Press, 2001.
———. *Suicide: A Study in Sociology*. Edited by George Simpson. Translated by John A. Spaulding. London: Routledge, 1952.
Ellmann, Richard. "The Big Word in *Ulysses*: Review of '*Ulysses*': A Critical and Synoptic Edition, by James Joyce, Prepared by Hans Walter Gabler, by Wolfhard Steppe, by Claus Melchoir." *New York Review of Books*, Oct. 25, 1984. http://www.nybooks.com/articles/archives/1984/oct/25/the-big-word-in-ulysses/.
———. *James Joyce: A New and Revised Edition*. Oxford: Oxford Univ. Press, 1982.
———. "*Ulysses*" *on the Liffey*. Oxford: Oxford Univ. Press, 1972.
Enright, Anne. *The Gathering*. London: Jonathan Cape, 2007.
———. *What Are You Like?* London: Jonathan Cape, 2000.
———. *The Wig My Father Wore*. London: Jonathan Cape, 1995.
Evans, E. Estyn. *Irish Folk Ways*. London: Routledge, 1956.
Faust, Drew Gilpin. *This Republic of Suffering: Death and the American Civil War*. New York: Random House, 2008.

Felman, Shoshana, and Dori Laub, eds. *Testimony: Crises of Witnessing in Literature, Psychoanalysis and History*. New York: Routledge, 1992.

Fleming, Marie. *An Act of Love: One Woman's Remarkable Life Story and Her Fight for the Right to Die with Dignity*. Dublin: Hachette Books Ireland, 2014.

Foster, John Wilson, ed. *The Cambridge Companion to the Irish Novel*. Cambridge: Cambridge Univ. Press, 2006.

Foucault, Michel. "What Is an Author?" In *Language, Counter-memory, Practice*, edited by Donald F. Bouchard and translated by Donald F. Bouchard and Sherry Simon. Ithaca, NY: Cornell Univ. Press, 1977.

Fraser, Theodore P. *The Modern Catholic Novel in Europe*. New York: Twayne, 1994.

Frawley, Oona, ed. *Memory Ireland*. Vol. 4, *James Joyce and Cultural Memory*. Syracuse, NY: Syracuse Univ. Press, 2014.

Freedman, Ariela. *Death, Men, and Modernism: Trauma and Narrative in British Fiction from Hardy to Woolf*. London: Routledge, 2003.

Freud, Sigmund. "Beyond the Pleasure Principle" [1920]. In *The Standard Edition of the Complete Works of Sigmund Freud*, edited by James Strachey, vol. 21. London: Hogarth Press, 1953.

———. "Civilization and Its Discontents." In *The Freud Reader*, edited by Peter Gay. New York: W. W. Norton, 1989.

———. "The Ego and the Id" [1924]. In *The Standard Edition of the Complete Psychological Works of Sigmund Freud*, edited by James Strachey, 19:1–66. London: Hogarth Press, 1961.

———. "Mourning and Melancholia." In *The Standard Edition of the Complete Psychological Works of Sigmund Freud*, edited by James Strachey, vol. 14. London: Hogarth Press, 1953.

———. *The Standard Edition of the Complete Works of Sigmund Freud*. Vol. 92, *"Beyond the Pleasure Principle," "Group Psychology," and Other Works*. Translated by James Strachey. 1920. Reprint, London: Hogarth Press, 1953.

———. *The Uncanny*. Translated by David McLintock. London: Penguin Books, 2003.

Friedman, Alan Warren. *Fictional Death and the Modernist Enterprise*. Cambridge: Cambridge Univ. Press, 1995.

Fuller, Louise. *Irish Catholicism since 1950: The Undoing of a Culture*. Dublin: Gill and Macmillan, 2002.

Gamble, John. "An Irish Wake." In *Irish Writing: An Anthology of Irish Literature in English, 1789–1939*, edited by Stephen Regan, 57–61. Oxford: Oxford Univ. Press, 2004.

———. *Sketches of History, Politics and Manners in Dublin and the North of Ireland in 1810*. London: Baldwin, Cradock, and Joy, 1826.

Garratt, Robert F. "History and Trauma in *Ulysses*." In *Memory Ireland*. Vol. 4, *James Joyce and Cultural Memory*, edited by Oona Frawley and Katherine O'Callaghan, 27–46. Syracuse, NY: Syracuse Univ. Press, 2014.

———. *Trauma and History in the Irish Novel: The Return of the Dead*. London: Palgrave Macmillan, 2011.

Gauthier, Tim S. *Narrative Desire and Historical Reparations: A. S. Byatt, Ian McEwan, Salman Rushdie*. New York: Routledge, 2006.

Gay, Peter. *The Freud Reader*. New York: W. W. Norton, 1989.

Gibbons, Luke. *Joyce's Ghosts: Ireland, Modernism and Memory*. Chicago: Univ. of Chicago Press, 2015.

Gifford, Don, with Robert J. Seidman. *"Ulysses" Annotated: Notes for James Joyce's "Ulysses."* Berkeley: Univ. of California Press, 1998.

Gill, Jo, ed. *Modern Confessional Writing: New Critical Essays*. London: Routledge, 2006.

Gorer, Geoffrey. *Death, Grief and Mourning*. Garden City, NY: Doubleday, 1965.

Gottfried, Roy. *Joyce's Misbelief*. Gainesville: Univ. Press of Florida, 2008.

Hallam, Elizabeth, and Jenny Hockey, eds. *Death, Memory and Material Culture*. Oxford: Berg, 2001.

Hamilton, Hugo. *Every Single Minute*. London: Fourth Estate, 2014.

Hand, Derek. *A History of the Irish Novel*. Cambridge: Cambridge Univ. Press, 2011.

Hansen, Jim. *Terror and Irish Modernism: The Gothic Tradition from Burke to Beckett*. Albany: State Univ. of New York Press, 2009.

Hansson, Hedi. "Beyond the Local in *The Wig My Father Wore*." In *Anne Enright*, edited by Claire Bracken and Susan Cahill, 51–66. Dublin: Irish Academic Press, 2011.

Harlow, Ilana. "Creating Situations: Practical Jokes and the Revival of the Dead in Irish Tradition." *Journal of American Folklore* 110, no. 436 (1997): 140–68. http://www.jstor.org/stable/541810.

Harper, Margaret Mills. "Flesh and Bones: Anne Enright's *The Gathering*." *South Carolina Review* 43, no. 1 (2010): 74–87.

Harrington, John P. *The Irish Beckett*. Syracuse, NY: Syracuse Univ. Press, 1991.

Harrison, Robert Pogue. *The Dominion of the Dead*. Chicago: Univ. of Chicago Press, 2003.

Harte, Liam. "Mourning Remains Unresolved: Trauma and Survival in Anne Enright's *The Gathering*." *Literature Interpretation Theory* 21. (2010): 187–204. doi:10.1080/10436928.2010.500590.

Hoffman, Fredrick. *The Mortal No: Death and the Modern Imagination*. Princeton, NJ: Princeton Univ. Press, 1964.

Hughes, Eamonn. "'All That Surrounds Our Life': Time, Sex, and Death in *That They May Face the Rising Sun*." *Irish University Review* 35, no. 1 (2005): 147–63. http://www.jstor.org/stable/25517246.

Inglis, Tom. *Moral Monopoly: The Catholic Church in Modern Irish Society*. Dublin: Gill and Macmillan, 1987.

Ingman, Heather. *A History of the Irish Short Story*. Cambridge: Cambridge Univ. Press, 2009.

———. *Twentieth-Century Fiction by Irish Women: Nation and Gender*. Hampshire: Ashgate, 2007.

Jacobs, Louis. *The Jewish Religion: A Companion*. Oxford: Oxford Univ. Press, 1995.

Jones, Ellen Carol. "Ghosts through Absence." In *Memory Ireland*. Vol. 4, *James Joyce and Cultural Memory*, edited by Oona Frawley and Katherine O'Callaghan, 125–44. Syracuse, NY: Syracuse Univ. Press.

Jordan, John. "Kate O'Brien: A Note on Her Themes." *Bell* 19, no. 2 (1954): 53–59.

Joyce, James. *Finnegans Wake*. 1939. Reprint, London: Penguin, 1992.

———. *Ulysses*. Paris: Shakespeare, 1922.

Joyce, Stanislaus. *My Brother's Keeper*. Edited by Richard Ellmann. New York: Viking Press, 1934.

Kelleher, Michael J. *Suicide and the Irish*. Dublin: Mercier Press, 1996.

Kelly, Dermot. *Narrative Strategies in Joyce's "Ulysses."* Ann Arbor: Univ. of Michigan Research Press, 1988.

Kennedy, Seán, ed. *Beckett and Ireland*. Cambridge: Cambridge Univ. Press, 2010.

Kenner, Hugh. *Ulysses*. London: George Allen and Unwin, 1980.

Kermode, Frank. *The Sense of an Ending: Studies in the Theory of Fiction*. Oxford: Oxford Univ. Press, 1977.

Kiberd, Declan. *Inventing Ireland: The Literature of the Modern Nation*. London: Jonathan Cape, 1995.

———. *Irish Classics*. Cambridge, MA: Harvard Univ. Press, 2001.

———. *"Ulysses" and Us: The Art of Everyday Living in Joyce's Masterpiece*. Chatham: Faber and Faber, 2009.

Kimball, Jean. "Love and Death in *Ulysses*: 'Word Known to All Men.'" *James Joyce Quarterly* 24, no. 2 (1987): 143–60. http://www.jstor.org/stable/25476793.

Kinsella, Thomas. "Death Bed." In *Contemporary Irish Poetry*, edited by Anthony Bradley, 159. Berkeley: Univ. of California Press, 1980.

Knowlson, James. *Damned to Fame: The Life of Samuel Beckett*. New York: Simon and Schuster, 1996.

Lacan, Jacques. *Écrits: A Selection*. Translated by Alan Sheridan. London: Tavistock, 1977.

LaCapra, Dominick. *Writing History, Writing Trauma*. Baltimore: Johns Hopkins Univ. Press, 2001.

Lang, Frederick K. *"Ulysses" and the Irish God*. London: Associated Univ. Presses, 1993.

Langer, Lawrence L. *The Age of Atrocity: Death in Modern Literature*. Boston: Beacon Press, 1978.

Laqueur, Thomas. *The Work of the Dead: A Cultural History of Mortal Remains*. Princeton, NJ: Princeton Univ. Press, 2015.

Lawrence, Karen. *The Odyssey of Style in "Ulysses."* Princeton, NJ: Princeton Univ. Press, 1981.

———. *Who's Afraid of James Joyce*. Gainesville: Univ. Press of Florida, 2010.

LeBlanc, Jim. "'The Dead' Just Won't Stay Dead." *James Joyce Quarterly* 48, no. 1 (2010): 27–39.

Lee, J. J. *Ireland, 1912–1985*. Cambridge: Cambridge Univ. Press, 1989.

Le Goff, Jacques. *The Birth of Purgatory*. Translated by Arthur Goldhammer. Chicago: Univ. of Chicago Press, 1981.

Lernout, Geert. *Help My Unbelief: James Joyce and Religion*. London: Continuum, 2010.

Levy, Eric P. *Beckett and the Voice of Species: A Study of the Prose Fiction*. Dublin: Gill and Macmillan, 1980.

———. *Trapped in Thought: A Study of the Beckettian Mentality*. Syracuse, NY: Syracuse Univ. Press, 2007.

Lewis, Pericles. *Religious Experience and the Modernist Novel*. Cambridge: Cambridge Univ. Press, 2010.

Liddy, Brian. "State and Church: Darkness in the Fiction of John McGahern." *New Hibernia Review* 3, no. 2 (1999): 106–21. http://www.jstor.org/stable/20557557.

Lightbown, Ronald. *Mantegna*. Oxford: Phaidon and Christie's, 1986.

Littleton, John, and Eamon Maher, eds. *Contemporary Catholicism in Ireland: A Critical Appraisal*. Dublin: Columbia Press, 2008.

Lloyd, David. *Anomalous States: Irish Writing and the Post-colonial Moment*. Dublin: Lilliput Press, 1993.

———. *Irish Times: Temporalities of Modernity*. Dublin: Field Day, 2008.

Long, Thomas G., and Thomas Lynch. *The Good Funeral: Death, Grief and the Community of Care*. Louisville, KY: Westminster John Knox Press, 2013.

Lowe-Evans, Mary. *Catholic Nostalgia in Joyce and Company*. Gainesville: Univ. Press of Florida, 2008.

M. L. "Review of Kate O'Brien's *The Ante-Room*." *Irish Book Lover* (Sept. 22–Oct. 1934): 120–21.

MacCabe, Colin. *James Joyce and the Revolution of the Word*. London: Macmillan, 1978.

Macintosh, Fiona. *Dying Acts: Death in Ancient Greek and Modern Irish Tragic Drama*. Cork: Cork Univ. Press, 1994.

Maher, Eamon. *"The Church and Its Spire": John McGahern and the Catholic Question*. Dublin: Columbia Press, 2011.

———. "Circles and Circularity in the Writings of John McGahern." *Nordic Irish Studies* 4 (2005): 157–66. http://www.jstor.org/stable/30001526.

———. *Crosscurrents and Confluences: Echoes of Religion in Twentieth-Century Fiction*. Dublin: Veritas, 2000.

———. "An Irish Catholic Novel? The Example of Brian Moore and John McGahern." In *Between Human and Divine: The Catholic Vision in Contemporary Literature*, edited by Mary R. Reichardt, 70–85. Washington, DC: Catholic Univ. Press of America, 2010.

———. *John McGahern: From the Local to the Universal*. Dublin: Liffey Press, 2003.

———. "Religion and Art." In *The John McGahern Yearbook*, 1:118–25. Galway: National Univ. of Galway, 2008.

———. "Tracing the Imprint: Catholicism in Some Twentieth Century Irish Fiction." *Studies: An Irish Quarterly Review* 100, no. 40 (2011): 489–500. http://www.jstor.org/stable/23209769.

Maher, Eamon, and Eugene O'Brien, eds. *Breaking the Mould: Literary Representations of Irish Catholicism*. Oxford: Peter Lang, 2011.

Malcolm, David. *Understanding John McGahern*. Columbia: Univ. of South Carolina Press, 2007.

Mays, J. C. C. "Young Beckett's Irish Roots." *Irish University Review* 14, no. 1 (1984): 18–33. http://www.jstor.org/stable/25477519.

McCarthy, Dermot. *John McGahern and the Art of Memory*. Bern, Switzerland: Peter Lang, 2010.

McDonald, Rónán. "The Ghost at the Feast: Beckett and Irish Studies." In *Beckett and Ireland*, edited by Sean Kennedy, 16–30. Cambridge: Cambridge Univ. Press, 2010.

McGahern, John. *All Will Be Well: A Memoir*. New York: Alfred A. Knopf, 2006.

———. *The Barracks*. London: Faber and Faber, 1963.

———. "The Country Funeral." In *The Collected Stories*. London: Faber and Faber, 1992.

———. *That They May Face the Rising Sun*. London: Faber and Faber, 2002.

Meaney, Gerardine. "Waking the Dead: Antigone, Ismene and Anne Enright's Narrators in Mourning." In *Anne Enright*, edited by Claire Bracken and Susan Cahill, 145–65. Dublin: Irish Academic Press, 2011.

Mercier, Vivian. *Beckett/Beckett*. Oxford: Oxford Univ. Press, 1977.

———. *The Irish Comic Tradition*. Oxford: Oxford Univ. Press, 1962.

———. "Kate O'Brien." *Irish Writing* 1 (1946): 86–100.

Mitford, Jessica. *The American Way of Death*. New York: Simon and Schuster, 1978.

Miyahara, Kazunari. "Why Now, Why Then? Present-Tense Narration in Contemporary British and Commonwealth Novels." *Journal of Narrative Theory* 39, no. 2 (2009): 241–68. doi:10.1353/jnt.0.0030.

Morin, Emilie. *Samuel Beckett and the Problem of Irishness*. New York: Palgrave Macmillan, 2009.

Morse, J. Mitchell. *The Sympathetic Alien: James Joyce and Catholicism*. New York: New York Univ. Press, 1959.

Moshenberg, Daniel. "What Shouts in the Street, 1904, 1922, 1990–93." In *Joyce and the Subject of History*, edited by Mark A. Wollaeger, Victor

Luftig, and Robert Spoo, 125–41. Ann Arbor: Univ. of Michigan Press, 1996.

Muir, Edward. *Ritual in Early Modern Europe*. Cambridge: Cambridge Univ. Press, 2005.

Murphy, Daniel. *Imagination and Religion in Anglo-Irish Literature, 1930–1980*. Dublin: Irish Academic Press, 1987.

Murphy, John. "Beckett's Purgatories." In *Beckett, Joyce and the Art of the Negative*, edited by Colleen Jaurretche, 109–25. Amsterdam: Rodopi, 2005.

Murray, Patrick. "The Shandean Mode: Beckett and Sterne Compared." *Irish Quarterly Review* 60, no. 237 (1971): 55–67.

Nixon, Mark. "'Writing Myself into the Ground': Textual Existence and Death in Beckett." In *Beckett and Death*, edited by Steven Barfield et al., 22–31. London: Contiuum, 2009.

Nolan, Emer. *Catholic Emancipations: Irish Fiction from Thomas Moore to James Joyce*. Syracuse, NY: Syracuse Univ. Press, 2007.

———. *James Joyce and Nationalism*. London: Routledge, 1995.

O'Brien, Kate. *The Ante-Room*. 1934. Reprint, Hamburg: Albatross Berlag, 1935.

———. *As Music and Splendor*. 1958. Reprint, London: Penguin, 2005.

———. Untitled review. *University Review* 3, no. 4 (1964).

———. *Without My Cloak*. 1931. Reprint. London: Virago, 2001.

O'Brien, Peggy. *Writing Lough Derg: From William Carleton to Seamus Heaney*. Syracuse, NY: Syracuse Univ. Press, 2006.

O'Connor, Sister Mary Catherine. *The Art of Dying Well: The Development of the "Ars Moriendi."* New York: Columbia Univ. Press, 1942.

Ó Crualaoich, Gearóid. "The 'Merry Wake.'" In *Irish Popular Culture, 1650–1850*, edited by James S. Donnelly and Kerby A. Miller, 173–201. Dublin: Irish Academic Press, 1998.

O'Faolain, Nuala. "The Saturday Interviews." Interviewed by Marian Finucane. RTÉ. *Irish Independent*, Apr. 13, 2008. htt://www.independent.ie/irish-news/nuala-o-faolain-interview-i-dont-want-more-time-as-soon-as-i-heard-i-was-going-to-die-the-goodness-went-from-life-26437188.html.

Ó hÓgáin, Dáithí. *The Sacred Isle: Belief and Religion in Pre-Christian Ireland*. Rochester, NY: Boydell and Brewer, 1999.

O'Mahony, Seamus. *The Way We Die Now*. London: Head of Zeus, 2016.

O'Rourke, Diane. "Mourning Becomes Eclectic: Death of Communal Practice in a Greek Cemetery." *American Ethnologist* 34, no. 2 (2007): 387–402. http://www.jstor.org/stable/4496813.

O'Shea, Michael J. "Catholic Liturgy in Joyce's *Ulysses*." *James Joyce Quarterly* 21, no. 2 (1984): 123–35. http://www.jstor.org/stable/25476572.

O'Shea, Shane. *Death and Design in Victorian Glasnevin*. Dublin: Dublin Cemeteries Committee, 2000.

Ó Súilleabháin, Seán. *Irish Wake Amusements*. Cork: Mercier Press, 1967.

Peters, Edward, ed. *The 1917 Pio-Benedictine Code of Canon Law in English Translation*. San Francisco: Ignatius Press, 2001.

Regan, Stephen. *Irish Writing: An Anthology of Irish Literature in English, 1789–1939*. Oxford: Oxford Univ. Press, 2004.

Reynolds, Lorna. *Kate O'Brien: A Literary Portrait*. Gerrards Cross, Buckinghamshire: Colin Smythe, 1987.

Ricks, Christopher. *Beckett's Dying Words: The Clarendon Lectures, 1990*. Oxford: Clarendon Press, 1993.

Riquelme, John Paul. *Teller and Tale in Joyce's Fiction: Oscillating Perspectives*. Baltimore: Johns Hopkins Univ. Press, 1983.

Robinson, Michael. *The Long Sonata of the Dead: A Study of Samuel Beckett*. London: Rupert Hart-Davis, 1969.

Robinson, Richard. *John McGahern and Modernism*. London: Bloomsbury, 2017.

Ross, Ciaran. *Beckett's Art of Absence: Rethinking the Void*. New York: Palgrave Macmillan, 2011.

Royle, Nicholas. *"The Uncanny": An Introduction*. Manchester: Manchester Univ. Press, 2003.

Sampson, Denis. *Outstaring Nature's Eye: The Fiction of John McGahern*. Dublin: Lilliput Press, 1993.

Sartre, Jean-Paul. *Being and Nothingness: An Essay on Phenomenological Ontology*. New York: Methuen, 1958.

Scarry, Elaine. *The Body in Pain: The Making and Unmaking of the World*. Oxford: Oxford Univ. Press, 1985.

———. *Resisting Representation*. Oxford: Oxford Univ. Press, 1994.

Schleifer, Ronald. *Rhetoric and Death: The Language of Modernism and Postmodern Theory*. Urbana: Univ. of Illinois Press, 1990.

Scott, Malcolm. *The Struggle for the Soul of the French Novel: French Catholic and Realist Novels, 1850–1970*. London: Macmillan, 1989.

Sheeran, Pat, and Nina Witoszek. *Talking to the Dead: A Study of Irish Funerary Traditions*. Amsterdam: Rodopi, 1998.

Sherman, David. *In a Strange Room: Modernism's Corpses and Mortal Obligation*. Oxford: Oxford Univ. Press, 2014.

Shovlin, Frank. *Touchstones: John McGahern's Classical Style*. Liverpool: Liverpool Univ. Press, 2016.

Shumaker, Jeanett. "Uncanny Doubles: The Fiction of Anne Enright." *New Hibernia Review* 9, no. 3 (2005): 107–22. http://www.jstor.org/stable/20558015.

Sicari, Stephen. *Joyce's Modernist Allegory: "Ulysses" and the History of the Novel*. Columbia: Univ. of South Carolina Press, 2001.

Smyth, Caroline, Malcolm MacLachlan, and Anthony Clare. *Cultivating Suicide? Destruction of Self in a Changing Ireland*. Dublin: Liffey Press, 2003.

Sobel, Zvi, and Benjamin Beit-Hallahmi. *Tradition, Innovation, Conflict: Jewishness and Judaism in Contemporary Israel*. Albany: State Univ. of New York Press, 1991.

Spain, John. Review of *Every Single Minute*, by Hugo Hamilton. *Irish Independent*, Feb. 22, 2014. http://www.independent.ie/irish-news/how-nualas-last-trip-restored-her-enthusiasm-for-life-30031750.html.

Spoo, Robert. *James Joyce and the Language of History: Dedalus's Nightmare*. Oxford: Oxford Univ. Press, 1994.

Staten, Henry. "The Decomposing Form of Joyce's *Ulysses*." *PMLA* 112, no. 3 (1997): 380–92. http://www.jstor.org/stable/462947.

Stewart, Garrett. *Death Sentences: Styles of Dying in British Fiction*. Cambridge, MA: Harvard Univ. Press, 1984.

Svevo, Italo. *Confessions of Zeno*. Translated by Beryle de Zoete. New York: Alfred Knopf, 1930.

Tait, Clodagh. *Death, Burial and Commemoration in Ireland, 1550–1650*. London: Palgrave Macmillan, 2002.

Tarlow, Sarah, and Liv Nilsson Stutz, eds. *The Oxford Handbook of the Archaeology of Death and Burial*. Oxford: Oxford Univ. Press, 2013.

Taylor, Jeremy. *The Rule and Exercises of Holy Dying*. London: R. Royson, 1651. http://gateway.proquest.com.eproxy.ucd.ie/openurl?ctxver=Z39.882003&res_id=xri:eebo&rft_id=xri:eebo:image:45783:157.

Taylor, Lawrence. "*Bás InÉirinn*: Cultural Constructions of Death in Ireland." *Anthropological Quarterly* 26, no. 4 (1989): 175–87. http://www.jstor.org.stable/33176614.

Teresa of Ávila. *The Life of Saint Teresa of Ávila by Herself.* Translated by J. M. Cohen. London: Penguin, 1957.

Tolstoy, Leo. *The Death of Ivan Ilych, and Other Stories.* Translated by Richard Pevear and Larissa Volokhonsky. 1886. Reprint, London: Vintage, 2009.

Tonning, Erik. "Beckett's Unholy Dying: From *Malone Dies* to *The Unnamable.*" In *Beckett and Death*, edited by Steven Barfield, Matthew Feldman, and Phillip Tew, 106–28. London: Continuum, 2009.

Townshend, Charles. *Ireland: The 20th Century.* New York: Oxford Univ. Press, 1998.

Ulin, Julieann. "'Buried! Who Would Have Buried Her?': Famine 'Ghost Graves' in Samuel Beckett's *Endgame.*" In *Hungry Words: Images of the Famine in the Irish Canon*, edited by George Cusack and Sarah Goss, 197–225. Dublin: Irish Academic Press, 2006.

———. "'Famished Ghosts': Famine Memory in James Joyce's *Ulysses.*" *Joyce Studies Annual* (2011): 20–63.

Vickroy, Laurie. *Trauma and Survival in Contemporary Fiction.* Charlottesville: Univ. Press of Virginia, 2002.

Walshe, Eibhear, ed. *Kate O'Brien: A Writing Life.* Dublin: Irish Academic Press, 2006.

———, ed. *Ordinary People Dancing: Essays on Kate O'Brien.* Cork: Cork Univ. Press, 1993.

Waters, John. *Beyond Consolation; or, How We Became Too Clever for God . . . and Our Own Good.* London: Continuum, 2010.

Watt, Ian. *The Rise of the Novel: Studies in Defoe, Richardson, and Fielding.* Berkeley: Univ. of California Press, 1957.

Weisberg, David. *Chronicles of Disorder: Samuel Beckett and the Cultural Politics of the Modern Novel.* Albany: State Univ. of New York Press, 2000.

Whyte, James. *History, Myth and Ritual in the Fictions of John McGahern: Strategies of Transcendence.* Lewiston, NY: Edwin Mellen Press, 2002.

Williams, Raymond. *Marxism and Literature.* Oxford: Oxford Univ. Press, 1977.

Wills, Clair. *The Best Are Leaving: Emigration and Post-war Irish Culture.* Cambridge: Cambridge Univ. Press, 2015.

Witoszek, Nina. "Ireland: A Funerary Culture?" *Irish Quarterly Review* 76, no. 302 (1987): 206–15. http://www.jstor.org/stable/30090860.

Wollaeger, Mark, Victor Luftig, and Robert Spoo, eds. *Joyce and the Subject of History.* Ann Arbor: Univ. of Michigan Press, 1996.

Woodman, Thomas. *Faithful Fictions: The Catholic Novel in British Literature.* Milton Keynes, England: Open Univ. Press, 1991.

Yeats, W. B. *Four Plays for Dancers.* London: Macmillan, 1921.

———. *Purgatory* [1939]. In *W. B. Yeats: Selected Plays,* edited by Richard Allen Cave, 255–62. New York: Penguin Books, 1997.

Ziel, Stanley van der. *John McGahern and the Imagination of Tradition.* Cork: Cork Univ. Press, 2016.

Index

Abbott, H. Porter, 104, 204n19
Adams, R. M., 45, 198n56, 199n69
American Wake. *See* wake
Anderson, Benedict, 196n16
Ariès, Philippe, 9, 124, 193n2, 194n13, 206n8, 208n43
Ars moriendi, 37, 41, 88, 95–97, 99, 100, 135, 182, 201n7
As Music and Splendor (O'Brien), 58
atheism, 12, 31; *The Barracks* and, 131–44
At Weddings and Wakes (McDermott), 186
authenticity, 120, 127, 134

Bakhtin, Mikhail Mikhailovich, 14–15, 194n20, 207n20
Barfield, Steven, 92, 203n12
Barry, Elizabeth, 92–93, 115, 205n57
Barry, Sebastian, 155, 166
Barthes, Roland, 53, 200n84
Beaty, Nancy Lee, 197n39, 201n7, 204n23
Beckett, Samuel, 89–91, 93–94; *Endgame*, 195–96; *Human Wishes*, 96; *Malone Dies*, 5, 19–20, 90–94; *Molloy*, 87, 89, 104–5, 204n30, 205n59; *More Pricks than Kicks*, 96; *Murphy*, 110; *Waiting for Godot*, 89, 203n3

Begam, Richard, 203n8
bildungsroman, 57, 117
Bixby, Patrick, 89, 203n5
Black Mass, 49
bodily pain, 3, 99, 112, 122, 125, 133–34, 138–42
Bracken, Claire, 210n35
Bronfen, Elisabeth, 13, 194n17
Brooks, Peter, 14–16, 28, 79, 93, 151, 194n19, 194n22, 195n9, 196n14, 204n16, 205n43, 205n50, 209n16, 211n42; *Troubling Confessions*, 159, 210n27
burial: *The Barracks*, 122; Catholic Church and, 8–9, 11, 193n9; *Endgame*, 113–14; Famine and improper, 13, 113–14, 198n46; Irish immigrants and, 14, 194n18; Jewish customs, 24, 41; major shifts in, 30, 157, 169, 185, 209n18, 209n20; *Riders to the Sea*, 158; *That They May Face the Rising Sun*, 149; *Ulysses*, 30–32, 39–40, 43, 44–45, 197n20

Cahill, Susan, 210n35
Canon Law, 7–8, 193n9, 194n12
Caruth, Cathy, 164, 208nn1–2, 211n40
Casanova, Pascale, 101, 204n35
Castle Rackrent (Edgeworth), 193n6

Catholic Church, 4–5, 7–9, 12–13; *The Ante-Room*, 57, 67–68, 74–77, 85; *The Barracks* and, 120, 126–27, 133–35, 139, 140–41, 145–46; Samuel Beckett and, 92, 101; as Catholic novel, 59, 200–201n5; death rituals, 4–11; *The Gathering* and, 159–60, 172–73, 178–79; James Joyce and, 24–25, 194n4; *Malone Dies* and, 97, 101, 105; John McGahern and, 123; Kate O'Brien and, 57–58; *Ulysses* and, 17–18, 31

Catholicism, 4, 11–12, 17, 24, 57, 60–62, 67, 68, 70–71, 75–76, 83, 85, 92, 144; *The Ante-Room* and, 56–61, 63, 65–68, 70–71, 74–75, 76–77, 82, 84–85, 200n4, 200–201n5; *The Barracks* and, 118, 124, 126, 134–35, 139–40, 145, 206n12; Beckett and, 92, 101; McGahern and, 148; *Ulysses* and, 29–38

"Celtic Tiger," 150, 160

Christ, Jesus, 44, 48, 62, 72, 75–76, 97, 106, 114–16, 133–34, 138, 140–41, 172–73

Civil War, Irish, 59, 185

Cleary, Joe, 124, 196n23, 206n10

colonial, 69, 90, 185

commodification, 169, 180, 189, 211n48

community: *The Ante-Room* and, 56, 59–62, 64, 83; *The Barracks* and, 6, 20, 127–28, 132, 135, 145–48; Catholic Church and, 56, 59, 64, 83; Durkheim's views on, 32; *The Gathering* and, 160, 172–73, 178; Irish, 125; *Ulysses* and, 26, 27, 39, 42

confession, 70–71, 159–61; *The Ante-Room*, 71–73, 77; *The Barracks*, 145; *The Gathering*, 159–61, 176–79; *Malone Dies*, 91–94, 97–100, 108–10

Connolly, Claire, 157, 210n23

Corish, Patrick, 193n8, 211n58

corpse, 8–10, 45, 54, 114, 157, 162, 170, 174, 188, 196n23, 199n63, 212n64; *The Ante-Room* and, 78, 82; "Finnegans Wake" (folk song) and, 193n6; *Finnegans Wake* (Joyce), 196n20; *The Gathering* and, 152, 157, 171–72, 174–77, 182, 211n49; *Malone Dies* and, 107; modernism and, 29–30, 43; *Ulysses* and, 29–33, 35–26, 39–41, 43–45, 181–82, *The Wire* and, 187–88, 198n46, 198n56

Cousineau, Thomas, 93, 204n14

Cré na Cille, 203n9

Croften Croker, Thomas, 187, 212n5

Cronin, Anthony, 203n2

Dalsimer, Adele, 63

Deane, Seamus, 89, 90, 195n7, 196n15, 197n24, 200n79, 203n5

death: acceptance of, 60, 128, 131, 138, 140, 188; aestheticizing of, 37–38; of author, 88; commodification of, 168; fear of, 5, 90–91, 111–13, 149, 163, 168, 170; history of, 2, 4–5, 9–10, 13–15, 185–86; of Irish culture, 17–18, 162, 195n3; novelistic narrative and, 15–17, 18, 21–22, 27–29, 50–51, 54–55, 58–59, 85–86, 87–88, 91–92, 95, 112, 113, 180–81; political, 8, 209n20; reality of, 1–4, 20, 82, 86, 94, 123, 169; representation and, 116–17, 123–24, 161, 181; sacrificial, 61–62, 72–73, 106, 140; secular, 1, 83, 184; Western attitudes toward, 3–4, 9–10, 13–14, 30, 88, 96–97, 168, 180–81. *See also* "good death"

deathbed, 3–5, 61–63, 79, 99–100, 104–5, 111, 145, 159–61, 201n7, 210n28; *The Ante-Room*, 56–63, 76–79; *Malone Dies*, 99–104, 108, 111; *Ulysses*, 32–37, 42–48, 195n2
death drive, 15–16, 28, 61–62, 83–84, 106, 107, 163–65, 167, 175, 212n67
Death of Ivan Ilych, The (Tolstoy), 111
Devotional Revolution, 7
Didion, Joan, 188–89, 212n7
disinterment, 157, 209n18, 209n20
Divine Comedy, The (Dante), 101
Dreaming of the Bones (Yeats), 158, 210nn24–25
Dubliners (Joyce), 24, 197n56; "The Dead," 24; "The Sisters," 24
Durkheim, Émile, 32–33
dying: *The Ante-Room*, 56–57, 60, 61, 75, 80, 85; *ars moriendi* and, 37, 41, 95–96, 99–100, 135, 182, 201n7; *The Barracks*, 5–6, 20, 119, 127, 132–34, 135, 139, 144, 148, 149; and bodily pain, 79, 117, 122, 124, 127, 148; Latin Prayers for, 34; *Malone Dies* and, 87–88, 89, 91–93, 103, 112–14, 203n9; modern attitudes toward, 3–4, 6–7, 9, 11, 21, 125, 180–81, 183; and mother, 6, 20, 56, 58, 105–6, 118, 120–21, 123; novelistic portrayals of, 5, 16, 55, 61, 85, 88, 93, 98, 116, 185–86; O'Faolain and, 1–4, 183–84, 193n4, 198n48

Easter Rising (1916), 59; Yeats's *Dreaming of the Bones* and, 158
elegy, 14; *The Ante-Room* as, 60
Ellmann, Richard, 37, 196n20, 197–98n43

Enright, Anne, 150, 152–53, 173, 208n4, 210n35, 212n67; *The Gathering*, 148, 150–53, 155, 159, 161–62, 177–79, 182; *What Are You Like?*, 163; *The Wig My Father Wore*, 152, 163
Eros, 15, 26, 28, 43, 52, 61, 74, 83–84, 95, 106, 153, 156, 202–3n56
Evans, E. Estyn, 201n18, 209n9
existentialism, 20, 120–21, 127–28, 131, 133–35, 137, 138, 139, 141–42, 148, 178

Famine, Great (1845–49), 2, 4, 13–14, 64–65, 114, 185, 198n46
Faust, Drew Gilpin, 204n24
Feldman, Matthew, 92, 203n12
Fleming, Marie, 183
folklore and belief, 8, 54, 65, 114, 157, 170, 176–77, 210n2
Foucault, Michel, 204n15
Freud, Sigmund, 15, 26, 28, 53, 61–62, 69, 74, 83–84, 95, 106–7, 153–54, 156, 162–63, 165–66, 167, 177, 195n8
Friedman, Alan Warren, 13, 41, 100, 198n48, 199nn58–59
funeral: *The Barracks*, 122, 123, 147; Catholic Church, 8; ceremony, 3–4, 9–11; *The Gathering*, 151–53, 167, 168–69, 175–77; Irish literary and cultural depictions of, 7, 161, 181–82, 186, 187, 195n3; *Ulysses*, 24, 27, 31–32, 36, 39–41, 42, 43, 51

Gamble, John, 187, 208n6, 209n9, 212n5
Garratt, Robert F., 166, 197n35, 208n6, 209n13, 211n43

Gibbons, Luke, 27, 69, 196n11, 198n49, 202n26
Gifford, Don, 34, 45, 197n32, 199n61, 200n76, 200n78
Glasnevin Cemetery, 39, 41–42, 44
God, 1–2, 20, 34, 71–73, 75–77, 82–83, 96–97, 102–3, 114, 130–32, 138–44; godlessness, 117; godlike, 70, 97; Lamb of, 49
"good death," 3–5, 25, 36–37, 41–42, 60–62, 92–93, 95–97, 101, 182–83
Gorer, Geoffrey, 9, 194n13

Hamilton, Hugo, 183, 184
Hand, Derek, 161, 195
Hansson, Hedi, 152, 209nn7–8
Harlow, Ilana, 54, 200n87
Harper, Margaret Mills, 153, 166, 209n10, 210n34, 211n34
Harte, Liam, 170, 210n34, 211n52
Heaney, Seamus, 101
heaven, 2–4, 31, 55, 60–66, 70–75, 80–83, 97–99, 101–6, 112–16, 119–22, 139–46, 204n33
Hoffman, Frederick, 13, 68, 140, 194n17, 202n23, 207n36
humanist, 4, 10–12, 21, 93, 178–79, 182

Inglis, Tom, 6
Ingman, Heather, 66, 203n33
Ireland: Devotional Revolution and, 7; Famine and, 2, 4, 13–14, 37, 64, 114, 185; folk tradition of, 8, 54, 64, 170; global position; 12, 176, 180; Literary Revival, 11; rural, 6–8, 20, 119, 121, 125–27, 134, 144, 180, 206n12

Irish culture, 1–4, 7, 11–13, 17–18, 55, 90–95, 100, 133–34, 152–53, 160–66, 173–74, 180–90, 194n16, 195n3, 196n23, 208n43
Irish language, 17, 24, 203n9

Johnson, Samuel, 96, 103
Jones, Ellen Carol, 198n54
Joyce, James, 24–25, 30, 37–38; Catholicism and, 25–26, 29, 55, 195n4, 196n17; *Dubliners*, 24, 198n56; *Finnegans Wake*, 25, 54, 193n6, 195n7, 200n89; *Ulysses*, 5, 17–18, 23–25, 29–30, 54, 88, 117
Joyce, Stanislaus, 37, 197n41
Judaism: burial customs and, 8, 24, 40–43, 49; *Ulysses* and, 18, 31, 48

Kennedy, Seán, 89, 203n5
Kenner, Hugh, 197–98n43
kenosis, 114–15
Kermode, Frank, 195n6
Kiberd, Declan, 60, 62, 86, 89–90, 95, 197n29, 200n4
Kimball, Jean, 38, 197n41, 198n44
Kings (film), 186
Knowlson, James, 203n4, 204n25

Lacan, Jacques, 212n67
LaCapra, Dominick, 195n8, 208nn1–2
Langer, Lawrence L., 30, 196n21
Lawrence, Karen, 27, 47, 49, 199n73, 200n77
Levy, Eric P., 111, 114–15
Lewis, Pericles, 25, 30, 195n5, 196n21
Liddy, Brian, 127, 131, 207n19, 207n25
Lloyd, David, 89, 203n5

Long, Thomas, 9–10, 187
Lowe-Evans, Mary, 195n2, 195n4
Lynch, Thomas, 9–10, 187, 211n48

macabre, 91, 114, 181–82, 201n15; Beckett's use of, 20, 89–94, 113–14, 118
Maher, Eamon, 127, 130, 137, 139, 194n21, 200n5, 206n12, 207n16
Malcolm, David, 125, 206n11
McCarthy, Dermot, 124, 130, 206n4, 206n6
McDonald, Rónán, 92, 203n10
McGahern, John, 5–6, 119–20, 123–26, 127; *All Will Be Well*, 119, 123–24; *The Barracks*, 20, 119–21, 124–25, 127–28, 133, 149; *That They May Face the Rising Sun*, 149
Meaney, Gerardine, 151, 208n4
memory: *The Ante-Room* and, 69, 73–74; *The Barracks* and, 131, corpse and "memory picture," 43, 199n63; cultural, 157, 161; *The Gathering* and, 151–56, 165, 168, 170, 172, 176–77, 179; *Malone Dies* and, 109, 115; trauma and, 166, 179; *Ulysses* and, 33–35, 38, 53, 195n2, 198n46, 198n49
Mercier, Vivian, 91, 114
metafiction: *The Gathering*, 153–55; *Malone Dies*, 95, 110
metaphor: death of Irish culture, 24; pain, 133–34; purgatory, 60; and trauma, 162
metempsychosis, 33, 46–47
Mitford, Jessica, 199n63
modernism: and *The Ante-Room*, 71; and *The Barracks*, 127–28; *The Gathering*, 151–52; *Malone Dies*, 89–102, 104; *Ulysses*, 30–33, 39, 196n19
modernization, 5, 30, 39
Morin, Emilie, 89, 90, 203n5
mortality, 10, 13, 15, 20, 22, 28, 30, 33, 41, 49, 60–68, 87–88, 99, 105, 113, 135, 151, 179, 186
mother, 20, 91, 105, 120, 163; and *The Ante-Room*, 56–64, 67, 77–84; and *The Barracks*, 6, 20, 118, 120–24, 129, 148; *Malone Dies*, 89–91, 102–8; *Ulysses*, 5, 18, 23, 28–39, 42, 44–50, 52–53, 195n2, 197n35, 199n58
mourning, 7–8; disinterment and, 157, 209n18; *The Gathering* and, 175, 208n4, 210n34; Irish wake tradition and, 114, 186–88; *Ulysses* and, 18, 26–28, 37, 52–53, 199n58
"Mourning and Melancholia" (Freud), 28, 195n8, 196n12, 199n70
Murray, Patrick, 110, 204n21, 205n48

narrative structure: *The Ante-Room*, 18–19, 65–66, 84; *The Barracks*, 20, 121–24, 125, 127–31, 136–37, 148–49; death and, 5, 10–11, 15–21, 26–27, 32, 113, 117–18, 125, 159, 170–72, 181–83, 190, 199n59, 201n7; *The Gathering*, 20–21, 150, 151–62, 166–68, 170–72, 174–79; *Malone Dies*, 19–20, 88–89, 91–95, 104–8, 110–12, 113, 115–16, 117–18; mythic, 9, 21, 25, 29–30; *Ulysses*, 17–18, 23–24, 26–27, 28–30, 32, 38–40, 50–55, 197n27, 198n49
naturalism: *The Barracks*, 121, 127–28, 129; *The Gathering*, 179
Nixon, Mark, 203

Nolan, Emer, 36, 197n27, 201n17
nostalgia: and *The Ante-Room*, 58;
  Joyce and Catholicism, 195n2; and
  Malone Dies, 104; and the uncanny,
  163
novel: and Catholicism, 59–60,
  200–201n5; as dialogic form, 14,
  184, 194n20, 207n20; Irish, 13–17,
  21–22, 55, 57, 86, 88, 90, 105, 117–
  18, 148, 155, 160–61, 179, 180–81,
  185–86, 195n3; and Protestantism, 96, 203n11; and secularism,
  5–6, 13–17, 28–29, 86, 160, 181;
  trauma and, 166–67, 209n13; Ian
  Watt's *The Rise of the Novel*, 14, 159,
  194n19, 210n31
Nowlans, The (John Banim), 157

O'Brien, Kate, 57–58, 63, 64–65,
  74–75, 126, 200n2, 206n12; *The
  Ante-Room*, 56–57, 59–60, 63–64,
  85–86; *As Music and Splendor*, 58;
  Without My Cloak, 59–60, 63
O'Brien, Peggy, 102, 205n36
Ó Cadhain, Máirtín, 203n9
Ó Crualaoich, Gearóid, 7, 171
O'Faolain, Nuala, 1–5, 183–85, 193n2
O'Mahony, Seamus, 181, 182, 187,
  208n43
Ó Súilleabháin, Seán, 187, 209n9,
  212n64

Parnell, Charles Stewart, 23, 42, 46
Peters, Edward, 193n9, 194n12
Playboy of the Western World, The
  (Synge), 193n6
plot: *The Ante-Room*, 56–58, 62–63, 72,
  84–85, 111; *The Barracks*, 120, 122,
  124, 131, 146, 148; *The Gathering*, 150–54, 156, 163, 165, 168–69;
  Malone Dies, 88, 90–91, 110–11, 118;
  novelistic, 14–17, 18, 28, 39, 49, 54,
  156, 163, 165, 168–169, 195n9; religious, 14; *Ulysses*, 23–24, 26, 28–29,
  38–39, 45–46, 49–50, 53–54
Pogues, The, 188, 193n6
postcolonial context: and Beckett,
  89–90
postmodernism: *The Gathering*,
  151–52, 155, 208n4
Protestant, 11, 14, 96, 101, 160,
  211n20; Beckett as, 92, 203nn10–11;
  Malone Dies, 92, 96; *Ulysses*, 31
purgatory, 60, 74, 80, 92, 101–3, 119,
  204n33. *See also* Yeats, W. B.

realism, 5, 14, 15, 17; *The Ante-Room*,
  61, 86; *The Barracks*, 125; *The Gathering*, 151, 179
religious belief systems and structures,
  4, 25, 38, 43, 59, 85, 88–89, 91, 95,
  97, 106, 116, 144
Reynolds, Lorna, 63, 201n16
Ricks, Christopher, 91, 203n7
Riders to the Sea (Synge), 158
Riquelme, Jean Paul, 199n74, 200n85
rituals: *The Ante-Room* and (*see* Catholic Church; Catholicism); *The Barracks* and, 120–23, 127, 136–37, 139,
  144, 149–50; death, 6–9, 10–11,
  21, 24–25, 181–82, 187, 189; *The
  Gathering* and, 155, 157–58, 163,
  169–71, 176; *Malone Dies* and, 91,
  95, 114, 117–18; *Ulysses* and, 32–36,
  39–49. *See also* Catholic Church;
  Catholicism
Robinson, Richard, 206n15, 207n18

romanticism, Irish, 157
Royle, Nicholas, 163, 210n37, 210n39

Sampson, Denis, 127, 130, 137, 207n17
Sartre, Jean-Paul, 131
Scarry, Elaine, 117, 122–23, 130, 133–34, 138–39, 141–43
Secret Scripture, The (Barry), 155, 166
secularism, 1–5, 8–12, 14–17, 28–29, 159–60, 180–82, 196n16; *The Ante-Room*, 19, 64, 65, 68–71, 83–86; *The Barracks*, 119, 133, 141, 148; *The Gathering*, 5–6, 21, 151, 172–73, 176, 178–79, 211n62; *Malone Dies*, 19, 89, 116; *Ulysses*, 5, 18, 28–29; wake, 187–89
Shadow of the Glen, The (Synge), 193n6
Sherman, David, 13, 29, 39–40, 43, 196n23
Shumaker, Jeanett, 163, 210n39
Sterne, Laurence, 90, 95, 110, 204n21
Stewart, Garrett, 13, 104, 109, 112, 201n12
suicide, 8–9; *The Ante-Room*, 57–59, 62–64, 71, 81–85; assisted, 183; *The Gathering*, 21, 150, 151–52, 164, 165–66; *Malone Dies*, 88; *Ulysses*, 28, 42, 55
Synge, J. M., 158, 193n6

Taylor, Jeremy, 19, 95–96, 99, 100, 103, 201n7
Taylor, Lawrence, 194n18, 109n20
Teresa of Ávila, Saint, 143–44, 208n42
Tew, Phillip, 92, 203n12
Thanatos, 15, 52, 61, 74, 95, 106, 153–54

Tolstoy, Leo: *The Death of Ivan Ilych*, 110
Tonning, Erik, 92, 96, 98, 103, 204n26, 205n38
trauma, 13–14, 21, 27, 48, 120–24, 125, 128, 134, 146, 147–48, 150–51, 154–55, 160–62, 164, 166–67, 170, 175–79, 195n8, 197n35, 198n49, 206n4, 208nn1–2, 209n13

Ulin, Julieann, 114, 198n46, 205n55
Ulysses (Joyce): "Circe," 26–27, 29, 32–33, 38, 45–50; "Hades," 24, 26, 31–32, 39–47; kinds of death in, 17–18, 23–24; style of, 26–28, 51, 53, 196n13; "Telemachus," 26, 32–39
uncanny, 154, 162–63, 168, 170, 210n39; and Freud, 162–63, 210nn37–38, 211n55

violence, 102, 138

wake, 4, 6–8, 12, 21, 161, 181–82, 186–90, 193n6, 195n3, 211n53; American, 14, 186–90; *Finnegans Wake*, 25, 54; *The Gathering*, 21, 150–54, 162, 167, 209n8; *Malone Dies*, 114; merry, 7, 171, 173, 187, 193n5, 193n7, 194n11, 209n9, 211n57, 211n59, 211n63; as symbols, 7, 161–62; *Ulysses*, 54
Waking Ned Devine (film), 186
Walshe, Eibhear, 57, 63, 200n2, 201n10, 201nn13–14
Watt, Ian, 14, 159, 194n19, 210n31
Weisberg, David, 89, 203n1, 204n18
What Are You Like? (Enright), 163

Wig My Father Wore, The (Enright), 152, 163
Williams, Raymond, 12, 194n16
Wills, Clair, 206n14
Winterwood (McCabe), 155
Wire, The (television show), 187–88
Without My Cloak (O'Brien), 59, 63
World War I, 9, 30, 185; interwar, 57

World War II, 20, 89, 97, 115, 118, 121, 131, 185

Year of Magical Thinking, The (Didion), 188–89, 212n7
Yeats, W. B, 11, 37, 158, 210n25; *Purgatory*, 101–2; "Who Goes with Fergus?," 32, 37, 48, 101

Bridget English holds a PhD in English from Maynooth University in Ireland. She researches and teaches Irish literary and cultural studies, modernism, and the medical humanities.